studies in jazz

Institute of Jazz Studies
Rutgers—The State University of New Jersey
General Editors: Dan Morgenstern and Edward Berger

1. BENNY CARTER: A Life in American Music, *by Morroe Berger, Edward Berger, and James Patrick, 2 vols., 1982*
2. ART TATUM: A Guide to His Recorded Music, *by Arnold Laubich and Ray Spencer, 1982*
3. ERROLL GARNER: The Most Happy Piano, *by James M. Doran, 1985*
4. JAMES P. JOHNSON: A Case of Mistaken Identity, *by Scott E. Brown;* Discography 1917–1950, *by Robert Hilbert, 1986*
5. PEE WEE ERWIN: This Horn for Hire, *as told to Warren W. Vaché Sr., 1987*
6. BENNY GOODMAN: Listen to His Legacy, *by D. Russell Connor, 1988*
7. ELLINGTONIA: The Recorded Music of Duke Ellington and His Sidemen, *by W. E. Timner, 1988; 4th ed., 1996*
8. THE GLENN MILLER ARMY AIR FORCE BAND: Sustineo Alas / I Sustain the Wings, *by Edward F. Polic;* Foreword *by George T. Simon, 1989*
9. SWING LEGACY, *by Chip Deffaa, 1989*
10. REMINISCING IN TEMPO: The Life and Times of a Jazz Hustler, *by Teddy Reig, with Edward Berger, 1990*
11. IN THE MAINSTREAM: 18 Portraits in Jazz, *by Chip Deffaa, 1992*
12. BUDDY DeFRANCO: A Biographical Portrait and Discography, *by John Kuehn and Arne Astrup, 1993*
13. PEE WEE SPEAKS: A Discography of Pee Wee Russell, *by Robert Hilbert, with David Niven, 1992*
14. SYLVESTER AHOLA: The Gloucester Gabrlel, *by Dick Hill, 1993*
15. THE POLICE CARD DISCORD, *by Maxwell T. Cohen, 1993*
16. TRADITIONALISTS AND REVIVALISTS IN JAZZ, *by Chip Deffaa, 1993*
17. BASSICALLY SPEAKING: An Oral History of George Duvivier, *by Edward Berger;* Musical Analysis *by David Chevan, 1993*
18. TRAM: The Frank Trumbauer Story, *by Philip R. Evans and Larry F. Kiner, with William Trumbauer, 1994*
19. TOMMY DORSEY: On the Side, *by Robert L. Stockdale, 1995*
20. JOHN COLTRANE: A Discography and Musical Biography, *by Yasuhiro Fujioka, with Lewis Porter and Yoh-ichi Hamada, 1995*
21. RED HEAD: A Chronological Survey of "Red" Nichols and His Five Pennies, *by Stephen M. Stroff, 1996*
22. THE RED NICHOLS STORY: After Intermission 1942–1965, *by Philip R. Evans, Stanley Hester, Stephen Hester, and Linda Evans, 1997*
23. BENNY GOODMAN: Wrappin' It Up, *by D. Russell Connor, 1996*
24. CHARLIE PARKER AND THEMATIC IMPROVISATION, *by Henry Martin, 1996*

Fifties Jazz Talk

An Oral Retrospective

Studies in Jazz, No. 47

Gordon Jack

The Scarecrow Press, Inc.
Lanham, Maryland • Toronto • Oxford
2004

SCARECROW PRESS, INC.

Published in the United States of America
by Scarecrow Press, Inc.
A wholly owned subsidiary of
The Rowman & Littlefield Publishing Group, Inc.
4501 Forbes Boulevard, Suite 200, Lanham, Maryland 20706
www.scarecrowpress.com

PO Box 317
Oxford
OX2 9RU, UK

British Library Cataloguing in Publication Information Available

Jack, Gordon, 1941–
   Fifties jazz talk : an oral retrospective / Gordon Jack.
      p. cm. — (Studies in jazz ; no. 47)
   Includes bibliographical references and index.
   ISBN 0-8108-4997-6 (pbk. : alk. paper)
      1. Jazz—1951–1960—History and criticism. 2. Jazz musicians—United States—
Interviews. I. Title. II. Series.
ML3508.G67 2004
781.65'5—dc22   2004005158

⊗™ The paper used in this publication meets the minimum requirements of
American National Standard for Information Sciences—Permanence of
Paper for Printed Library Materials, ANSI/NISO Z39.48-1992.
Manufactured in the United States of America.

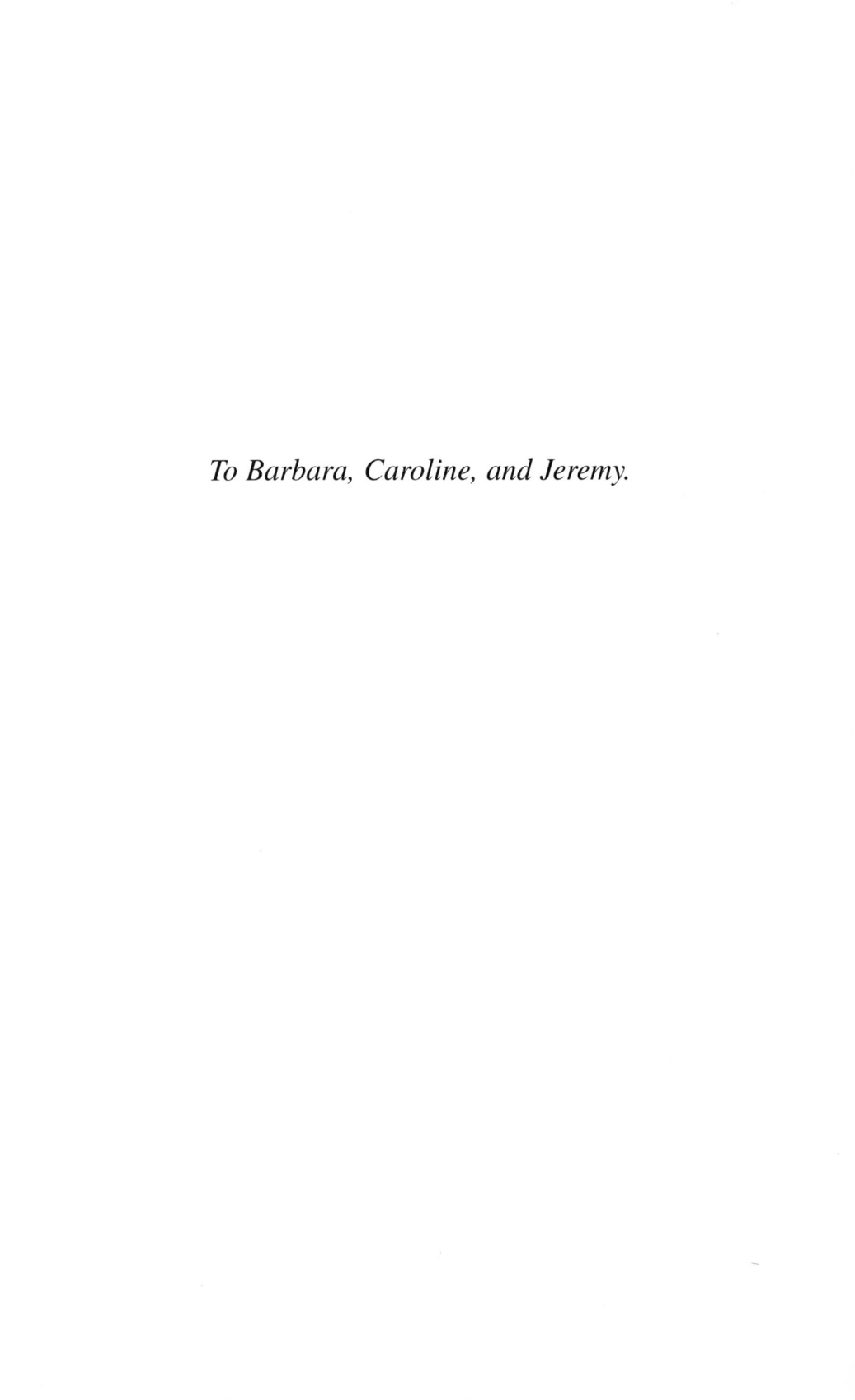

To Barbara, Caroline, and Jeremy.

Contents

Foreword, by Alun Morgan

Because so much of what happens in jazz is ephemeral, it is essential to place on record, and in the correct chronology, the events which led to the creation of so much outstanding music. The fifties saw many changes, including the premature death of Charlie Parker, the fountainhead of so much that had happened in the previous decade. There was also the launch of the long-playing record, a piece of technology which was to have a considerable effect on jazz, for it enabled the "three-minute limit" of the 78 rpm disc to be overcome. In the United States the polarization of jazz centers to the East and West Coasts (and principally to New York and Los Angeles) gave rise to a dichotomy eagerly pounced upon by journalists and critics. Some were quick to come up with slick titles such as "Best Coast Jazz," "Worst Coast Jazz," and "White Coast Jazz." The musicians involved in the divisions were more resilient. Drummer Shelly Manne, for example, would often announce the names of the men in his group followed by their place of birth, proving that none of them actually came from anywhere near California, yet the band was hung with the "West Coast" tag.

For this considerable contribution to the oral history of jazz, Gordon Jack has for several years made it his business to interview many of the survivors from the fifties. He is ideally qualified for the task. Firstly, he speaks from the standpoint of the musician, having played the baritone semi-professionally for a number of years. Secondly, his knowledge of the period and the recordings it produced is unsurpassed. Thirdly, his actual interviewing technique has unlocked the memories of his subjects, many of whom were asked to recall events which took place nearly half a century before. I have known Gordon for some years and have admired the way in which he prepares himself for a meeting. He researches the musician's biography, picks out any discrepancies in published facts, such as recording discographies, and acquaints himself with the parallel careers of colleagues who worked with his subject. Many musicians have been amazed at Gordon's diligence when he undertakes an interview but we, the readers, benefit because invariably we learn something new.

Sadly, a number of important musicians passed away before Gordon had the opportunity to interview them. Nevertheless, he has captured many of consequence in his net, men who played a vital part in the development of jazz or who were central to particular phases. Stan Levey, for example, was a young man when he was swept along by the excitement of bebop, working with the greatest in the field, including Charlie Parker and Dizzy Gillespie. Trombonist Eddie Bert has worked with many of the finest big bands, including those of Woody Herman, Stan Kenton, Thad Jones, and Mel Lewis, and Benny Goodman. But Eddie has also kept diaries of every gig and record date he has played on, making him a vital source of information. At least four of the musicians who told their stories to Gordon had never properly been interviewed: Gene Allen, Joe Dodge, Don Ferrara, and Frank Isola. But I guarantee that any readers who thought they knew all there was to know about the thirty musicians featured in this book will be in for a surprise.

Acknowledgments

My thanks first of all to Jerome Klinkowitz and Alun Morgan, who encouraged me to find a publisher for these interviews. Jerome and I became acquainted when he was researching his book on Gerry Mulligan, and Alun of course is one of the foremost writers on jazz today.

The project would probably never have got off the ground without the computer skills of my daughter, Caroline, who regularly talked me through any number of self-created problems.

I offer another deep bow and a doff of the cap to my old friend John Bell. He is a trombone player about town, but when I first knew him in the late 1950s, he was studying proofreading at the London School of Printing. His considerable knowledge of jazz, and especially grammar, has been invaluable.

Dick Bank in Los Angeles has also been very helpful. He not only tracked down some difficult-to-find musicians but has also allowed me to use some of the photographs he commissioned for his excellent Fresh Sound recording projects.

Many others have helped in generously sharing information, loaning photographs, or reading the final manuscript: Arne Astrup, Russ Chase, Bill Crow, Gerald Dugelay, Jim Gavin, Kellie Hagan, Math Herman, Chris Hitchcock, Raymond Horricks, Frank Howling, Don Jordan, David Lands, Tony Middleton, Arlyne Mulligan, Franca Mulligan, William Schrickell, Putter Smith, Shirley Smith, Michael Sparke, Michael Stallion, Les Tomkins, Joe Urso, Peter Vacher, Steve Voce, Malcolm Walker, Bob Weir, John Williams, and Valerie Wilmer. Once again, many thanks.

Introduction

Most of this material has already appeared in an edited form in *Jazz Journal International* and is reproduced with kind permission of the editor, Eddie Cook. The only exception is the chapter on the Gerry Mulligan Quartet 1952–1953, which was first seen in *Crescendo and Jazz Music* and, once again, is republished with the permission of the editor, Dennis Matthews.

I grew up listening to the music of people like Gerry Mulligan, Zoot Sims, Clifford Brown, Miles Davis, Bob Gordon, and Paul Desmond, and for more than thirty years I wrestled with the baritone saxophone in an unsuccessful attempt to duplicate some of the sounds I heard on my hi-fi. There was a time back in the sixties when I flirted for a while with what seemed to be the "big time"—the rock 'n' roll big time, that is. I was working with a rhythm 'n' blues band, playing mostly James Brown material, and Bruce Talbot, the author of Scarecrow Press's *Tom Talbert—His Life and Times* (Studies in Jazz, No. 45) was on tenor. We occasionally shared the stage at London's 100 Club or the Establishment or the gloriously named Eel Pie Island with artists like Jimi Hendrix, Eric Clapton, the Kinks, Jimmy Witherspoon, and Stevie Winward with Spencer Davis. My saxophone now remains in its case, but I like to think that I am still available for Bar Mitzvahs, Italian weddings, or Buffalo Lodge dinners.

Soon after I stopped playing, Steve Voce, who knew of my admiration for John Williams, told me that the pianist was visiting London and suggested I give him a call. John could not have been nicer, and we had a long talk about his career in New York during the fifties, when he played with giants like Charlie Parker, Stan Getz, and Bob Brookmeyer. Herb Geller, another of my heroes, then came to town and I contacted him to ask for an interview, and over the next several years I met or corresponded with the musicians highlighted here. They all became well known during the fifties, with the exception of Pete Christlieb and Hod O'Brien, who of course emerged a little later. I have included them both because I love their playing and it *is* my book!

I have tried to replicate Ira Gitler's approach in *Swing to Bop*, where the musicians are allowed to talk freely with the very minimum of interjections from the interviewer. My questions have therefore been removed and any input from me is generally confined to the notes at the end of each chapter. Of course each piece has been edited to avoid repetition and to ensure events follow chronologically, but I hope the reader feels that each musician is talking to him or her without a third party getting in the way. My main contribution was to find the "play and record" button on my tape recorder, leaving center stage to the musicians, who have all proved to be highly articulate and quite happy to talk frankly to a complete stranger.

In some cases where it was impossible for me to meet the interviewee, the musician in question sent a cassette with his answers to my written questions. The chapter on the Gerry Mulligan Quartet does have a number of personal comments because it is a four-way interview with Larry Bunker, Chico Hamilton, Carson Smith, and Bob Whitlock. A road map seemed necessary to avoid possible confusion. Finally, the chapters on Joe Dodge and Frank Isola are reproduced here as articles and not interviews, which is how they originally appeared in magazine form.

Chapter One

Gene Allen

*Gene Allen was born on December 5, 1928, in East Chicago, Indiana, which
is on Lake Michigan. His real name is Eugene Sufana. He modestly refers to
himself as a freelance journeyman, but he has a résumé that reads like a
"who's who" of the postwar big band scene. He fit perfectly into a variety of
musical settings. Tex Beneke, Tommy Dorsey, Benny Goodman, Woody Herman, Gerry Mulligan, Louis Prima, and Claude Thornhill are just a few of the
bandleaders who benefited from the rich sound of his baritone in their saxophone sections. This interview took place in December 2000, when Allen
replied on cassette tape to my written list of questions.*

My parents, who emigrated from Romania, had nine children, and there
were always musical instruments around the house because one of my elder
brothers was a sax player who ran a dance band. For professional reasons he
called himself George Allen, and while I was growing up, his band used to rehearse in our living room. From an early age I was exposed to the sound of a
big band as I lay on the floor absorbing everything I could. When I was eight
I started clarinet lessons, and later I learned about orchestrating from a German music teacher, who revealed the secrets of Glenn Miller's reed voicing,
which I found fascinating.

My first job was with my brother's band on tenor, and when I was fifteen
I joined Louis Prima on alto. Young players were getting into the bands during World War II because a lot of older guys had been drafted, so bandleaders were looking around for young players with potential. My parents were
not too keen, but they let me go. Just like Jack Teagarden, who was Stan
Getz's guardian, Louis Prima became mine, and he threatened to send me
home if I didn't behave. After a few months the baritone player left, so Louis
asked me to make the switch. It was around that time I started using the name

Gene Allen because the paymasters didn't seem able to spell my name correctly on the checks.

The band already had a minor hit with "Robin Hood," and in June of 1944 Louis recorded his first million-selling record, "Angelina," which was an Italian-flavored song in 6/8 time and something we had to play all the time after that.[1] Prima was from New Orleans, so we played in a Dixieland style with a swing feel, and he was a very good musician, able to rehearse the band well and impart some education along the way. He was a fine soloist, but by the time I joined he had been forced to promote his showmanship more, so he could make some money and stay in the business. Sonny Berman, Al Porcino, and Charlie Kennedy were in the band, and Edgar Battle and Earl Bostic wrote some of the arrangements. Earl was a fine gentleman who encouraged me a lot, and I got to know him well. He wrote some of the flag-wavers like "Chinatown My Chinatown" that we used to open stage shows. It was taken at a breakneck tempo, with some interesting saxophone parts, which allowed Louis to do his high-note trumpet work over the closing choruses, with the band storming away. Another one of his charts was an old waltz called "I Love You Truly," which was played in double-time and was very "notey" for the saxes—one of those arpeggiated up-and-down things that gave the section a real workout. It was like practicing while working.

The first trombonist was Milton Kabak, who also arranged for the band. As he was a fan of the Stan Kenton orchestra, some of his writing was in that idiom. He later played with Kenton, and he was there for quite a while, as Stan's trombone sections got bigger and bigger. When we played the RKO Theater in Boston, I was hospitalized, and Louis not only arranged my surgery but sent all my paychecks while I recovered. I never saw that happen in any other organization.

Prima was a good boss, but by 1948 I had saved some money, so I decided to leave the band. I had been playing oboe and bass clarinet and had recently bought a bassoon, and I wanted to stay in New York to study. I started hanging out at a musicians' bar called Charlie's Tavern on Seventh Avenue, where I met other baritone players like Danny Bank, Sol Schlinger, and Manny Albam, who were all very helpful. Funnily enough, I was thrown out of Charlie's once on a case of mistaken identity, when a barman thought I was Gene Roland. Gene sometimes had a sharp tongue and had probably upset someone there. Manny Albam, who had played with Charlie Spivak and was writing for Charlie Barnet, agreed to give me lessons in musical structure, and he introduced me to the twelve-tone scale. To this day I don't know why people get so shook up about it. If you look at a piano keyboard, the black and white keys consist of twelve notes in each scale, so why not use them? A lot of arrangers at that time, like Pete Rugulo, Stan Kenton, George Handy, and Ed

Finckel, were assimilating new approaches and tonalities and doing adventurous things in expanding the language.

Gene Williams had been a singer along with Fran Warren in Claude Thornhill's Orchestra, and for a while in the late forties he had his own band. Manny Albam did most of the writing, and we made one record which became a mild jukebox hit in the New York bars; it was called "Just Goofin'." He also did an arrangement of "Allen's Alley" which featured me on the baritone. Don Joseph was in the band, along with Frank DeFranco (Buddy DeFranco's cousin) on lead alto, and Buddy Arnold had the solo tenor chair. Buddy Arnold's girlfriend was Arlyne Brown, the daughter of songwriter Lew Brown. She had been to college and, being very clever, tried to educate all the jazz musicians about their behavior. She later married Gerry Mulligan, and I remember their small son Reed coming to the Village Vanguard on a Sunday matinee and doing a little dance in front of the Concert Jazz Band, which was very charming.[2]

I left Gene in late 1948 and auditioned for Claude Thornhill. He was re-forming again after disbanding the band that had included Mulligan, Brew Moore, and Red Rodney, and I met Gerry for the first time when we were playing at the Glen Island Casino. I was playing baritone with the band, and he brought in two of his orchestrations, "Jeru" and "The Five Brothers." We still had some of his other charts in the book, like "Poor Little Rich Girl" and "Rose of the Rio Grande," which we enjoyed playing. Gerry was in the same boat as other arrangers who were also instrumentalists, because there was always a conflict in finding time to do both. Hal McKusick was Claude's lead alto and clarinet player, and he was very influential and significant in my education. He was already a veteran of several bands and very conscientious about passing on his knowledge of bebop. He had written out a lot of Charlie Parker's solos, and when we were on the road we would play them together. I learned a lot about that idiom; it was a many-sided education to be in Claude's band. It had an entirely different sound and tone quality to anything else at that time, and his piano fill-ins gave the arrangements a certain flavor because they always related to the warp and weft of what was being played. He was not playing a constant solo throughout a piece, like so many other pianists did, which was something that always bugged Mulligan.

Claude was a hands-off bandleader and a man of very few words, leaving the musicians to their own devices; either you did the job or you left the band. Gene Roland was on trumpet, and he and Gerry would sometimes rehearse us, although when we were on the road, Gene would often pass out new parts to the guys during an intermission. We would run them down cold, and they would usually be fine except for some clinkers or copying errors—and if there was a train wreck, that was your problem! Musicians could read very well, and the younger arrangers wanted the bands to play in a more relaxed, laid-back way, which suited me fine. We all fell into that loose, Woody Herman, "Four Brothers" feel. Sadly, most of Thornhill's charts were stolen when the band bus was robbed in Chicago in the late fifties—can you imagine that?

I got married in 1950, which is when I left Thornhill, because I wanted to settle down. I wasn't sure about staying in the music business, so I attempted to become a salesman, selling vacuum cleaners, but I was not too successful. I was still visiting Charlie's, which is where I met Marion Evans, who was very knowledgeable about orchestrating. In his Alabama accent he would hold forth in a booth there, and I was fascinated, listening to his approach. He recommended me to Tex Beneke because he was writing for the band, and I joined them for a three-week engagement on New Year's Eve 1951. This is when I first met Mel Lewis and Buddy Clark, and lo and behold, Bob Brookmeyer was on piano. Bob switched to the trombone section later and played the solos on valve, but Tex asked him to use the slide; I guess the sound was not what he wanted. He also asked me to change from metal to a rubber mouthpiece, which is what he used, and when I did, he said, "Good, I like that." Tex was a very professional and congenial gentleman, and although we played a lot in the Glenn Miller style, he hired other arrangers who wrote in a different manner, without the clarinet lead.

After I left Tex, I did some casual work around New York, which included recording with Tony Fruscella and Phil Urso[3] and working in a strip club on 52nd Street. I played tenor there with just drums and piano, which gave me a chance to carry the ball for a change. Then in late 1953 I joined the Sauter-Finegan Orchestra. It was a happy band because they were not conventional bandleaders, and for the first few weeks I was pretty high with the stimulating sounds that engulfed me. There was a cross section of players from symphonic backgrounds, veterans from big bands like Nick Travis, Joe Ferrante, and Mousey Alexander, and young guys just out of the conservatory. By the mid fifties, just about everything that could be done with a standard big band had been tried, but Eddie and Bill wanted to do things differently—and they sure did, because there was a lot of adventure in the writing, which kept the musicians interested. The reed section had two baritones, and Wally Kane, who was twenty-one years old, sat next to me, playing the heavy utility chair—second baritone, flute, clarinet, bass clarinet, and bassoon. In fact, the five saxes doubled about thirty woodwinds between them, and we also had a harp and two percussionists. Mundell Lowe was the guitarist, and his book had a lot of written parts, not just chords.

When Sauter-Finegan disbanded early in 1956, I had a call from Tino Barzie, who was Tommy Dorsey's manager, because their baritone player Teddy Lee was leaving and they wanted me to take his place. Dorsey's band was in the middle of a ten-year contract at the Statler Hotel, where they were resident for most of the year, and they were also featured on a CBS nation-wide T.V. show called *Stageshow.* The Statler had formerly been called the Pennsylvania Hotel, which inspired Glenn Miller's big hit, "Pennsylvania 6-5000." Funnily enough, about an hour after Tino telephoned, Stan Kenton called to ask me to join him, but I decided to go with Dorsey, as I could stay in New York and not have to relocate. I'm not sure how it would have worked out with Stan, because his band seemed a bit too physical for me, although I enjoyed listening to it.

When I joined Dorsey, the billing was *The Fabulous Dorseys—Tommy and Jimmy*, and I stayed until Tommy passed away in November 1956. There were no rehearsals; I just met the guys on the bandstand at the Statler. It meant a lot of sight-reading for me, but that's the way it goes. The trick is to keep looking about four bars ahead, because things move along very quickly. The first night we did three radio broadcasts, but I was experienced by then and just did my job, although Teddy Lee had clued me on some tricky spots where the baritone was exposed. We had an extensive library from way back, with more than 1,300 numbers in the book, including Paul Weston and Bill Finegan charts. Tommy also liked the Basie band, so he had Ernie Wilkins write some new material in that style, and with people like Charlie Shavers and Louie Bellson, it was a terrific band. Tommy was always pretty mellow, and most of the time he sat in the trombone section instead of standing out front, but Jimmy could be temperamental, because I think what he really wanted was a Dixieland band of his own. Jackie Gleason and Tommy were very close, and Jackie often came to the Statler to raise a little ruckus. When he did, Tommy would just turn the band over to him.

Gerry Mulligan called me for a big band recording in 1957,[4] and I remember the parts were written in pencil. He walked around the band, rewriting or erasing certain measures, although I felt that what he removed was just fine. I liked playing his charts, and I was disappointed when the album was not released for about twenty years—probably because of Gerry's "pickyness"! In 1958 I joined Benny Goodman for a European tour, which included a week at the Brussels World's Fair. I always stayed out of disputes in the bands I played with, and as far as Mr. Goodman is concerned, he had his eccentricities but he should be remembered as a terrific musician. He was also a great clarinetist, although my all-time favorite has to be Buddy DeFranco, who should have got much more attention through the years. In the late fifties I worked with Richard Maltby and Warren Covington, and I did some weekends with Boyd Raeburn. Once again it was all sight-reading, which was not that easy with Boyd, because the baritone book had some tenor parts which had to be transposed at sight. Try that sometime, and it will keep you awake nights!

In January 1960 I ran into Mulligan again on 49th Street, and he invited me to join the Concert Jazz Band, which had started rehearsing at Lynn Oliver's studio on 89th Street. Nick Travis was there, and he really wanted the jazz chair, but Gerry persuaded him to play lead. The CJB was an adventure, and Gerry was hip to where musicians were at, because he would cut you some slack when necessary, and sometimes *he* needed it too. He was easy to play for, and having been through the mill himself, he knew how the guys liked to work. He never imposed the fact that he was *the* Gerry Mulligan, and he was always very friendly to me. The only temperament I saw from him sometimes was at conditions in a club or onstage, but never at musicians. He surprised us all by using ordinary metal music stands instead of the normal music desks with the leader's initials or logo, because he thought that they muffled the sound. He also made us sit on drum stools so we didn't get too relaxed or laid back. With my heavy baritone around my neck, I found those small stools pretty uncomfortable.

Some of the bebop fans were a little disappointed when they first heard us, because they expected a big powerhouse ensemble, whereas Gerry's approach was far more subtle. He paid a lot of attention to dynamics, and the arrangers achieved some startling textures and original sounds with just four reeds and six brass. As a soloist he was very creative, but I don't think he was totally interested in the baritone *per se*. Just like Al Cohn and Bob Brookmeyer, for instance, you could always sense the composer's wheels in operation. He often said that we should do something together on baritone, but I didn't push it because it would have been like "taking coals to Newcastle." But sometimes on club dates, he would open up the arrangements so we could all get to play a little and stretch out. The only recorded solo I had with the CJB was a bass clarinet feature on "Chuggin,"[5] which was a cute original by Gary McFarland, and I would like to buy that particular take back. On the previous one I had played more in the higher register, not exactly Eric Dolphy you understand, because I was not very experienced in soloing on the instrument, but it was a better solo. On the same album we did George Russell's long and complicated "All about Rosie," which was challenging, but I was used to not being intimidated by parts. I made it a point to get things under my fingers as quickly as possible so that I was making music and not just playing the notes. George was very enthusiastic about the CJB and often came to hear us.

Towards the end of the band's life in 1964, I sometimes sent in a substitute like Sol Schlinger or Tony Ferina if I had a booking with Les Elgart or a jingle recording. Along with Richie Kamuca, who was the tenor soloist by that time, I was also working at the Copacabana, which helped pay the rent. One night, though, when we were packing up at the Village Vanguard, Gerry said,

"You know, you can't make any money in jazz music," and he called it a day very soon afterwards with the CJB.

A highlight for me was touring the Soviet Union with Benny Goodman in 1962. Soon after we got back, I went to hear Woody Herman at the Metropole. They were stomping away there, with Bill Chase leading a five-man trumpet section and Sal Nistico breaking it up on tenor. I figured that this would be my swan song with a road band, so I joined Woody for about eight months, and surprise, surprise, after a couple of weeks the rest of the saxes had left and I found myself breaking in new players on one-nighters; a typical Woody Herman experience. While I was with Herman I played on Mulligan's last recording with the CJB.[6] The night before, I had been playing full throttle at the Metropole with Woody; the next day, I had to shift gears into the Mulligan mode, which meant trimming down my sound. Nat Pierce was Woody's musical director, and I don't think he was too crazy about Mulligan's band, because he didn't want things to get too complicated or symphonic—he just wanted to swing. He used to say, "Listen, really blow that baritone and pump it out." In other words, let it vibrate like Harry Carney or Charlie Fowlkes. Harry had a wide range of dynamics, and he was the grandaddy of the baritone. He had a lot of freedom in Duke's band, because individual sound qualities and playing styles were big factors in their success, but if I had adopted that style in most of the bands I played with, I would not have been too popular with the leader. All the writers of the cool school, like Billy Byers, Johnny Mandel, and Al Cohn, wanted the saxes to have a light, breezy feel and to be very "fly" rhythmically.

Getting back to Woody's band, I liked the "Four Brothers" sound with the tenor lead, although it was not much fun for the baritone, because you are in the upper register a lot, rather like a tenor harmony part. I much prefer the conventional sax line-up where the baritone plays double lead or has a contrapuntal role. This gives the arranger greater flexibility and far more tone colors. While I was there, Nat Pierce did a lot of the charts. He got Woody back to playing the saxophone, so we had a lead alto on some numbers.[7]

In December 1963 I was in the band that accompanied Thelonious Monk at Lincoln Center.[8] I was a little worried in case Monk or Charlie Rouse said, "He's not much of a swinger—who is this stiff?" But that didn't happen. A lot of the pieces, like "Four in One," were difficult to play until you had the pattern under your fingers, but the challenge was fascinating. At the start of the concert he threw us a curve, because we had the charts set up in order but Monk sailed straight into the introduction of another tune, which had us scrambling through the music to catch him up.

As a freelance journeyman musician, you have to be ready for anything in a city like New York or Los Angeles, so for the rest of the sixties I grabbed whatever work I could find, like playing in the pit for the Broadway show *Folies Bergère* for six months. I was also at the Copacabana a lot, backing acts like Nat Cole, Peggy Lee, Eydie Gorme, and Jane Russell, as well as playing with Fred Waring Jr., Ray Eberle, Urbie Green, Rusty Dedrick, Johnny Mince, and Marshall Brown. I was occasionally called in by the Metropolitan Opera Orchestra if there was a baritone sax part, as there was on some Villa-Lobos pieces. I would be the only sax player there, and sitting with that large orchestra close to the cello section was really something to be experienced. It can get pretty stressful, chasing around town with your horns from date to date, and around 1969 some long-running physical problems caught up with me, which meant I had to cancel a lot of work and take a long rest. It took me years to recover, and I never got back to working full-time as a musician, even though I wanted to. I used up a considerable amount of money, but I learned a lesson: we all need to slow down and meditate a little and not get too depressed when the world doesn't follow the beat of our baton.

From about 1950 onwards I played a Conn saxophone, partly because some leaders wanted the big sound that the Conn provided. I tried the Selmer, with the low A, and it certainly had a faster action which I liked, but I never made the switch because it was too much extra weight for just a semi-tone. The Conn was a very serviceable horn and could take more punishment on the road than the Selmer, and of course Harry Carney used one all his life. On a blowing instrument, the mouthpiece is very important, and Jack Jenney's brother George was an expert. He had designed the facing on Harry's big rubber job, and although it was supposed to be a military secret, he did the same for me.

The best thing about music is playing it. Looking back, it was a great trip for me. Now that I am retired, I listen to a lot I missed the first time around, like Red Allen, Benny Carter, McKinney's Cotton Pickers, and the Don Redman Orchestra. These things are a shot in the arm when you hear them, and I bet a lot of people have forgotten the bandleader Isham Jones. He also wrote some great songs, like "It Had to Be You," "Spain," and "(There Is) No Greater Love." Both Woody Herman and singer Tony Martin played in his saxophone section. I listen to everything except for rock 'n' roll, and I can't stand rap. There's too much good music around to waste time on that stuff.

NOTES

1. Louis Prima was still playing "Angelina" in the 1950s, when he had a highly popular nightclub act in Las Vegas with his wife Keely Smith, together with Sam Butera and the Witnesses.

2. In *Meet Me at Jim and Andy's* by Gene Lees (Oxford University Press), he reveals that Gene Williams eventually left the music business and worked quite happily at Charlie's Tavern, where he could meet and socialize with his old friends from the band days.

3. Tony Fruscella, *Complete Studio Recordings*. Jazz Factory JFCD 22808.

4. Gerry Mulligan, *Mullenium*. Columbia CK 65678.

5. Gerry Mulligan, *A Concert in Jazz*. Verve V-8415.

6. Gerry Mulligan, *Mulligan '63*. Verve VLP 9037.

7. Gene Allen has a fine solo on Horace Parlan's "Blues for J.P." on *Woody Herman '63*. Philips (Verve) PHS 600-065. (He could shed no light on the identity of "J.P.")

8. Thelonious Monk, *Big Band and Quartet in Concert*. Columbia 476898 2.

Chapter Two

Mose Allison

Mose Allison was born on November 11, 1927, in Tippo, Mississippi, which is in Tallahatchie County, a location immortalized by Bobbie Gentry in her 1967 hit, "Ode to Billy Joe." Before recording his famous Back Country Suite *in 1957, Allison had played in the rhythm sections of Brew Moore, Al Cohn, Stan Getz, and Gerry Mulligan. During his December 1994 engagement in London's Pizza Express, he reminisced about those days.*

Brew Moore was from Indianola, Mississippi, and he was a great hero to all the southern guys because he was the first one of us to work and record in New York. I started playing with him in 1951 when I was attending the Louisiana State University, studying for my B.A. in English and working at the Flamingo in Baton Rouge in the evenings. He had left New York by that time and was appearing down in New Orleans, but he came up to the Flamingo to play a couple of weeks with me. I heard him in many different situations, but even on the dumbest gig with people that could barely play, he always sounded terrific, because Brew meant every note. He was a very bright, sensitive, and colorful character, and he also wrote poetry. I would say he was one of my favorite players of all the Lestorians. Of course Zoot, Al, and Stan Getz were great, too, but Brew was the most determined Lestorian of them all. He even sometimes played his tenor at an angle, just like Lester.[1]

You probably know that Brew died in Copenhagen in 1973 at a party he gave to celebrate an inheritance, but there is another part of the story that isn't too well known. It concerns one of my favorite Southerners, Carmen Massey, who is a fine bass player and a real good friend. He and Brew used to hang out a lot together, and Brew was staying at Carmen's house in Biloxi, Mississippi, when he heard that he had inherited all this money. Now you have to remember that Brew had been scuffling on the fringes of the jazz world all his life, and he had never made much at all, so Carmen, who is very sensible and businesslike, said, "Let me invest the money to take some of the pressure off you." But Brew decided that now he could afford it, he wanted to go to Europe, and when he got there he discovered that he had lost the good luck charm he had been carrying around for years. He wrote to Carmen asking him to check if he had left it at the house. The next thing that Carmen hears is that Brew had died, and a few days later one of Carmen's children found Brew's lucky charm. That story sounds like something out of Truman Capote.

I first went to New York in 1951, and I remember taking some arrangements to Buddy DeFranco when he was rehearsing a big band, but I don't think he used them. I played at sessions in town, but I never did get a job. In fact, nobody seemed to be working, and most of the people I had been reading about in *Down Beat* just wanted to borrow $5 from *me*! I remember everybody getting very excited because Gerry Mulligan got a gig, but when I went to see him, it was just a one-nighter in some bar over in Queens. I was in New York in the summer, which is always a slow time, but I decided not to stay.

I returned to New York in 1956 and have been there ever since. Just before coming back I had met Al Cohn's wife, the singer Marilyn Moore, when I was playing down in Galveston, Texas. She sang with the group one night, and because she liked the way I accompanied her, she told me that if I ever came back to New York I should give Al a call. When I telephoned him, he was really nice. He had me over to his house right away and used me on little one-nighters, which were usually just Al and a rhythm section. He wasn't doing that much playing because he was pretty busy with writing and recording, but he was great, and he is one of my heroes. Of course it's well known that he had a marvelous sense of humor; you could write a book of Al's jokes. He and Zoot were made for each other, and if there was a leader, I suppose it was Al, because he wrote the arrangements and usually decided what to play.

A couple of friends of mine, southern guys, owned a loft at 335 East 34th Street where there was always plenty of music going on, with people like Al, Zoot, Phil Woods, Fred Greenwell, Clyde Cox, Buddy Jones, and Al Haig.[2] I first met Frank Isola there, and one of the mainstays was Jerry Lloyd (formerly Jerome Hurwitz), who seemed to be there all the time. He was very friendly with Ralph Hughes, a trumpeter from Mississippi who also played drums and had worked a lot with me down South. Ralph had played with Brew as well as going on the road with some big bands.[3] Getting back to Jerry Lloyd, he'd recorded with Zoot, George Wallington, and Mulligan and had played with Charlie Parker, but he wasn't working regularly. In fact, at the time, he was driving a cab to make ends meet. He was a character and a hero to all those in the know, rather like Tony Fruscella, because they could really play. Another guy in New York who never really became well known except to other musicians was Dave Schildkraut, but he was one of the premier Bird-influenced altoists.

It was Frank Isola that recommended me to Stan Getz. I didn't audition for him because he never really auditioned anybody; the job was the audition, and if he was satisfied with you on the night, you stayed with the band. While I was with him he probably used about ten or twelve drummers, often for one night only, but he used Frank a lot. I know all the stories about Stan, but I never had any problems with him at all because he was always nice to me, and it was a real thrill to work with him. I saw how he was with some people, but you have to remember that Stan Getz was a matinee idol when he was sixteen years old, and having that much adulation so early does something to you. I really enjoyed working with him because he was a fantastic player, and nobody is going to refute that.[4]

Stan didn't use any of my material, but sometimes during the evening he would let me play with just the trio. For instance, on that broadcast from the Red Hill Inn,[5] I play an original of mine called "Ain't You a Mess" with Jug Taylor and Paul Motian. Of course, Jug Taylor was a nickname for Taylor La-Fargue, who played bass on *Back Country Suite*.[6] Frank Isola was on that album, and he was a terrific drummer. At his best he was as good as any drummer I've heard, and whenever I go to his hometown in Detroit, I always ask about him because I loved his playing. He was unique and quite different to most of the others, playing in a quieter, much more subtle way, with more touch. The whole idea about drums for me is momentum without magnificence, or to put it another way, momentum without volume. A lot of good drummers get the momentum but there's too much volume. I like the guy who can get momentum without excess volume, and Frank was the master of that.

It was thanks to George Wallington that I recorded *Back Country Suite*. One night I was at a party at his house and I played some sketches from the suite, which he liked, and when I told him I had a tape of it, he arranged for Bob Weinstock at Prestige Records to hear it. Frank Isola, Taylor LaFargue, and I had made the tape at the loft on 34th Street, and although the piano there wasn't very good, the tape was ten times better than the recording we did for Prestige. I don't know what happened to that tape, but if you could hear it, you would know what the suite was supposed to sound like. None of us felt we did a good job on the record date; we felt uneasy and uptight. It was my first time as a leader, and Taylor's first recording of any consequence, and we weren't prepared for stopping and starting, playing things over and over. I still don't feel comfortable recording, because it's a chore and I feel too self-conscious. You start playing and something breaks down and the whole situation becomes clinical, unlike the feeling I get in a club. I was really disappointed when I first heard the recording, and I couldn't wait to forget about it, but then the reviews started coming out and I thought maybe it wasn't so bad after all. It was quite different to what was happening in New York at the time, which was one of my goals to get across. There was so much experimental stuff being done that was getting away from the essence of jazz and blues.

Bob Weinstock gave me a contract, which was a thrill, even though it was only for $250 an album for six albums over two years. I have never made any money from artist's royalties on records; the only real money I made was from copyrights of my songs, and when the Who recorded "Young Man Blues," I made more from that than all my royalties put together. Pete Townshend was nice about it, because he used to give me credit when they performed it at live performances. I influenced some of the British rock groups, but everyone was working from the same sources; the rock 'n' roll thing came from the blues anyway.

Taylor LaFargue also played with my first trio in 1950, which we called the Nat Garner Trio because we were trying to avoid paying union dues! Having a fancy name seemed like the thing to do at the time, and as Nat Cole and Erroll Garner were two of my heroes, we used that name on our first job in Lake Charles, Louisiana. I saw Taylor last year when I was playing in Mississippi, and although he is older, he hasn't changed; I don't think that anyone does after about twelve years old or so. You learn more and get a different perspective, but essentially you have the same attitudes. He doesn't play bass much anymore, but he says he is going to get back into it. The drummer with the Nat Garner Trio was Dale Hampton, and like Taylor, he was from DeWitt, Arkansas. He was actually a trombone player, but he had good time, so we went to a music store and bought him a very modest kit; no bass drum, just a snare and hi-hat.

In 1958 I played with Gerry Mulligan, and I was one of the few piano players he used at that time. We did some sessions at a studio he had access to in Carnegie Hall, and we had such a good time, he hired me, although it was just a few gigs. We played at the Cork 'n' Bib out on Long Island, which was one of the places everybody worked, and we were supposed to have six weeks in the Midwest, but he cancelled the tour after three weeks and I can't remember why. We did a date in Detroit with Zoot, Henry Grimes, and Dave Bailey, which was fun, and I seem to recall playing trumpet at a session with him along with Lee Konitz, Joe Benjamin, and Dave Bailey. I like to play an economical type of rhythm piano when I'm playing behind a horn, and with Gerry I probably played a little less than I would normally. I didn't play too much, just minimal rhythm to make it swing, and just like Stan, I got along fine with Gerry. He was another one of the greats, with probably a little more of an intellectual approach than Al or Zoot. I was still playing some trumpet in those days, and I remember going to Don Ferrara's place once or twice to play with him. Eventually the trumpet was stolen on a gig, and for a while after that I used a cornet, but I didn't persevere with it. Gerry had been using Henry Grimes, who was a good friend of mine, and we often played together. He was very active at the time, and everybody wanted to use him because he was a master bass player with a big sound. I don't really know what happened to him. I remember Cecil Taylor once asking me for his telephone number, but I think by that time he might have gone into the Church and become a Reverend.

Chet Baker had played a date with Stan Getz when I was with the group, and as a result Chet asked me to play with him, but it only lasted a short while. He had a couple of fine charts by Richard Twardzik that were very busy and complicated, and he wanted them played exactly as written. I told him I was not a great sight-reader, so in the end he hired someone else. Of course Dick Twardzik was a great talent. He was a fantastic pianist, and I love that trio album he did for Pacific Jazz. Another one of my favorites was Lennie Tristano, which may surprise you. He and Bud Powell were the founders of modern piano playing, since nearly everyone was influenced by one or the other of them. I also like Sal Mosca very much.

In 1958 *Esquire* magazine took a photograph that became very famous. It showed a crowd of well-known jazz musicians standing outside a brownstone in Harlem, and I was supposed to be in it. Unfortunately I was late, but I did have a photo taken that day with the other latecomers, who included Ronnie Free, Oscar Pettiford, Charlie Rouse, Lester Young, and Mary Lou Williams.[7] Ronnie Free lives in South Carolina. I played with him last year, and he is still playing great, because he is one of those guys who never loses it.

Thanks to the success of *Back Country Suite*, I started getting bookings for my trio in New York. Our first gig was at the Café Bohemia in 1958 with Addison Farmer and Paul Motian, opposite Horace Silver's quintet and Herbie Mann's group. I remember Art Farmer was with Horace, and Herbie Mann was playing bass clarinet rather than flute. I no longer play some of those early songs of mine, like "Eyesight to the Blind," "V8 Ford Blues," "One Room Country Shack," and "Parchman Farm," because they reflect a sharecropping scene in the South that has disappeared. Of course I still get requests for them, especially "Parchman Farm," but I haven't played it in over twenty years. The story is about a man serving time in prison, and in the last line of the song he says, "All I did was shoot my wife." It started out as a joke, but I didn't like the idea of singing about such a violent act. It seemed that whenever I sang it, everyone was waiting for that line, so I started to feel uncomfortable performing it. One of my early songs that I still perform, although I do it differently now, is "Ask Me Nice," and it happens to be my mother's favorite, too.

NOTES

1. Regarding Lester Young, Brew Moore famously once said, "If you don't sound like Prez, you're wrong!"

2. Patti Jones, in *One Man's Blues: The Life and Music of Mose Allison* (Quartet Books), devotes several pages to the loft on East 34th Street. Other regulars at these sessions included Sonny Rollins, Henry Grimes, John Williams, Stan Getz, and Dave Frishberg. Bud Powell also visited but did not play.

3. Ralph Hughes was married to Mose's cousin, Susan Staton, and had grown up with Brew Moore. Some of the bandleaders he played for in the late fifties included Tex Beneke, Claude Thornhill, Billy Butterfield, and Urbie Green. He died in 1997.

4. In Patti Jones's book, Mose says that the adulation showered on Stan Getz was "Completely overwhelming to me because down South where I had been playing, musicians had about the same status as a bus boy!"

5. Stan Getz, *Stan and Shelly Live in 1956/57*. Jazz Band EB-407.

6. Mose Allison, *Back Country Suite*. OJC 075.

7. In 1992 this picture appeared in the *Al Cohn Collection of Photographs* published by the Music Department at East Stroudsburg University.

Chapter Three

Dave Bailey

During the fifties and sixties, when Gerry Mulligan was leading a variety of pianoless groups, he employed some of the finest and most sympathetic drummers in jazz. Larry Bunker, Chico Hamilton, Frank Isola, Gus Johnson, and Mel Lewis all made significant contributions to the success of his music. However, one drummer in particular, David Samuel Bailey, is closely associated with Mulligan during this period and worked with him from 1955 to 1965. Bailey was born in Portsmouth, Virginia, on February 22, 1926, but he was raised in Philadelphia, where his family moved when he was quite young. This interview took place in January 1997, when he replied on cassette tape to my list of written questions.

During World War II, after flight training in Tuskegee, Alabama, I served as a Pilot Officer in North Africa and Italy. When I left the service in 1946, the G.I. Bill helped me to study drumming at the Music Center Conservatory in New York. From 1951 to 1955 I played off and on with Lou Donaldson, and we have had a professional and personal relationship ever since. Peck Morrison and Herman Foster were in the group, and sometimes Lou added Donald Byrd. In 1952 I was with Charles Mingus for a few months in a pianoless quartet with Teddy Charles and J. R. Monterose, and the following year I spent about nine months with Johnny Hodges when he had a septet, and that was a wonderful experience. Shorty Baker and Lawrence Brown were in the band, and John Coltrane was with us for a while.

I joined Gerry Mulligan in 1955. He was rehearsing a tentet at Nola's Studios on Broadway, and Peck Morrison begged me to go along with him—not to get a job, but just to listen to the music, because we had all been impressed by Gerry's writing for the Miles Davis nine-piece group. Oscar Pettiford and Osie Johnson were supposed to be there, but when they didn't show, Idrees

Sulieman, who was in the band, introduced Peck to Gerry. Peck mentioned that I played drums and that is how we ended up in Gerry's sextet, which opened in Cleveland the following week. A little later, when the group became popular, Oscar and Osie both wanted the gig back! Idrees was an excellent musician, and he stayed with us for about two months, but Gerry was looking for someone with a more Chet-like approach. Idrees had a big, warm sound rather like Clifford Brown, which didn't really blend with Gerry, so he left. A little while later, Peck moved on because of the additional stress that came with a pianoless group. Gerry put a lot of pressure on bass players, which I don't think that Peck was able to deal with, and his wife probably didn't want him to travel as much as the Mulligan group was travelling.

As a matter of fact, I almost quit playing around that time, and it was Christopher Columbus (Sonny Payne's father) who talked me out of it. Gerry's sextet was booked at Basin Street East with the Clifford Brown/Max Roach group, and Gene Krupa was also on the bill. Max was playing so much drums, it was just incredible, and we were swinging and taking care of serious business with Gerry. Then Gene came onstage with those single-stroke rolls that every drummer can do, and the crowd went crazy. I don't mean any criticism of Gene, but the audience just didn't appreciate how well Max Roach was playing, and it was really disheartening to see their lack of reaction to him. I felt like giving up. On my way home, I stopped by Small's Paradise, where Chris was playing with "Wild Bill" Davis, and luckily he persuaded me to carry on.

Jon Fardley had replaced Idrees on trumpet, but he had some very serious problems that often prevented him from playing up to par, and with his horrendous drug dependency, we couldn't always be sure that he would show up for the gig. Eventually he left and went back to Florida, which is when I recommended Oliver Beaner as his replacement. He was with us for a few weeks and did the sextet's last booking at the Preview Lounge in Chicago. He was a marvelous musician who sight-read the parts, and if Gerry had carried on with that group he would have kept Oliver, because he sounded like a cross between Chet and Miles. After the sextet broke up, Gerry went back to a quartet with Bob Brookmeyer, and on the early records I played mostly brushes, which was my decision—Gerry rarely dictated what I should use. He was very liberal in that regard and would not have wanted to confine me to brushes.

Mulligan taught me something very early in the game about getting people's attention; you can either play very loudly or very softly. I remember once we had a rowdy customer sitting in front of the bandstand at Storyville, which was an intimate club in Boston. We gradually brought our volume down until the only thing you could hear was the guy talking and shouting.

Gerry then chastised him for spoiling things for the audience who had paid to
hear us. He used that strategy quite a few times in clubs over the years.[1] When
Brookmeyer left in 1957 I stayed with Gerry, who was working with Lee
Konitz at places like the Village Vanguard. Sometimes he added Mose Allison, and having a piano at that time with Mulligan was a little unusual.

In 1957 I made a lot of records with Gerry. On the "Sax Section" date with
Lee Konitz, Zoot Sims, Allen Eager, and Al Cohn, he decided to use a rhythm
guitar.[2] He asked my opinion about the rhythm section because saxes are
noted for making tempos drag a little, and as he wanted a really solid sound
but without a piano, Freddie Green was the next best thing. When he did the
album with Chet Baker, I think that he wanted the two of them to get back together, which is why the L.P. was called "Reunion."[3] Gerry respected Chet,
but he always said that he had taken the fall for him when he was incarcer-
ated in 1953. Gerry didn't tell the authorities that the controlled substances he
was accused of owning actually belonged to Chet. The album with Annie
Ross, which included Chet on some numbers, was a fun date when she was
in her prime.[4] Despite all this recording activity, Gerry tended to work spo-
radically, usually about six months a year. When I was free I played with people like Ben Webster, Billie Holiday, Chris Connor, Coleman Hawkins, Billy
Taylor, and Lou Donaldson—just group after group.

In 1958 Mulligan put together the quartet with Art Farmer, which he always said was the best group he ever had. I seem to remember him asking me
to recommend a trumpeter who would fit, and I immediately suggested Art.
He was a consummate musician who stepped right in and played the parts im-
maculately, and we had just one rehearsal before making our debut at Newport that year.[5] Gerry always had very professional musicians who were able
to interpret his ideas easily, so he didn't have many rehearsals with the quartet or sextet, although he would sometimes get together with the bass player
to decide on a certain background or accompaniment. Occasionally he would
bring in sketches, but we would all contribute, so it was the group's input you
heard. Of course things changed later with the Concert Jazz Band, when he
had a lot of rehearsals. The studio date with Art—*What Is There to Say?*[6]—
was sheer joy and excitement, and in my opinion Gerry's best album bar
none. I was glad to be a part of that group because they were happy times for
me and I hoped we would stay together forever, although we only lasted a
year. But what a year! It didn't feel like work because we loved to play, and
nobody was ever late, but all good things must come to an end—*c'est la vie*.

When I first joined Gerry Mulligan, his wife Arlyne was also his personal
manager, and she took her job very seriously, being very protective of him,
which some people mistook for bossiness. Martha Glazer had taken Erroll
Garner from being an unknown pianist to the top of the world, and Arlyne

perceived a similar role for herself with Gerry. She had helped him get out of jail in 1953 and stuck by him when it was necessary, and whatever her faults, she was primarily concerned about Gerry at the expense of everything else. After they broke up, I became the road manager, dealing with the agency about transportation and accommodation, etc. I also handled the money, and I was the one he would ask about hiring new players, but there were a lot of other drummers who were trying to get *my* job, and he used to kid me about it. They would call him and say, "What are you doing with that Dave Bailey?"—and we are not talking about "Joe Blow" here; these were superstars trying to get the gig with Gerry at my expense.[7]

Henry Grimes joined the quartet at my recommendation, and he was a hometown guy, because we had both been raised in Philadelphia. He eventually left because he was a very sensitive person and, as I said before, there was a lot of pressure on bass players in Mulligan's groups. I think that it affected Henry, who wanted to play a certain way, but Gerry wanted something different. I don't know what happened to him, but I heard recently that he had become a minister.[8]

In the summer of 1959 I traveled to L.A. with Gerry and Art to record André Previn's music for *The Subterraneans*.[9] Although we only worked two days a week on the film, we spent several months in California, which gave me plenty of time to visit local clubs like the Lamp. It later became known as Shelly's Manne-Hole, and holding forth there was an unknown pianist called Les McCann, who had a duo with Leroy Vinnegar. I often used to take my snare and sock cymbal along to sit in, and when I got back to New York, I told Blue Note how saleable he would be if he were recorded—and the rest is history. I also mentioned him to Dick Bock at Pacific Jazz, so I take a little credit for helping to launch Les's career.

In 1960 I played on the single "I'm Gonna Go Fishin'" with Gerry's CJB,[10] and I loved that band, although initially we didn't work that often. Our first engagement was at Basin Street East, and Blue Mitchell and Charlie Rouse were on the gig, but they didn't stay with the band. They were excellent soloists and fit perfectly, but they already had steady work with people like Monk and Horace Silver, so they were not committed to Gerry for the major part of their employment. Playing with Gerry was my principal job, but I had to leave the CJB because I was getting a lot of record dates: jazz, blues, pop, gospel, you name it. I was making good money, so I saw no reason to be on the road with the band when I could stay in New York.

Towards the end of 1959 I became a founding member of the Jazztet with Benny Golson, Art and Addison Farmer, Curtis Fuller, and McCoy Tyner. It started as a cooperative group with everyone sharing equally, rather like the MJQ, and it worked very well. We had a wonderful time, and unlike Gerry's

small groups, everything was written out. I remember when we were rehearsing "Killer Joe," I added an accent on the fourth beat which was not
written. Benny immediately said, "That's a killer," and although my name
isn't "Joe," he always tells people it was titled as a tribute to me. It was Curtis and I who thought of the name Jazztet, but some outside forces convinced
Art and Benny that it should become the Art Farmer/Benny Golson Jazztet,
which was not the original plan. I left because of the name change, but it is
all water under the bridge now.

In 1961 I worked with Tubby Hayes at the Half Note, and we also recorded
with Clark Terry.[11] I had already played with Tubby in London when I had
toured there with Gerry, and I was shocked at how good he was. I think that
he was the very best of the non-American jazz musicians, closely followed by
Niels-Henning Ørsted Pedersen, and that is an opinion shared particularly by
Afro-American players. The following year I produced *Jeru*[12] for Gerry Mulligan on my own record label, which was later sold to Columbia. The album
featured a number of ballads which he really excelled at, and I wanted him to
exploit that particular strength. Ballads allowed his compositional skills to
come to the fore, because he could improvise new melodies on the spur of the
moment, which is what jazz is all about. He agreed to my choosing the repertoire and the musicians—Tommy Flanagan and Ben Tucker—and he didn't
charge me for playing on the date, because he wanted to do something for me
as a sort of payback.

Around that time I was also working with Clark Terry and Bob Brookmeyer, and they were happy, happy times. Clark was the star of the *Tonight
Show* band with Johnny Carson, and after recording the show, he would come
down to the Half Note and play all night with us. He is a real quality person
and one of the most generous musicians in the world. Very often at the end of
the week he would give me the money and say, "Dave, pay the guys. I don't
want any money." Bob Brookmeyer has discussed his drinking problems, but
it was never an issue all the time I played with him, because he was always
ready to perform. I knew he drank, but if he was out of it, it was not obvious
to me.

After he broke up the CJB I went back to Gerry's quartet and worked with
him until around 1965, which is when I dropped out of the jazz scene. Chris
Columbus had advised me that I should stop playing when music became
work, and that is what it had become. I had other interests, and the flying bug
had hit me again. During the years I had been with Gerry, I regained the flying licenses I had given up when I left the Air Force in 1946. I started flying
professionally for F. Lee Bailey, the famous attorney, as his pilot for about
five years, and as you know, he had some very high-profile clients over the
years, like Patty Hearst and O. J. Simpson.

Looking back on my time with Gerry Mulligan, I would say that he was a wonderful saxophone player with a unique sound and approach to the instrument. With his soft tone coupled with the masculinity of the baritone, he would sometimes blow your mind, especially on ballads. He was a stand-up guy, and I had no complaints playing with him, because he was always straight and never deceptive or difficult to work for. Some others surrounding him could be difficult from time to time, but not Gerry. He said what he felt, occasionally to his own detriment, which could lead to misunderstandings with other people. He was always very generous and protective of his musicians, and a good example of that occurred back in 1956. The sextet was booked into a Baltimore club, and Peck Morrison and I arrived early to set up. Afterwards we sat in the body of the club, but the owner sent someone over to tell us to wait in the kitchen, because musicians were not allowed in the club when they were not performing. When Gerry arrived, he saw the owner, and it turned out that the policy related particularly to the black players, so he came back to tell us to pack up; we were leaving. Now the place was sold out because Gerry was hotter than a firecracker at the time, and the owner knew he would lose a whole bunch of money if he didn't play. The policy changed immediately that night, thanks to Gerry's economic power.

I have already said that he only worked about six months a year, because if he worked more often, all the money would go to the federal government in taxes. We always flew first class whenever possible, because he could write that off as a business expense, and he bought our clothes, which were classed as uniforms, although they weren't. He paid well because he said he would rather give the money to his musicians than the government.

Apart from working for F. Lee Bailey, Dave taught flying at Westchester County Airport for a number of years after he stopped playing. He also succeeded Billy Taylor as a director of Jazzmobile, which organizes jazz performances in Harlem, Brooklyn, and the Bronx. He came out of retirement on February 12, 1996, at St. Peter's Church in Manhattan when, along with Art Farmer, Joe Temperley, and Bill Crow, he performed "Festive Minor" at Gerry Mulligan's memorial service.

NOTES

1. On a CD recorded at Storyville, Mulligan can be heard losing patience with a noisy customer who insists on whistling during a performance of "Limelight." He threatens to take him outside, which must be a first on a commercial recording! Pacific Jazz CP32-5358CD.

2. *The Gerry Mulligan Songbook.* Pacific Jazz 7243 8 33575 2 9.

3. *Gerry Mulligan Quartet Reunion with Chet Baker*. Pacific Jazz CDP8 38263-2.

4. *Annie Ross Sings a Song with Mulligan.* Pacific Jazz CDP 7243.

5. Gerry Mulligan Quartet. JUCD 2052.

6. Gerry Mulligan, *What Is There to Say?* Columbia CK 52978.

7. Dave was reluctant to name names, as some of the drummers are still alive, but he did say that Art Taylor and Osie Johnson were both keen to join the group.

8. One of Grimes's last appearances with Mulligan, Farmer, and Bailey was on a CBS Timex T.V. show on April 30, 1958. Radiola Video MR 1095. His playing took a new direction in the sixties, when he started working with Cecil Taylor, Albert Ayler, and Don Cherry. He retired from music in 1967.

9. *The Subterraneans* original soundtrack. Sony AK 47486.

10. Gerry Mulligan, *Concert Jazz Band*. Verve CLP 1432.

11. Tubby Hayes, *New York Sessions*. CBS 4663632.

12. Gerry Mulligan, *Jeru*. Columbia COL 473685 2.

Chapter Four

Chuck Berghofer

Chuck Berghofer was born in Denver, Colorado, on June 14, 1937, although some jazz reference books incorrectly quote a different date. The list of his credits includes some of the very best in jazz and popular music because it features, among others, Ray Charles, Ella Fitzgerald, Peggy Lee, Shelly Manne, Art Pepper, Frank Rosolino, Zoot Sims, Frank Sinatra, and Barbra Streisand. During a 1996 holiday in London Berghofer talked about his career, which has included playing on the soundtrack of more than four hundred films. Sadly, a number of the artists mentioned in the interview, such as Conte Candoli, Frank Sinatra, and Mel Tormé, have now passed away.

My grandfather played cornet with John Philip Sousa, my uncle played tuba with the Saint Louis Symphony, and my cousin John Banbridge played saxophone with the *Johnny Carson Show* for years, so you can see that I came from a musical family. We moved to southern California when I was eight years old, and the following year I took up the trumpet. Later on, I also played the trombone, tuba, and mellophone, until in 1954 I switched to the string bass.

I used to listen to Ralph Peña play with Pete Jolly, and the duo sounded so good, I persuaded Ralph to give me lessons. He was also playing with the Jimmy Giuffre Trio, and I would often stay on after my lesson while they rehearsed with Jim Hall, which was a real education. Ralph had a retarded child, which made his home life difficult, but he was the sweetest man, and I didn't realize how much he had taught me until the album with Pete Jolly came out later.[1] Some titles had Ralph on bass and others had me, and it is difficult to tell us apart. I studied regularly with him for about eight months. I also spent a lot of time with Red Mitchell—not studying, just hanging out at his place, where he would play the piano with me on bass. A mutual friend,

Kenny Hume, who was with Patti Page for years, played the drums. Those were great days, and Red was a sweetheart, too, but I was about ten years younger than most of the guys who were associated with the "West Coast School," although I played with all of them at one time or another.

There were a lot of good bass players in L.A. at the time, like Wilfred Middlebrooks, who used to work with Paul Smith, but I haven't seen him around much lately. Bob Whitlock was another great player, who I met when I was working at Shelly's Manne-Hole. He was going out with Ruth Price, who sang with Shelly's group, but he seemed to disappear sometime in the sixties.[2] Don Prell was very good, and he often played with Bud Shank and Claude Williamson before moving to San Francisco, where he was with the Symphony Orchestra for many years. I knew Don well, and he was a really strong player who was into "legit" bass playing, and whenever I visited him in Venice, I could hear him practicing with the bow two blocks away. Carson Smith was wonderful, but he lived in Vegas; I knew his brother Putter Smith better, and he is another fine player who often works with Alan Broadbent.

My first professional experience was with the Skinnay Ennis Orchestra, which I joined when I was nineteen years old. I don't suppose anyone under fifty will remember him, but he was a singer and a bandleader whose biggest hit was "Got a Date with an Angel." He wasn't such a good singer, but it was a fine band, with some Gil Evans arrangements, which unfortunately we didn't play very often. We played at dances, and we had Bill McDougal on tenor, who was a good player, and Fred Otis on piano, who had been in Woody Herman's band, where he and Serge Chaloff were very close; in fact, he was always talking about him. He had a style similar to Jimmy Rowles, and he took me under his wing, teaching me a lot about music. When Skinnay telephoned offering me the job, which paid $60 a week, I had no idea who he was, but my dad knew him and he was very impressed. I remember getting on the bus at the Union building and travelling for about three days out to the Midwest before we did a job. The whole time, I was worried in case I couldn't read the parts, but I was too embarrassed to look at the book until we finally got to the first gig. It was just quarter note, rest, quarter note, rest, etc., etc.; all very easy and no problem. We toured the Midwest and the South, and I was with the band on the road for about six months.

Shortly after I left Skinnay Ennis, Bobby Troup called and asked me to come over, and although he didn't use the word "audition," I knew that's what it was. I used to listen to Bobby when I was in high school because he was one of my idols. Driving over to his place, I was so nervous, I had to keep stopping to go to the bathroom. After the audition, with the beautiful Julie London there as well, Bobby seemed happy, so we started working at Kirkwood's Bowling Alley with Herb Ellis. I had already worn out my copy of

Herb with the Oscar Peterson Trio at Stratford,[3] so to be actually playing with him was a big event for me. Just like Fred Otis, I learned a lot from him, and we were soon off and running. I stayed with Bobby Troup for several years, off and on, and sometimes when we were on the road with Julie London, we had Jack Sheldon with us, who was a scream, especially back then. Once when Julie was ill, Jack did the show for her, and he was so good, he was booked for a return appearance. Unfortunately he brought Joe Maini with him and, needless to say, he wasn't asked back! Of course they were both part of the wild group of jazz musicians that used to hang out with Lenny Bruce.

Joe Maini lived next door to me, and he was such a sweet guy, but he was nuts. He would do *anything*. His apartment overlooked my barbecue in the backyard, and he would shout out, "What are you having for dinner?" If it was something like hamburgers or hot dogs, he'd say, "Oh no you're not!" and he would go down to the store for cigarettes, but he would hide a couple of steaks in one side of his coat and something else in the other side so we could have a *real* barbecue! My other neighbors were Jack Nimitz and Mike Melvoin, who was a wonderful jazz pianist, and every day the four of us would get together and play in Mike's garage. Joe Maini was an excellent lead alto player, who sadly killed himself in 1964. Although it was said to be an accident, he was playing Russian roulette at the time, so I don't know how much of an accident it really was.

Getting back to Bobby Troup, Jack Sheldon would do a couple of numbers with the rhythm section, and then Julie would come out and he would play behind her. Onstage she seemed a little shy, but after the show she was anything but; she would give Bobby a hard time, using real truck-driver's vernacular, if anything had gone wrong during the act. While I was with Bobby, I often went to Sherry's on Sunset Strip to listen to Pete Jolly with Ralph Peña, and when Ralph eventually left to go with Frank Sinatra, I took over. Right from the first night Pete and I clicked musically and socially, and we played at Sherry's for about two years without a drummer, which was really good training. He had such great time that we didn't need one, and when a drummer sat in, it wasn't so good, because our groove was perfect. Eventually Nick Martinis started playing with us, and he was the kind of drummer who puts the frosting on the cake. The three of us have been together now for thirty-five years, and we made an album a little while ago called *The Twenty-Fifth Anniversary*;[4] we lied a little bit!

I was sitting at home one day in 1960 when the telephone rang, and it was Shelly Manne. He was opening his new club, the Manne-Hole, and needed a bass player because Monty Budwig was leaving, and would I mind coming down? Just like Bobby Troup, he didn't say that it was an audition, but that's what it was. I played one tune with the group—Jack Sheldon, Richie Kamuca, and Russ Freeman—and Shelly said, "You've got the gig." We didn't have written parts for the quintet except when Ruth Price worked with us, because she sang a lot of obscure songs, and still does. Russ Freeman had a lot to do with working on the arrangements, although it was pretty much of a cooperative thing between him and Shelly. The routine would be for the group to play a set and, after a break, we would come back to support Ruth. I worked three nights a week with Shelly and other nights with different musicians who came through. The money was $16.50 a night, and I suppose I did about five nights a week at the club, but by this time I had a wife and a five-year-old stepson to support. Shelly Manne was one of the greatest, not only as a person but also as a musician who gave 120 percent on every performance. Even though he was very busy in the studios during the day, he would still be at the club every night, and at the end of the set he would always say, "Do I sound O.K.?" We only made one road trip when I was with the group, and I can't remember all the places we played, but we did play at Steptoe, Idaho, which became my nickname. To this day, whenever I see Conte Candoli, who had replaced Jack Sheldon, he always says, "Hey, Steptoe."

All of these people we are talking about are the nicest people you can imagine, especially Conte. I have never heard anyone say a bad word about him, ever—he and his brother Pete both. I think he is the best jazz trumpet player there is, and playing with him is like being on a magic-carpet ride, which is just how it was with Zoot Sims. I worked with him at Donte's in 1970, and there is a video of it with Roger Kellaway and Larry Bunker where the sound is amazing.[5] The music just flowed, and he was so relaxed and laid back that you couldn't miss. He didn't need a band behind him because he could do it all on his own, and with Zoot it was happy music. I looked forward to going to the club every night, and I hated when it ended, because he would create and you would just go along for the ride, and Conte is the same. I must mention Larry Bunker, because even though he played with Bill Evans for a couple of years, he is still underrated. But in L.A., he is the busiest studio percussionist. He is the greatest timpani player, and really, he is the greatest everything.

Frank Rosolino was someone else that I often played with; in fact, I was raised playing with him. He was a fantastic trombonist and a real comedian who always seemed so happy. I was on a quartet album he made in 1961 for Reprise[6] with Victor Feldman and Irv Cottler, where he plays and sings on every number, but unfortunately it has been deleted. When I was with Sinatra, I talked to some of his people to see if it could be reissued, but now that Reprise has been sold, it would be very difficult. I found out about his suicide from a headline in the morning paper, which just said: "Jazz musician dies." I had seen him a few days before, and he seemed very depressed and strange, and I thought it was because he hadn't been working enough. Frank's life had been tragic because one of his former wives had committed suicide, another one had left him, and his current girlfriend was pretty strange. There was obviously a dark side to Frank that nobody was aware of, and one night when his girlfriend was away, he took a gun, shot the kids, then turned it on himself. One of the children died and the other one is paralyzed; it was all so terrible.[7]

I worked with Roland Kirk at Shelly's Manne-Hole and also with Philly Joe Jones, which was quite an experience. The first time I played with him, he turned to me as we left the bandstand and said, "I am going to make a bass player out of you." At that time none of us used amplifiers and, being young, I used to attack the bass, trying to play as loud as I could. Philly Joe told me to back off a little and relax, which I did, and suddenly it started flowing and I thought: "Wow! I don't have to work so hard anymore." During that period I was wearing out the records of Miles Davis, and I have never heard a better rhythm section than the one he had with Red Garland, Paul Chambers, and Philly Joe Jones. Paul used to solo a lot with the bow, which I never did, because I didn't like the sound. I thought it best to leave that to the "legit" guys who could really get a sound. And anyway, you need a different set-up, because a jazz bass is not really suitable. Of course I make my living these days from playing "legit" music with big orchestras, because that is all there is. I do plenty of jazz for fun, but not to make a living.

Shortly after I left Shelly Manne, I started working for Jim Bowen, who was a big record producer in L.A. He had worked with Frank Sinatra, but at that time he was handling Nancy, and I played on her first big hit, "These Boots Are Made for Walking," which really put me on the map. That little semi-tone figure on the bass seemed to make the record, and as a result I started doing about three pop record dates a day all over town. Nancy recently did a *Playboy* spread, and she is back on the road again, trying to make a comeback. I still see her off and on. Frank was also trying to get a hit at that time, and I made some records with him, but not the good ones, unfortunately. I was on "Strangers in the Night" and "Somethin' Stupid," and whenever I recorded with him, the orchestra would rehearse in the studio from 8 p.m. until 10 p.m., mostly to eliminate copying errors. As you know, the musicians are so good that, if old arrangements are being used that had already been corrected, we would probably make a "take" the first time. Then Sinatra would make his entrance, and when he comes into a room, it is like the president of the United States has arrived, only more so. He would clap his hands, saying, "Right, let's go," and everyone would be on edge because you didn't dare screw up. At the end of each number he would just shout "Next," but he would always be very gracious to the band, because he likes musicians. Many years later, when I toured with him, I found that he doesn't like the accompaniment to change, because being older he latches onto certain things so that he knows where he is. On the other hand, he makes the whole band come alive, unlike most singers, where the band makes *them* sound good. His voice obviously isn't what it was, and he can't always remember the lyrics, but his timing and phrasing are absolutely incredible; he's like one of the great jazz instrumentalists.

During the sixties I recorded with the Everly Brothers, Bobbie Gentry, Elvis Presley, and a lot of other pop stars, and I would go home with a headache because a lot of it was such terrible music, but it was good money. In 1965 I went from making $6,000 to $25,000 a year. I still played string bass, but on the pop records, they used an electric bass in unison, because they wanted the click sound from the Fender and the resonance from the double bass. I worked on the Glen Campbell T.V. show under Marty Paich for a couple of years, and then I did the Carol Burnett show for eleven years, with Peter Matz as conductor, and it was probably through him that I worked with Barbra Streisand. I played on the soundtrack of *Funny Lady*, and she can be difficult because she is pretty tough. She backs it up, though, by being a terrific singer, but she is relentless with whoever is the orchestra leader. Peter was her conductor for a long time, but with Barbra, it was always "Change this, do that." You could end up working on one arrangement for four days until you couldn't stand it anymore. She has gone through a lot of conductors where they just give up and say, "Forget it."

I used to sub in the *Tonight Show* all the time, and Pete Christlieb, Bill Perkins, Ed Shaughnessy, Ross Tompkins, and Snooky Young were all in the band. The only chance we really got to play, though, was when they took a break for commercials. If Tommy Newsom was the leader, it would be a straight-ahead jazz thing, but if it was Doc Severinsen, it would be more rock oriented.

Over the years I have played on the soundtracks for over four hundred films, like *The Graduate*, *Planet of the Apes*, *French Connection*, *Rocky 1* and *2*, *Fabulous Baker Boys*, and *On Golden Pond*, which was written by one of my favorite film composers, Dave Grusin. After the orchestra played the first piece of music, the whole ensemble just stood and applauded Dave because it was so lovely. Something that I am really proud of is winning the NARAS, which is the National Academy of Recording Arts and Science Award, as the most valuable bass player for four years in a row in the mid eighties, the judges being other musicians.

Despite all this commercial activity, I was still playing a lot of jazz. There was a time in the late sixties when I was part of what was virtually the house rhythm section at Donte's, along with Frank Strazzeri on piano and Nick

Ceroli on drums, and in 1968 we recorded a live album there with Art Pepper and Joe Romano.[8] I have played a lot with Buddy Collette over the years, who is a real sweet guy, and I see his name everywhere because he does a lot of commercials as an actor. Bob Cooper was another lovely guy. I know that the jazz world is full of people who aren't so nice, but Buddy and Bob, when he was alive, were two of the nicest people you could meet. Bob was one of the last of the real tenor players, and Pete Christlieb is carrying the torch now. I often work with Pete, and we are currently on *Star Trek* together, although there is no jazz playing on it. Some time ago, a big art dealer who likes jazz got married in L.A., and he asked me to form a band to play at the wedding. I phoned Plas Johnson, Snooky Young, Ross Tompkins, and Jake Hanna, and I call it "The Wedding Band" because that's how it started. We have done several other gigs, and Pete has been on tenor just lately, and he is incredible. His hobby is racing dragsters, which are the cars that have parachutes to stop them. He's well over six feet tall, so he doesn't drive the cars, but he works on them because he is such a great mechanic.

I mentioned Nick Ceroli, who unfortunately died at the age of forty-six just when he was becoming *the* drummer in town. He often worked with Bob Florence, and of course he was with Herb Alpert's Tijuana Brass for years, as were a lot of other jazz musicians, like John Pisano, Bob Edmondson, and Dave Frishberg. I often played with Dave before he moved to Seattle, because he did a lot of studio work until he said to the contractor one day, "Please don't call me for this anymore." Studio work is particularly hard on pianists because of all the sight-reading they are expected to do, and he just felt that he couldn't take it anymore. In 1988 I did a couple of albums with Mel Tormé, and besides being a wonderful singer he is also an arranger who just wants to get the music right. He might step on your toes or hurt your feelings, but the bottom line is that he gets what he wants. The real bottom line, though, is hearing his voice on the monitor back where I play; he sounds absolutely fantastic, just a great musician. If he wasn't so good, you might not put up with his demands, but he covers himself by being such a great performer. He leads a very clean lifestyle, and he doesn't drink at all, so his voice hasn't deteriorated like Sinatra's. He's overweight because he likes to eat, but I don't think eating destroys your brain cells.

I did a concert in Colorado Springs with Stan Getz before he died, together with Pete Jolly and Nick Martinis. On one number Stan said to me, "Just you and me for the first chorus," and I suddenly realized that I am standing onstage with Stan Getz, and it is just the two of us; it was like I had died and gone to heaven! He was a total genius, and he might have been tough in his early years, but he was very nice to me and easy to play for. Gerry Mulligan was another one of the jazz greats from that era, and I played with him when he appeared at Shelly's New Manne-Hole in the seventies, with Dave Grusin, Harvey Mason, and John Guerin. I was also with him when he was a guest soloist with the New American Orchestra in L.A. in 1982, and working with him was fantastic, but he was very straight-ahead and positive. He told you exactly what he wanted, which made him a little scary, but musically it was incredible because nobody played the baritone like that. He was a wonderful player, and I enjoyed working with him very much. In 1982 he wanted me to go on the road with him, but unfortunately the money wasn't right, and I think he was a little offended when I turned him down.

We should talk about my influences, and the first one was Leroy Vinnegar, because the *My Fair Lady* album[9] he did with André Previn and Shelly Manne really turned me on to the walking bass. I have already mentioned Paul Chambers, and of course everyone listened to Ray Brown. Scott LaFaro took the instrument to another level, although I wondered what he was doing when he used to sit in at Sherry's when I was with Pete Jolly. He sounded so far out because he was all over the bass, which was a new thing then, but when you listen to the records he made with Bill Evans, he sounds absolutely marvelous. He was like the John Coltrane of the bass because, after him, guys like Gary Peacock and Chuck Israels started playing in a different way. The best soloist on the instrument was Red Mitchell, although I didn't care for the way he played a walking bass line in the rhythm section, but melodically speaking, as a soloist he was the best. Bass and drum solos are often there to give the pianist a rest, but when Red was playing, it was something you waited for, because his solo was often the highspot of a performance. I *loved* to hear him solo.

I have four instruments, which I use for different types of music. My jazz bass is about one hundred years old, and I bought it from Joe Mondragon about six months before he died. I have an older instrument with the low C extension that I use for "legit" work, and I have another bass that I take on the road, when I am with Sinatra for instance. I also have a plywood bass that I can play out in the sun, which sounds really good; in fact I played it when I was on Mel Tormé's album in Japan.[10]

NOTES

1. Pete Jolly Trio, *The Red Chimney and Sherry's Bar Recordings*. V.S.O.P. 91.

2. After graduate work at the University of California, Bob Whitlock was awarded a Fulbright grant in 1961 to study with Pierre Boulez in Paris for a year. While there he worked with Kenny Clarke, Bud Powell, and Zoot Sims, among many others. Returning to the States he played with Joe Albany, Victor Feldman, Terry Gibbs, and Peggy Lee before spending five years with the George Shearing Quintet.

In 1976, as a result of personal problems, he entered Tuum Est, a therapeutic community in Venice Beach modeled along the lines of Syanon. Some years later he decided on a career change and formed his own successful retail computer business. He retired in 1997.

3. Oscar Peterson Trio, *Live at the Stratford Festival*. Verve 8024.

4. Pete Jolly Trio, *The Twenty-Fifth Anniversary*. Holt HRCD 3303.

5. *Zoot Sims Quartet at Donte's*. Video KJ002.

6. Frank Rosolino Quartet, *Turn Me Loose*. Reprise 960106.

7. Talking about Frank Rosolino in *Meet Me at Jim and Andy's* (Oxford University Press), Gene Lees quotes Roger Kellaway saying, "When somebody cracks four jokes a minute, we all should have known there was something wrong."

8. Art Pepper Quintet, *Live at Donte's*, vol. 1. Fresh Sound CD 8.

9. Shelly Manne, *My Fair Lady*. Fantasy CDCOPD 942.

10. Mel Tormé, *In Concert—Tokyo*. Concord CCD 4382.

Chapter Five

Eddie Bert

Eddie Bert was born in Yonkers, New York, on May 16, 1922, and has a well-deserved reputation of having played with just about everyone in the music business. He has an excellent memory and a written record of every musical engagement he has played, in more than fifty years as a professional trombonist. At the 1998 "Kenton Rendezvous" in Egham, near London, Bert looked back on some of the highlights of his long and varied career.

When I was young, I used to fool around with a tenor sax, and Lester Young was a big influence on me, which is why I try to play "tenor" style on the trombone. I love that feeling he had, which sax players seem to achieve better than anyone, and I particularly liked his playing on those 1936 "Jones-Smith Incorporated" recordings.[1] When I found out that he was in Basie's band at the Famous Door on 52nd Street, I went along to listen. I met Benny Morton there, who had a great knowledge of the trombone, and he agreed to give me some lessons. I used to study with him after the band finished rehearsing at the club. I was there when they and Jimmy Rushing rehearsed "London Bridge Is Falling Down," "Stop Beatin' Around the Mulberry Bush," and "Jumpin' at the Woodside" before their 1938 record date.

Around this time I was playing in a kid's band led by Hal Gill, with people like Shorty Rogers and Manny Albam, who played baritone. They were both neighbors of mine because I lived in Mount Vernon and they lived in the Bronx. I played my first union job with Sam Donahue's band in 1940, and although he liked my soloing, my reading wasn't good enough. "Tak" Takvorian took my place, and that's when Trummy Young sent me to Miff Mole, who taught me how to read. I also used to jam with Herbie Fields at a place called George's near where Sweet Basil's is now. One night Red Norvo and Mildred Bailey came in, and Red asked me to join his new big band, which opened on December 6, 1941, in Armonk, which is about 30 miles north of New York. Of course the next day the Japanese bombed Pearl Harbor. I finally get a steady job and they start a war! We managed to do a twelve-week tour with Jimmy Durante, travelling by train because of gas rationing, but eventually the band got hit by the draft. Red broke down to a small group with Aaron Sachs, Clyde Lombardi, and Specs Powell, and as he needed a jazz trumpeter, I recommended Shorty Rogers, who joined us at the Famous Door.

By 1943 I was getting all sorts of offers from different bandleaders, but I decided to join Charlie Barnet, because Trummy Young was in the band and he had been a favorite of mine since I had heard him with Jimmy Lunceford. Al Killian, Howard McGhee, Buddy DeFranco, and Dodo Marmarosa were all there—it was a wild band. We had two basses for a while, Chubby Jackson and Oscar Pettiford, until one night Chubby told Oscar that they were going down front to do a feature and a dance, which is when Oscar said, "I'm a bass player—bye!" I left Charlie to go with Woody Herman, until I got drafted along with Nick Travis.

After the war I went back with Sam Donahue for a while, but Kai Winding, who was a friend of mine, told me that he was leaving Stan Kenton, who was reorganizing in California. Stan had heard me back in 1942 with Red's group, and as I knew his band was coming to New York to play at the Commodore Hotel and the Paramount Theater, I wrote to him in 1947 and said, "How about a gig?" I stayed with him for about nine months while he worked in the East, but when he started returning to California I dropped off in Chicago, because my wife was expecting our second child. The band was like one big family, and when the baby was born in March 1948, I got a card signed by everyone saying, "Congratulations." While I was with Stan, I roomed with Art Pepper, who was very studious because he wanted to be the world's greatest saxophone player. A little later when he was given a recording contract by Discovery Records, I thought that maybe I could get one, too, so I said, "Hey, I used to room with Art Pepper!" They gave me a contract, and my first date as a leader was in 1952, with Sal Salvador, Harry Biss, and Clyde Lombardi.[2] I asked Clyde who we should use on drums, because if the bass player and drummer don't get along you're in trouble. He recommended Frank Isola, who was great.

When I left Stan's band, I used to visit Nola's Studios, which was on the other side of the street from Birdland. Nola's was where you would meet people and get your gigs, and I also started rehearsing there with what became known as the Miles Davis "Birth of the Cool" nonet. I made four rehearsals, but when I showed up for the fifth, Kai Winding was there. I didn't find out what had happened until about twenty years later when I ran into Junior Collins. He played French horn in the band and he had told Miles that I'd said they were out of tune, which was quite untrue, but Junior liked to stir things up. Anyway, Miles was always very friendly to me after that and never mentioned it. I also rehearsed with Benny Goodman at Nola's when he had a be-bop band with people like Doug Mettome, Buddy Greco, Wardell Gray, Sonny Igoe, and Eddie Wasserman, but it wasn't very successful, and the band folded in 1949. Benny could be tough, but it was work, and I played with him off and on over the years until he did the last T.V. show *Let's Dance*, just before he died.

Also in 1949 I worked with Bill Harris, when he had a group with a three-trombone front line. Milt Gold was the other horn, and we played at the Blue Note in Chicago with Lou Levy, Bob Carter, and Shelly Manne. In 1950 I re-hearsed with another band at Nola's organized by Gene Roland as a feature for Charlie Parker. It was an enormous band with eight saxes, five trombones, eight trumpets, and four rhythm, but Gene was like that; he liked to be different. It became known as "The Band That Never Was" because it never worked; we just rehearsed.[3]

In the early fifties I worked at the Paramount Theater with Buddy Rich's band, backing Frank Sinatra. Frank's career had taken a big dive, so audiences were small, because this was just before he made *From Here to Eternity* in 1953. His voice was sometimes hoarse, and we didn't always know if he was going to show up; it was really weird. Harry Edison, Zoot Sims, and Davey Schildkraut were in the band, and Ava Gardner was there too. I used to ride up in the elevator with her, and even without makeup she looked fantastic.

A little later, in 1955, *Metronome* magazine nominated me as one of the Musicians of the Year, along with John LaPorta, Bud Shank, and Barney Kessel. I figured I would use that title on an album[4] with Hank Jones, Wendell Marshall, and Kenny Clarke, and there is a funny story behind it concerning J. J. Johnson. He wanted to make a two-trombone album for Savoy with Bennie Green, who was unavailable, so he called me, but I was contracted with Discovery, who wouldn't let me do the date. J. J. then called Kai Winding, which is when they made their first album together, and although the name "Jay and Kai" sounds better, it could have been "Jay and Eddie"! Getting back to my album, a month after Discovery refused to let me record with J. J. they went bankrupt, so Ozzie Cadena of Savoy called and asked if I would do a two-trombone album myself, only I would be the only horn because they were going to overdub. Remember that this was 1955, so I didn't know what overdub meant. Anyway, I went to Rudy Van Gelder's studio and put down the basic track with the blowing and added another part later when Rudy figured out how to do it. On "Stompin' at the Savoy" I played open and with a solo tone mute, which was the type of mute Tommy Dorsey used for that commercial sound. When Jimmy Cleveland heard it on a Leonard Feather *Blindfold Test*, he said it sounded like Jay and Kai at their best and gave it five stars. I did get to record with Jay and Kai later, when they did their octet album.[5]

Around that time I was working with Charles Mingus, who I had first met in San Francisco when I was with Benny Goodman. I remember Clyde Lombardi saying that we just had to see this bass player who was at the International Quarter in a group with four basses, and there was Charlie, playing lead bass. When we both got back to New York, I started rehearsing and working with his "Jazz Workshop" along with Art Farmer, John LaPorta, Teo Macero, and Teddy Charles, and I found that as long as you did the right thing, you could get along with Mingus. In 1955 I recorded with him at the Café Bohemia,[6] when he was starting to formulate his ideas, and George Barrow, Mal Waldron, Willie Jones, and I would go to his house, where he would play something on the piano which we had to learn by rote, because he wouldn't write it down. He said that you could get more feeling into a piece when you have it in your head instead of just reading it.

The funny thing is, when Fantasy included the Bohemia material on a twelve-CD box set, there were eleven previously unissued titles, so I called them and asked for a cassette to be made of the unissued material, but they wouldn't do it. They wanted me to buy the whole set for $175, which I really didn't want to do. Eventually they agreed to sell me the box set for $60, and when I checked what I had made on the original date it was $60, so I came out even! I've kept a written record of everything I have ever done, and people often telephone asking if they were on a date and did we get paid? If I was there, I know who was on it and what we played. I also have all my records. I get them when they come out, as you never know when they will be deleted.

While I was with Mingus, I also had my own group playing Monday nights at Birdland as well as at the Café Bohemia, and I usually had Vinnie Dean, Duke Jordan, and Clyde Lombardi, with a variety of drummers like Ed Shaughnessy, Gus Johnson, or Osie Johnson. Osie of course was a great drummer, and for a while he was part of what became known as "The New York Rhythm Section," with Milt Hinton and Hank Jones. My group did an album for Savoy with Joe Morello on some tracks, and it may be Joe's first recording.[7]

In 1954 I recorded with Coleman Hawkins and Emmett Berry.[8] Hawk had just flown in with his horn stored in the luggage compartment, where it gets very cold. At the date, he was oiling his tenor, and I remember the producer complaining that we had been in the studio for forty-five minutes without recording anything because he was fooling around with his sax. I only mention this because there is a good picture of Coleman and me taken at the session by Milt Hinton, and you can see it in Milt's book.[9]

In 1956 I subbed for Jimmy Cleveland in Seldon Powell's group. Seldon and I were good friends, and he was a very busy guy. Years later, he got me into the band for *Ain't Misbehavin* on Broadway, because he was the contractor. The band played onstage, and the music sounded like Fats Waller's band jamming, but it was all written. Everyone had their own part, so if you lost your place, you were hung! I sight-read the show, but the producer, who was Richard Maltby's son, said, "He sounds fine but he's white. It's supposed to be a black show." Seldon just said, "Do you want a prop or do you want a trombone player?" So I kept the job.

I should mention that for most of the fifties, I was also studying for my master's degree in music. Back in 1951 I decided that I really wanted to stay home because I had a family, but it was difficult breaking into the New York scene because I had the reputation of being a road musician, having played in a lot of bands. I had been in the Army, so my wife suggested I enroll at the Manhattan School of Music using the G.I. Bill. At the time it was almost like a jazz school, because some of my fellow students were Joe Wilder, John Lewis, Max Roach, and John LaPorta. While I was there I did some one-nighters with the Sauter-Finegan Orchestra, and I sometimes went out of town with Charlie Barnet. When I was on the road, the school would send me homework to complete, and I finally graduated in 1958. Once I had my degree, contractors knew that I was established in town and unlikely to be going on the road with every band that came to New York, so I started to do a lot of commercial work.

I was still playing in the clubs, and in the late fifties I worked a lot with Gil Mellé, the baritone player, who was scuffling around trying to get gigs and earn a living. One night at the Bohemia we had a pianoless quartet with Tommy Potter on bass, who really took care of business, even though Gil wrote way-out changes on practically every beat, which Tommy had to make. Every now and then he would say, "Can't you guys afford a piano player!" I was on one of Gil's first albums in 1952,[10] which actually helped me get my own contract with Discovery. Eventually he went to California and made a lot of money writing film music, and when I visited him at his home in Malibu, he had four Rolls-Royces, a Morgan, and an Alfa-Romeo. But he is still a New Yorker at heart; he hasn't fallen for that plastic stuff out there! He is a great guy and still into jazz, messing around with a soprano and manzello because he wants to get back into playing.[11] I also often worked with Cecil Payne in those days, and he has a completely different sound to any other baritone player because he sounds as though he is dancing while he is playing. He lives in lower New Jersey, and he is still playing and sounding wonderful, although he has trouble seeing and walking now.

In 1959 I played on Thelonious Monk's Town Hall concert.[12] We had originally met in 1955 when we were guests on Steve Allen's show. When I was packing my trombone away after the broadcast, I heard Monk say to Steve, "What do you mean, scale?"[13] which is when I left, before the knives came out! He asked for me on the Town Hall date as well as a concert at Lincoln Center in 1963.[14]

In 1960 I was working weekends with Elliot Lawrence when he decided to take the band into the pits of some Broadway theaters. We did a whole series of hit shows, like *How to Succeed in Business without Really Trying* with Rudy Vallee, *Golden Boy* with Sammy Davis, and *Golden Rainbow* with Steve and Eydie, and I was always able to take off and put in a deputy if something else came up. Elliot had a fine band, with people like Aaron Bell, Jimmy Crawford, Kenny Burrell, Art Farmer, and Frank Wess, and this lasted until the eighties, which was wonderful, as I could do my commercial work in the daytime and the show in the evening. I also did an album with Elliot called *The Trombone Scene*, with Jimmy Cleveland, Sonny Russo, Jimmy Knepper, Urbie Green, and Willie Dennis.[15] Now Willie had a unique style and sound, playing some notes out of the usual positions and doing something we call "crossing the grain." The trombone has seven positions, and each one has a series of overtones starting with an octave, then a fifth, a fourth, and a third, and as you get higher, the intervals are smaller. If you move quickly from the first to the fourth position, for example, you can play these overtones up high and "cross the grain," which Willie did a lot. I saw him the night he was killed, on July 8, 1965, because we were both in Joe Harbor's bar across the street from Birdland. There was a sailor there who was pretty juiced and kept asking if he could take Willie home, even though Willie didn't want to go. Eventually they left, and the sailor was driving so fast in Central Park that he lost control and hit a tree, sending Willie through the windscreen, killing him instantly.

In the late sixties I worked with Thad and Mel at the Village Vanguard, which I could do after my theater gig, and I did the European tour with them in 1969.[16] That was a great band, but one night Thad had a meeting in the Vanguard kitchen and told us we had to go on the road if the band was going to function, which is when a lot of guys like Snooky Young, Eddie Daniels, and myself left, because we had commitments in town. It was never the same when Thad and Mel split up later on, because Thad knew how to run a band. He was out front, and even though we played the same arrangements every night, they sounded different because he could change things around on the spot. That was something Mel couldn't do from behind the drums.

While I was working in the theaters, I also did the *Dick Cavett Show* for four years, with Bobby Rosengarden, which unfortunately prevented me from taking up an offer to join Duke Ellington for a Far Eastern tour. During the fifties and sixties I worked a lot with Lena Horne, and I was on her album *At the Waldorf Astoria*,[17] which won an award. We had first met back in 1941 at the Café Society, because she was there one night when my friend J. C. Higginbotham persuaded me to sit in with Red Allen's band. Lena was truly amazing, but she was always just one of the guys.

I said earlier that saxophone players like Lester Young were very important to me, and two more influences were Willie Smith, who taught me a lot about phrasing, and Budd Johnson. I used to work and hang around a lot with Budd, who had a great knowledge of music. My early influences on trombone were Trummy Young, Vic Dickenson, and Benny Morton, and my favorite writers are people like Bill Finegan, Ernie Wilkins, and Sy Oliver. I must mention, though, Duke Jordan, who I have worked a lot with over the years, because he is my favorite pianist. He plays great solos that sound like a horn, and when he accompanies you, it is like an arrangement, never getting in the way—just goosing you. He played on my Fresh Sound album, along with Jerry Dodgion, Carmen Leggio, Ray Drummond, and Mel Lewis, and it is one of Mel's last recordings. Mel and I first worked together years ago in Boyd Raeburn's band, and his playing might have seemed laid back, but the time was always going on underneath like a drone—it was fantastic. We called the album *The Human Factor*[18] because there were no electronic tricks or splices, and we did the entire CD in one day, from ten in the morning until five in the afternoon.

I'm still very busy, and in 1997 I did a European tour and an album with T. S. Monk, who is a fine drummer. We did a lot of Thelonious's new material that T. S. had found around the house, and he hired me because I had played with his father. If you hang around long enough, you find that you've played with everyone's father!

NOTES

1. This group featured Lester Young with Carl Smith, Count Basie, Walter Page, and Jo Jones. It was actually a group drawn from the Basie band, and producer John Hammond had wanted Buck Clayton for the session. He was not available, so Carl Smith took his place. These recordings contain two of Young's most famous solos: "Lady Be Good" and "Shoe Shine Boy." *The Lester Young Story*. Properbox 8.

2. Eddie Bert Quintet. Vogue EPV 1097.

3. Some fine photographs taken by Eddie at one of the rehearsals are in Ken Vail's book *Bird's Diary: The Life of Charlie Parker 1945–1955* (Castle Communications).

4. Eddie Bert, *Musician of the Year*. Savoy CD SV0183.

5. *Jay and Kai Plus 6*. Columbia COL 480990 2.

6. *Charlie Mingus Quintet at the Café Bohemia*. Original Jazz Classics OJC 045.

7. Eddie Bert Quintet, *Kaleidoscope*. Savoy SJL 1186.

8. Coleman Hawkins. Jazztone J-1201.

9. *Overtime* by Milt Hinton (Pomegranate Artbooks).

10. Gil Mellé, *The Complete Blue Note Fifties Sessions*. Blue Note 7243. In his notes for the CD booklet, Mellé refers to Eddie as a "lifetime close friend."

11. Gil Mellé was a fine baritone player whose quartet appeared at the first Newport Jazz Festival in 1954, where it was billed as "The most promising new group of the year." He is featured in a 1997 German film documentary on the Blue Note label, which includes reminiscences by Johnny Griffin, Lou Donaldson, and Max Roach, among others.

12. *The Thelonious Monk Orchestra at Town Hall*. Riverside 12-300. In an interview with Bill Crow, Eddie said that prior to the concert the band rehearsed at Hall Overton's apartment on Sixth Avenue. Monk was apparently in another room dancing, and when Hall asked him if he was ever going to play the piano, he said, "When the tempo's right!" This interview was published in *Allegro* by Local 802, Associated Musicians of Greater New York.

13. A reference to minimum payment, or union scale.

14. Thelonious Monk, *Big Band and Quartet in Concert*. Columbia 476898.

15. Elliot Lawrence, *The Trombone Scene*. Vik LX 1087.

16. Thad Jones and Mel Lewis Orchestra, *In Paris 1969*. Jeal RJD 511.

17. Lena Horne, *At the Waldorf Astoria*. RCA Victor LOC 1028.

18. Eddie Bert Sextet, *The Human Factor*. Fresh Sound FSR 5005CD.

Chapter Six

Bob Brookmeyer

I don't know if Bob Brookmeyer has read The Go Between, *but he would surely agree with L. P. Hartley's opening statement that "the past is a foreign country," as he is far more interested in the next project rather than retrospective discussions about former glories. Luckily, when we met at his London hotel early in 1995, Brookmeyer was willing to indulge in a little nostalgia and talk frankly about what he called "the old days."*

I was born in Kansas City, Missouri, on December 19, 1929, and became a trombone player by default, because my father, who had been very encouraging about music, started me on an old clarinet when I was about eight years old. Later on, though, I had problems with my teeth, so I had to change to another instrument. I really wanted to be a drummer, and one summer I worked as a day laborer, theater usher, and all manner of jobs to buy the kit I had picked out. Then a band director appeared at my house just before school started, and I wound up being the new sixth trombone player at Central Junior School, Kansas City. I went to an old German teacher every Sunday morning who spat in my face while he taught me to tongue, but he also wrote music. He wrote marches in a lovely hand, and I saw all these wonderful pages full of handwritten music, which made me think that writing music would be a nice thing to do. In the school band I also played baritone horn, and I learned the fingering by watching the trumpets.

My earliest recollection is listening to the Basie band on the radio, and when I finally heard the band live when I was eleven years old, I knew that was what I wanted to do.[1] I had the same feeling a little later when I was about fifteen and I first heard Debussy's *Nocturnes* and Stravinsky's *Firebird Suite*. I couldn't believe that could be done in music, and as soon as I left high school, I enrolled at the Kansas City Conservatory to study composition. By that time I had an old gutted piano and knew enough to get by, so I studied piano as a minor instrument. There wasn't a lot of work for trombone players, but I was kept pretty busy playing piano, as I was determined to put myself through school and pay my own way. I played jazz piano for people like Wingy Manone, Vido Musso, and Ben Webster, and I also coached some singers. While I was at the Conservatory, I met Urbie Green for the first time, and I did some writing for him when he had a band down South. I was about eighteen or nineteen, and there were rumors that I was going to join Woody Herman, and I remember Stan Kenton calling, but I wasn't ready to go on the road yet.

In 1948 Kai Winding came to Kansas City with Red Rodney, Gerry Mulligan, and George Wallington to play at Tootie's Mayfair. Tootie was famous for once hitting Charlie Parker, and it was here that I first met Gerry, when I sat in with the group. I remember they were playing numbers like "All God's Chillun Got Rhythm" and Red said it sounded like I knew the arrangements. Kai and his wife were very nice to me, and they both came to my house for lunch. I'd had a couple of awful valve trombones, but by the time I sat in with his group, I was playing a Reynolds, which was my first really good horn, and it was then that I decided to concentrate on the trombone. I'm still a frustrated drummer, but I'm getting over it.

By 1950 I was taking all sorts of subjects at the Conservatory, some master's and some doctorate, and I was even teaching there, but things were getting a bit too easy, so I left to go on the road with Orrin Tucker's band. We went to Chicago for three months, which is where I met Red Lionberg, who hardly anyone knows today. He is either dead or crazy by now, but he was a wonderful drummer—just like Mel Lewis, only more loose! I enjoyed playing with him even more than with Tiny Kahn in those days. While we were in Chicago, I organized jam sessions every week at the Aragon Ballroom by telling the manager that we were having a rehearsal for the Tucker band. That's where I met Max Bennett, Tiny Kahn, Lou Levy, Ira Sullivan, and a lot of other Chicago musicians, and I remember Frank Rosolino used to come, as he was in town with Herbie Fields. I left the band to join the Army, which was a six-month mistake on both our parts, and a little later, the Tex Beneke band came through Kansas. Mel Lewis had me sit in for the last set on piano, and Tex hired me straight away. That was in December 1951, and we were on our way to New York, where I left the band and began freelancing around town with people like Claude Thornhill, Woody Herman, and Louis Prima. I also played with Ray McKinley, who had a nice band, playing Eddie Sauter's music, which was quite a challenge for me on piano. I was in Howard McGhee's group with Charlie Rouse and Elmo Hope, and I became fast friends with Pee Wee Russell after we worked together.[2] When I was with

Thornhill, I was playing slide trombone as well as second piano because Claude liked to go home early. This was when I made the complete switch to the valve instrument, because one of the guys in the trombone section had a 78H Conn, which was much too loud for the band, so I sold him my slide, and his name was Ace Laine. Up until then I had been using the slide as well as the valve instrument.

The first time I played with Stan Getz was in December 1952, when we played a week's engagement at the Hi-Hat in Boston with Duke Jordan, Bill Crow, and Frank Isola.[3] Stan was a wonderful performer, and his hero was Al Cohn. If he could have been Al Cohn, he would have been very happy. Jimmy Raney had left the band, and Frank Isola had recommended me because we had been playing together in jam sessions, so sight unseen I went to Boston for a week with Stanley. He didn't audition people. If you couldn't play well, he didn't keep you, but he liked my playing and he wanted me to stay—but I had sort of promised to join Woody Herman's band, which had been one of my dreams. Woody had become interested in me when he heard me play trombone in Chicago, because he thought I sounded like Bill Harris, who of course was one of my idols. I joined them early in 1953, but it was not a good band at that time, so I quit after the first night. I had to stay, though, for about six weeks, until Urbie Green returned, which is when I went back to Stan.

The Getz group worked on the East Coast until May. Then we went to Los Angeles with John Williams and Teddy Kotick to play at the Tiffany club and Zardi's. We'd been using Al Levitt, but he didn't come to California and I can't remember why, so for the Tiffany date we had Richie Frost on drums. Gerry Mulligan and Chet Baker were still at the Haig, and every intermission we used to go there to listen, but eventually we got fired. We kept getting back late, until the Tiffany owner said, "If you like the Haig so much, I think you had better go over there." That is when I left Stan to go back to Kansas City, because at that time I was going through a personal crisis. I had been reading Emerson and Thoreau and I wanted a quiet life. I planned to do a series of jobs I had lined up and save some money so I could buy a cabin in the Ozarks, which is a lake in Central Missouri, and stay there the rest of my life. Stan, John, and Frank Isola, who by this time was in California, kept calling me to come back, which I finally did, and we spent the next three months at Zardi's. Jimmy Giuffre used to sit in with us on Mondays, which was his night off from the Lighthouse. There was just a little corner on the bandstand, and there would be Jimmy, playing his baritone.[4]

While we were at Zardi's, we played a lot with Gerry and Chet after work, and in fact Gerry wanted to add me to his group as a part-time soloist and arranger when he and Chet went on the road. The idea really was for Stan, Gerry, Chet, and me to form a band, although there have been different stories about that.[5] Gerry said that Stan wanted to be the leader, and of course you had two conflicting temperaments with both of them, but whatever the reason, things didn't work out. Chet and I didn't care; we just wanted to play. Gerry had to go away for a while,[6] and after Stan disbanded, I went back to New York. It was then that Richard Bock advised Chet to form his own group, which for Chet was an unwise thing to do at that time. I believe he should have stayed with Gerry for a couple of years, touring and getting some experience of the rest of the world; New York is not Los Angeles.[7]

A little later, around Christmas 1953, Gerry telephoned and invited me to join the quartet he was reforming in California. I was to bring a rhythm section with me from New York, and he particularly asked for Frank Isola, who was an exceptionally good drummer. He had heard Frank with Stan's band, and the new quartet with Bill Anthony on bass rehearsed at a recording studio at Capitol, L.A. We did a concert with the quartet and Gerry's tentet in L.A., followed by a booking at the Blackhawk in San Francisco, and this was the official start of Gerry as a well-dressed, successful bandleader. When he first arrived in California, he just wanted to play and write, but when he went on the road with the quartet, he became a *bandleader*.

When Gerry and I first started working together, he used to make a lot of announcements saying he was insecure as the band did not know the music well enough, but I think he just enjoyed being an M.C., because we were well prepared. I liked the pianoless concept because it set off the linear aspect very well, rather than having to respond to the harmonic situation from the piano all the time. With Stan's group, we were getting known for immediate improvisation or counterpoint, which was something he had never done, because he hadn't had another horn to work with. Gerry and I had the same capacity because we were both writers and knew the right color notes to play. There was a problem, though, as the baritone and trombone are in a similar register, and during the first months I was drinking heavily and I used to quit every night. I knew how good the group had sounded with Chet, and I thought it really needed a trumpet, not a trombone. In other words, somebody higher up, because Gerry and I were so close in sound. One night when we were in New York, I didn't say anything about quitting. I got a telephone call at six the next morning, and Gerry said, "Are you alright?" I said, "Yes, why?" and he said, "Because you didn't quit tonight!" I finally did quit when we were in Paris for the Jazz Fair in June 1954. Gerry was having temperamental problems, and I was not able to deal with explosive anger at that time. We had a big argument at the airport in Paris, and I quit right there on the first night, and I think Frank Isola did too.[8]

After I left Gerry, I went back to New York, where I met and fell in love with a lady from Philadelphia who unfortunately was to become my first wife. We moved out to L.A., where I had a booking for my band at the Haig with Zoot Sims, Kenny Drew, Buddy Clark, and Lawrence Marable, but I left after a few nights because I wasn't happy. We stayed in California during the rest of 1954, while I did some writing, recording, and freelancing, and I subbed for Conte Candoli at the Lighthouse, where Howard Rumsey had the band. Howard was not the best bass player in the history of music, and the newest people had to stand next to him, which is where I stood. At that time I was an unbalanced and unhappy man, because I didn't find the same sense of community spirit in L.A. that I found in New York, where all the jazz musicians lived and worked in a four-block area of Manhattan. I never felt that I belonged in California.

I came back to New York in February 1955 and rejoined Stan Getz, who was organizing a sextet with Phil Sunkel, which was not the greatest idea in the world, but I needed a job. Phil didn't really fit in with Stan and me, although he was a nice writer and an O.K. player, but it didn't seem to work. His cornet playing was a little choppy, with more of a Dixieland base, whereas Stanley and I had a very fluid approach, so I wasn't happy with the group. Eventually Stan disbanded, and I did some small group work with Oscar Pettiford. He and I were good friends, and we did an album called *The Oscar Pettiford All Stars*, with Donald Byrd, Gigi Gryce, and Jerome Richardson,[9] and we also did a T.V. show.

In the summer of 1955 Gerry decided to form a pianoless sextet, and Don Joseph, who was Gerry's favorite trumpeter after Chet, was going to be in the group. He didn't show up for rehearsals, so we started with Idrees Sullieman, Zoot Sims, Peck Morrison, and Dave Bailey. For some reason Idrees struck out, so we got Jon Eardley, who was O.K. We worked a lot on the East Coast, and we also visited Europe, which included a lovely month at the Paris Olympia Theatre in the spring of 1956. Jon left when we got back to the States, and when we eventually did our last engagement in Chicago, Oliver Beaner was on trumpet. Gerry was happy with the sextet, but by then, I had decided to form a band with Zoot, because we wanted more room to play. The sextet was never my favorite group, but I haven't heard the records for forty years, so I may change my mind. Zoot and I had a recording contract with George Wein's company Storyville, but when that didn't come to anything, I went back to Gerry, who was reforming the quartet.

I left Gerry in August 1957 and, during that fall, freelanced with some half-assed bands of my own, with people who are unknown today, but I did use Bill Evans for a while. I really didn't know how to be a bandleader, and I didn't want to be one, but I had to work. By that time Jimmy Giuffre had come to New York with Jim Hall and Ralph Peña, and they were working at the Village Vanguard, which was my neighborhood bar, about a block and a half from where I was living. I was enchanted with the trio, and we all became very good friends and had many happy dinners together. I taught Jimmy how to drink cocktails and gave him a taste for martinis he still has. Ralph was leaving, so he started asking me about joining the group, but I thought it was crazy to have a band without a bass, drums, or piano. Jimmy kept asking and I kept refusing; then one night in late November he came by my apartment unannounced and rang and rang. I'm famous for not answering my door, but when I finally did, he barged in and insisted I have dinner with him. We went to a Spanish restaurant in the Village, and after a long dinner I became the newest member of the Jimmy Giuffre Three. That really was a happy year, and although we didn't realize it and it is not documented on record, we were probably one of the first performing *avant-garde* ensembles. We did a lot of group improvisation, and sometimes when I played piano, it sounded more like Webern than jazz. We did all sorts of free improvisation, plus Jimmy's music, and although I wrote a couple of pieces, I was not writing much.

Gerry's Concert Jazz Band started as a week at Basin Street East in January 1960. We hadn't been in touch during 1958 or 1959, when I had been freelancing in New York as a studio trombone player. Manny Albam had been a great help in hiring me and convincing contractors that I could be a viable member of a studio orchestra, because in those days nobody thought that the valve trombone was worth anything. When Gerry dropped by in early 1960, he asked if I would be interested in writing some music for the Basin Street date. I wrote a couple of arrangements, we had some rehearsals, and that was the beginning of the CJB. We did some recording with the New York band and then went to California, which is where we heard Terry Gibbs's band, with Al Porcino and Mel Lewis. I told Gerry that we had to make some changes, because Terry's band was clearly a better band than ours. I was the hirer and firer, what we call the "strawboss," so after we talked it over I hired Conte Candoli, Buddy Clark, and Mel Lewis, who had been a friend of mine for a long time. We originally had Dave Bailey, but he was not really a big band drummer, and there was nobody like Mel—he was one of a kind. The only track from the New York band that was issued was Bill Holman's arrangement of "I'm Gonna Go Fishin'," and the rest is from the replacements. Gerry's idea was a good one, because he wanted to build the band up from the quartet and have a small brass section—and for me, it was one of the more successful bands. It was probably the only one that I was physically involved in, and I talked Gerry into keeping it, even when he wanted to drop it. I wanted that band to succeed because I felt it was partly my band.

Gerry wasn't writing much, because being a bandleader, player, and writer are three distinct jobs. Although he had started out as a writer rather than a player, by the time the quartet was successful in California, he had become more of a player.[10] He was a wonderful songwriter, but being a big band arranger is a lot of work, so he brought in Bill Holman to do some charts, who wound up playing in the band because we couldn't find a good enough tenor player. Bill did write some, and so did Al Cohn, but I wrote the majority of the music, and later on Gary McFarland contributed some arrangements. Gary came to my apartment, I think it was a "cold" visit, and asked if I would take one of his charts to Gerry. It was a marvelous piece called "Weep," which went very well at rehearsal and was recorded by the CJB. He didn't have a normal jazz background, so he didn't sound like anybody else. Gary was a uniquely gifted man who didn't have enough history to be an imitator, and he became one of our resident composers.

We had Willie Dennis in the trombone section, and he and I loved to work together. We tried to give him all the solo room we could on pieces that suited him, bearing in mind that I was the second banana and featured soloist. Willie was a very unusual player because he didn't seem to tongue at all, and I don't know how he did that, but he was wonderful to work with. Later on when Clark Terry and I had our little band, Clark would be quite happy if I sent Willie in when I had to have a night off. Of course Willie Dennis and Don Ferrara, who was also in the band, came from the Lennie Tristano school, and all his students had a very individual voice. I wish that I had paid more attention to what Lennie was doing, although I remember dropping by at a couple of sessions, but it seemed very scholastic to me. I think that if I had been more mature and a little less of a "good time Charlie," I would have been more interested in Lennie, because I did a lot of playing with other musicians from that school, like Sonny Dallas, Peter Ind, Lee Konitz, Warne Marsh, and Dick Scott.

By the end of the CJB's first year, I was very excited. George Russell had brought in "All About Rosie," and we had a piece from Eddie Sauter, which was not recorded and I can't remember its name, but anyway, I was very much for the band moving on, doing newer music. In the beginning of 1961, my personal life got messed up because I was involved with a very destructive woman, and then Judy Holliday became sick. Her cancer had been diagnosed in the fall of 1960, and when we were on the road, Gerry was flying back every night to be with her, which of course upset him. We all loved Judy. In fact, anyone who knew her loved her very much, but because of these problems there was a dip in the energy level when we should have started 1961 with a big roar. I think also, to a small degree, there was the beginning of a philosophical difference between Gerry and me about where the band should go. At the time, Gerry's personal life was extremely difficult because of Judy's problems, and mine was troubled because I was a troubled man. In 1962 I had an offer to join Duke Ellington's Orchestra, which I deeply regret not being able to do, but I was getting divorced and I needed too much money. By their standards, I was making a lot with Gerry, and they couldn't afford to pay me what I needed for lawyers and ex-wives. If I didn't pay them, I went to jail! Gerry and I started working again with the quartet when we didn't get bookings for the CJB; the band actually became an adjunct to the quartet. The CJB's last job was at Birdland, which was closing down, and we closed the club in grand style in December 1964.[11]

I was now married again, for the third time, to a very nice woman, certainly a far better choice than the prior two, and I was beginning to get interested in a more stable life. Jim and Andy's was our local musicians' bar, and people there were talking about grown-up things like mortgages and investments, which really sounded like something. Clark Terry had joined Skitch Henderson's band on the *Johnny Carson Show*. I also had the offer of a job there, which I turned down because I was asked to write a Broadway musical, so Willie Dennis took my place. That was when I left Gerry, and I was going to bring in Rob McConnell, who had been playing around New York, as my replacement. I auditioned him one night at the Village Vanguard and told Gerry that he would be O.K., and as the CJB had become a dead issue by January 1965, Rob was to join the quartet. Getting back to the musical, Dizzy Gillespie was going to be in the show, and it seemed to be an attractive deal, but I didn't like the songs at all, so I left and rejoined the quartet before Rob McConnell had a chance to play with Gerry. I "unquit."

Later on in 1965 I made one of the worst decisions of my life when I finally left Mulligan to take a studio job on the *Merv Griffin Show*, which was a sort of minor-league *Johnny Carson Show*. I thought previously I had been living in a childlike world and was now joining the adults, but I found out on my first night I had been in the adult world all along. I was now in a world of incompetent, angry children, which television is, so after the first show I went out and tried to get as drunk as I possibly could. My marriage was already in trouble and so was I, although my drinking had not been publicly acknowledged by me at that time. I was a very successful drinker because I didn't appear drunk, but I had a bad alcohol problem and was becoming dysfunctional. I kept busy, and the small group that Clark Terry and I had formed in 1961 was still working. I was also involved with the Thad Jones and Mel Lewis Band, and then, in 1967, Jimmy Giuffre and I discussed the possibility of getting back together again. We rehearsed for a while and did a couple of jobs with Don Friedman, Chuck Israels, and Steve Schaeffer, and Jimmy was serious about the group, but I was not capable of being serious about anything. He really wanted it to happen, because he liked working with me, and I love Jimmy, but I just couldn't get interested, so the group was very short lived.

Inside me, I was an angry child and very unhappy with the choices I had made in life, but I was unable to correct them. I decided to leave New York in September 1968 and went to California, where I met a nice lady who loved me very much.

The seventies were a washout for me. I stayed in California, gradually taking care of my problems, and when I eventually returned to New York in 1978, I found a whole new language had sprung up in jazz, with people like John Coltrane, Dave Liebman, and John Scofield. I decided to rethink, because I hadn't learned anything new in a long time and my approach was now old fashioned. I wanted to do some writing, and I started studying scores and going to a lot of classical concerts. My favorite writers are people like Berio, Boulez, Morton Feldman, Ligeti, Lutoslawski, Shostakovich, and my good friend Earle Brown. Over the next couple of years after Thad Jones left, I became the musical director of Mel's band. I was becoming very experimental and giving them music that was not suitable for them, so by 1982 I had written myself out of Mel's band.

In 1979 Mel and I came over to Europe, and I did my first conducting job in Helsinki. In 1981 I did a four-week tour of Cologne, Helsinki, and Stockholm, and I talked to producers there about writing something for the symphony orchestra. I received some commissions and began doing a lot of experimental work, learning as I went along. Every year I went to Cologne, and it became clear that for what I wanted in my life, Europe was better for me than America, because I had "done" America. I had played all the jazz clubs, concerts, and festivals, and that was no longer what I wanted to do. I wanted to be a composer, study, and learn how to conduct, and eventually, Europe became my musical home to the point where I decided to start a new music school in Rotterdam. Unfortunately that became a dead issue when I lost my partner, who was the president of the conservatory there. However, the recovery from that has been very nice, to the extent that 1993 and 1994 have been two of my busiest years ever, both writing and playing. While in Rotterdam, I found a wonderful young pianist, Kris Goessens from Belgium, who was a student of mine and actually got me interested in playing again. In 1992 Gerry asked me to do the "Rebirth of the Cool" tour, but I was working on my opera and I just didn't have the time. I liked the people involved, and if we had been doing new music, I would have been more interested, but I wasn't keen on recreating something that was done perfectly in 1949.

To some extent it was my wife who persuaded me to accept the post of chief conductor to the Danish Radio Big Band. I had initially declined the offer from Peter Larsen, who is their producer, but she felt I had been teaching and writing too much, all "inside" work. She saw that I was much happier when I conducted, so I have now taken up Peter's offer, and from January 1996 I will be their chief conductor. I have just built a new house in the woods of New Hampshire, so the schedule will now be six months in Europe and six months in America. I have to complete the opera, and I will also be working with my quartet, including Kris Goessens, who is my pianist of choice. I am going to be doing things that are creative and forward-looking and working with people that I enjoy.

After a short break for refreshments, I asked Bob if he had ever been aware of an anti-white feeling from some musicians and critics during the sixties, what became known as "Crow Jim."

With most musicians, it was never an issue. In the fifties, all the jazz musicians lived in a four-block area of Manhattan, where everybody knew everybody. We all loved music, and color might have been important outside of our little world, but in New York we were all brothers and sisters together. Dizzy had Mel on drums, and Basie wanted him, but they were going South so they couldn't take him, and of course Miles had Bill Evans. By 1954 I was on speaking terms with Count Basie, Duke Ellington, and Dizzy Gillespie, and I remember playing piano for Charlie Parker at a rehearsal. If you played well, you were in the club, and it didn't matter what color you were. Even though we were aware of the racial situation, there really was a bond between us that transcended racial barriers. Then in the early sixties, a necessary movement started called Black Power or Black Pride, which unfortunately had a negative side. In 1961, for instance, when Clark and I had our little group with Milt Hinton, Osie Johnson, and Hank Jones, I got flak from some people for being the only white guy in a black band. Young black musicians would stop me in the street and say, "You tell Clark Terry from me that he is an Uncle Tom M-F!" I would reply, "I suggest you tell him yourself, because he has arms like redwood trees and he trains with Archie Moore!" When Gerry formed the CJB, we made a determined effort, for musical and social reasons, not to have an all-white band by hiring Blue Mitchell and Charlie Rouse. Dave Bailey was on drums with the CJB, and of course the quartets had never been chosen by race.[12] We did our best, but Blue and Charlie didn't stay, and Mel Lewis eventually took over from Dave.

The CJB once played a major network television show hosted by Mike Wallace, who can really be a pain. He was very nice in the pre-show warm-up, but during live transmission he said to Gerry, "I see a lot of white faces. How come there are no black faces in the band?" I meanwhile had come up front to do a quartet thing with Gerry, who was nonplussed, not knowing what to say. I pointed to Mel and said, "We've got a Jewish drummer. Is that a help?"

As I said, the Black Power movement was necessary because America had segregation until 1964, and segregation is a form of slavery. I don't think white people will ever accept anyone else as an equal member of society, although given human nature, if the colors were switched and black people had the power, the situation might be the same. I do, however, have more faith in the black race than the white, so possibly there might be an improvement. White men have run the world for the last 10,000 years and made a horse's ass out of it, and my theory now is, on a good day God is a black woman! I had a huge amount to learn from the history of black music, and I certainly wouldn't be able to play if it were not for black musicians. There are, though, certain techniques in so-called "white" European music that you need to learn before you can move on. These skills are not given automatically, and whether you like it or not, we are dealing with music and not sociology. You must have these skills and there are requirements that must be met if you are to successfully function as a player and a writer.

The other problem we have in the United States is political correctness, which cuts out dialogue. You can't sit down and talk honestly with someone because you are afraid of hurting their feelings, but I don't find it solvable, and I don't have time to worry about it. I'm not happy with America and probably wouldn't be with any government I lived under. Among civilized nations, we're eighteenth in health care, but I have to go outside an airport to smoke. I can buy a gun without a problem, but I have to watch where I smoke! The reason I live in the woods in New Hampshire is because it looks like Norway and not America.

There is currently a "back to the future" movement in jazz, which I find depressing. I mean 1955 was O.K., but if you are going back, then try 1946, when Dizzy Gillespie and Charlie Parker were playing; go back to the masters. I would rather play like Dizzy Gillespie and not like someone copying Dizzy Gillespie. As far as my own instrumental influences are concerned, three of the major ones are Al Cohn, Zoot Sims, and Gerry Mulligan. The list of favorite arrangers is long and would include Al and Gerry along with Duke Ellington, Gil Evans, Buster Harding, Fletcher Henderson, Jimmy Munday, Eddie Sauter, Billy Strayhorn, and especially Bill Finegan.

To sum up, while it's O.K. to talk about the old days and I had some good musical experiences then, I enjoy my life now much more. It's more than eighteen years since I stopped drinking, although that sounds negative, but it's like having a new life and I'm doing things that I wanted to do when I was seventeen. I'm very interested in what's going on today and tomorrow, unlike some of my contemporaries who sadly are only happy with what went on earlier in their life. I think I'm playing my best now, although I am not writing my best, but I'm working on it. I feel a great sense of beginning rather than ending.

NOTES

1. On the sleevenote that Bob wrote for his fine 1958 album *Kansas City Revisited*, he enlarged a little on his earliest exposure to the Basie band. "When I was one of the youngest jazz fans in the country, my dad and I would cheat on the parson a Sunday or two and stay by the radio to wait for the fifteen minutes of Basie over KCKN (now a country and western station, bless their souls). Then too, Basie would come through town at the Tower theater five or six times a year and I got to be a real pro at forging passes from school, to catch three shows and two bad westerns before there would be some salt from the home kitchen." The album features numbers associated with the Basie band like "Jumpin' at the Woodside," "Blue and Sentimental," "Doggin' Around," and "Moten Swing." This United Artists LP UAL-4008 is long overdue for reissue on CD.

2. Other musicians Bob played with at this time, while trying to obtain his New York union card, were Coleman Hawkins, Buck Clayton, and Ben Webster. His website also mentions "One memorable night with George Wallington, Pops Foster, and Zutty Singleton—a rhythm section to remember! That period included my first performance with Charlie Parker which was a rehearsal with 'Bird and Strings' subbing for Walter Bishop, and my first ever engagement at Birdland playing piano with my hero, Bill Harris."

3. Music from this engagement has been issued on Fresh Sound FSCD 1014 and 1015—*Stan Getz Quintet at the Hi-Hat, Boston*. There is some confusion about the drummer. The sleevenote says it is Al Levitt, and Arne Astrup's Getz Discography mentions Roy Haynes. However, Frank Isola has confirmed to me that he is on drums.

4. In a 1961 *Down Beat* profile on Brookmeyer by Bill Coss entitled "Strength and Simplicity," Jimmy Giuffre is quoted saying, "That band with Getz and Brookmeyer is my favorite of all the jazz groups I have ever heard." When I reminded Bob of this, his comment was, "Jimmy said that? Bless him."

5. Stan Getz told *Down Beat*, "I am going to the coast and when I return I intend to bring with me Gerry Mulligan and Chet Baker. With guys who can blow as much as Gerry, Chet, and Bob the band should be the end." This was news to Mulligan, who wrote to the magazine saying, "I don't know what Stan has in mind here when he talks about adding me and Chet to his combo, joining me or whatever it is, but it is not for me. For years I stayed in the background and wrote arrangements for many bands. Now in the quartet, I have something that is all mine. I can see no reason for sharing it with anyone."

6. Bob's reference to Mulligan "going away" is explained more fully in the chapter titled "Gerry Mulligan Quartet, 1952–1953."

7. In a 1987 interview in *Crescendo*, Mulligan expressed similar views to Les Tomkins: "Chet had never been on the road with a band and was totally inexperienced. He had no idea what it felt like and it takes some learning."

8. Bob of course was to rejoin Mulligan many times over the years. Frank Isola remained with the group until November 1954.

9. Oscar Pettiford, *All Stars*. Bethlehem BET 6017-2 CD.

10. In a conversation with Nat Hentoff for the album *The CJB at the Village Vanguard* (Verve CD 314 589 488-2), Mulligan said: "So far as my own participation is concerned, my stamp is on the band and I'm the featured soloist, but up to now I have been more of a supervisor of the writing than a very active contributor." In Bill Crow's book *From Birdland to Broadway* (Oxford University Press), he confirms how Gerry would successfully edit other writers' arrangements. Bob would often tell the band, "We're having a rehearsal tomorrow; bring your erasers!"

11. Bob's website says: "We closed the original Birdland in grand style—scotch, cocaine and Santa Claus!" A few months before, in the April 1964 issue of *Down Beat*, Ira Gitler, who was reviewing the CJB at Birdland, said: "If this band cannot work when it wants to, there is something very wrong with the state of music in the United States." The personnel that so impressed him included Thad Jones, Clark Terry, Nick Travis, Brookmeyer, Willie Dennis, Alan Raph, Bob Donovan, Phil Woods, Richie Kamuca, Tony Ferina, Mulligan, Bill Crow, and Mel Lewis.

12. One example will suffice. In 1958 Mulligan was the only Caucasian in the quartet that included Dave Bailey, Art Farmer, and Henry Grimes. This group appeared on a CBS Timex show that was recorded on Radiola Video, MR 1095.

Chapter Seven

Pete Christlieb

Despite his nearly forty years in the business, it is still one of the very best kept secrets in jazz that Pete Christlieb is one of the music's most exciting and inventive tenor players. He has worked with Count Basie, Louie Bellson, Bob Florence, and Woody Herman. When we met in 1999, he was a featured soloist with the Bill Holman band at a party to celebrate Vic Lewis's eightieth birthday.

I was born on March 16, 1945, in Los Angeles. My father was a professional bassoon player at Twentieth Century Fox, and as a youngster I listened with him to Boulez, Schoenberg, Stockhausen, Stravinsky, and Villa-Lobos, because our house was full of classical music. Stravinsky often came over to rehearse with my dad, so it is not surprising that I took up the bassoon and, a little later, the violin. It wasn't until I was about thirteen years old that I first heard some jazz. We had a few Gerry Mulligan Quartet albums lying around the house, and that's when I decided to learn the saxophone, which turned out to be a lot easier than the violin; you press a button and you get a note. When I was about sixteen, I played in a Saturday morning rehearsal band with some other kids my age, and occasionally somebody good would sit in, to show us how the charts should *really* sound. The great Joe Maini once visited and played the lead alto chair, and he was so good, it was frightening. He more or less said, "You follow me, kid, and try to stick close to my ass, because we're going down the road and we're going fast!" Man, what authority. It was just fantastic to play in the section with him.

The first road band I played with was Sy Zentner, who gave me a call when I was about eighteen and flew me to Chicago. Although it was a dance band, they had a lot of nice arrangements, and being the solo tenor, I had the opportunity to play a little bit. Of course I wanted to be like Gerry Mulligan and play in a small group, but before you can do that, you have to pay your dues and go to "boot camp" on the road in a bus, just like everyone else. Sy told me there were also some clarinet parts, so before I left town, I had to take lessons real quick with Russ Cheaver, who was wonderful. He was at Fox with my father and had played many fine clarinet solos in motion pictures over the years, and he was also the lead soprano with the Hollywood Saxophone Quartet.[1] In just three lessons he taught me enough for my chair, which was really "industrial strength" clarinet, where you don't play any lead or any jazz, just a lot of whole notes. Gene Goe, who was the lead trumpet with Basie for a long time, was in the band. The bass player was Jeff Castleman, who had recommended me to Sy. Jeff eventually went with Duke Ellington and married the singer Trish Turner. When we were playing opposite Harry James at Lake Tahoe, I used to sit in with his band when Sy's gig finished, because Harry's last set was a jam session. We stood next to each other, and he was just outstanding. Even though he was a hell of a drinker, he could always function, and he was such a great instrumentalist, he could play every part in the book. Harry was wonderful, and there was a camaraderie in his band rather like a bunch of guys fighting a war.

I was still too young to get into most of the jazz clubs, where you had to be twenty-one because of the drinking laws, but the Lighthouse served food, which gave them a loophole. Teenagers could go and listen, and that's where I asked Bob Cooper for some lessons. It turned out that he lived a block from our house and knew my father by reputation, and although he was not a regular teacher, I went to him for a couple of years for fine-tuning. If Lester Young had lived that long, I think he might have sounded like Coop, because Bob was such a fluent player. He started me thinking about new possibilities and other avenues for improvisation, and we studied the old Nicolas Slonimsky book on scales and melodic patterns that everybody has.[2] If you really listen, you will hear people quoting from that book all the time. You know, the more I listen to Al Cohn and Zoot Sims from those days, the more I realize how much they influenced me, because they were both highly lyrical "Song in My Heart" type players, just like Bob. When I was in New York in the early sixties, I used to visit the Half Note and watch Zoot go through his routine of looking away from the bartender and dropping his empty glass fifteen feet from the bandstand. The guy would catch it, fill it up, and pass it right back up to him. Zoot was a clever guy; he was like the Will Rogers of the tenor. Al was also clever and very funny, and together they were pretty wild. I got to know Al well a few years later at the Dick Gibson Jazz Parties in Colorado, and I told him what a pleasure it was playing with someone I idolized as a child. I used flattery as my opening approach, and it worked!

It was thanks to Bob Cooper that I became one of the Lighthouse All-Stars. He was playing on the *Dean Martin Show* at NBC, so he used to send me to the club as his substitute. I played with Sonny Criss there, and going toe-to-toe with him was like standing in front of a wheat-eater. I mean, he was geared to play with guys like Sonny Stitt, which I wasn't at the time, and I got beat-up pretty good. He was impressed that I was willing to get up on the stand with him, so we became buddies and he was like a father figure to me. I also played a few weeks with Hampton Hawes, who was a sweetheart. And Frank Butler, another genius, was the drummer. This was around 1965, but it wasn't too long before they changed the format and the Lighthouse All-Star era sort of "uglied" away into the sunset, collapsing in a heap of dust.

Soon afterwards, Chet Baker called me for a gig with Terry Trotter, Ray Brown, and Colin Bailey at one of those unattractive little bars near L.A. airport, the Boom-Boom room or some such name. It was a strange part of town, but people were flocking there to hear the great Chet. There was nothing written; he just called tunes and we played. After that, he had another date in Pueblo, Colorado, and he asked me to go with him. If I had been a little older and wiser, I would have asked for the money up front, because at the end of the week I didn't get enough from him to pay my hotel bill, let alone get home. This is what happens when you work for a junkie, so you really have to watch out for yourself. Musically it was the best because he was playing beautifully, but everything else was a tragedy! I did some tunes alone with the rhythm section that I wanted him to play, and after a couple of times he had them down—he had great ears. Anyway, my wife and I had only been married a couple of months, and here we were in this little hotel in Colorado Springs; eventually I had to wire for money to get home, and that was the end of my career with Chet Baker. I think Phil Urso took my place.

I went back to L.A. and got a call from trumpeter Bobby Bryant, who was in town and making a big impression with Gerald Wilson's band. He wanted me for his steady gig at Marty's down on 58th and Broadway, which featured a hot organ and two-tenor group, along with Bobby. This was around the time of the big riot in Watts, and the club was located at ground zero there. I waltzed on over, and the first thing they told me to do was to take the battery out and put it in the trunk so I could start my car after the job. I was replacing Herman Riley for six weeks while he went on the road with Louie Bellson and Pearl Bailey, and the other tenor was Hadley Caliman, who was quite an exponent of the John Coltrane approach. Now I was from the tough "Lockjaw" Davis school, with some Gene Ammons, Coleman Hawkins, and Zoot Sims thrown in, so we went at it like a sword fight in a pirate picture every night! Bobby was on staff at NBC, so he would come in later and get in the middle, saying something like, "O.K., you guys—cool down!" It was a wonderful experience. I learned the technique of how to really work a rhythm section on the bandstand—what to do and what not to do, and if you are going to play more than two choruses on *anything*, you had better have a good reason. That job lasted a couple of years, because when Herman got back, Hadley took off.

In 1966 I was at the Flamingo in Las Vegas, backing Della Reese with another two-tenor and trumpet group. Buddy Childers was the leader, and the other tenor was Jimmy "Night Train" Forrest. Della was a big star, but she was a real sweetheart, and it was fun working for her because she didn't act big time at all—just a great gal and one of the guys. Woody Herman was at the Tropicana, and Buddy used to hang out there all the time, and when our job with Della finished, it was Buddy who recommended me to Woody, because Joe Farrell was leaving. Bill Byrne, who played trumpet and was the band manager, called and asked me to join them at the Chez Club in West Hollywood. I had all the records with Sal Nistico and the '63–64 band, so I was already familiar with the music, and I was like a young lion ready to take on the world—let me have at it! I really roared through the stuff, and Woody was pretty cool. At the end of the first week, we had a party at his house in the Hollywood Hills, which used to be Humphrey Bogart's old place, and he gave us the "Cook's Tour." We got to this beautiful bathroom, which looked like the municipal plunge. It was like a big swimming pool about eight feet deep, and it would have taken about two hours to fill it up. I said something like, "Hell, Woody, what do you need that for?" and he said "To soak a sore ass, kid. Now keep moving and don't loiter!"

The word was that we were going to Europe, and two days before we were due to split, Woody said he wanted to talk to me. I thought that I had been doing pretty well and he wanted to give me a raise, but he told me that I was not going, which was like a harpoon to the old ego. Apparently Sal Nistico wanted to come back, and Woody needed him for his big name and crowd appeal, because he would be a big draw in Europe. The deal in those days with big bands was that if they let you go, they had to give two weeks notice or two weeks pay, and as they were leaving straight away, I was supposed to get the money, which was $300. At the time, everyone was making $150 a week, unless you were on Basie's band, for instance, where some of those guys were on about $500, and Sonny Payne was probably getting $2,500 a week. Woody said to go and see his personal manager, Abe Turchen, and you can guess exactly what happened; I got nothing but a promise. About a week later Bill Byrne phoned from Switzerland and told me that, as soon as the plane landed, Sal disappeared and wasn't seen again.

They had been using some other guy, but Woody wanted me back. Now I had just had a call from one of the trombone players who was booking for

Buddy Rich's band, and he offered me $175, so I told Bill I would come back for $225 clear. In other words, they could pay the tax. He replied, "$225 clear? I'll have to ask Woody." I could hear Woody in the room with Bill saying, "Christlieb that S.O.B.! Stan Getz didn't get $225 clear." Then Bill says, "Well, that'll be fine with Woody!" I rejoined the band in Oklahoma City, and by this time it was a completely different band; everyone had left. Cecil Payne was on baritone, and the other tenors were Steve Lederer and Steve Marcus. With Woody, if you played first tenor, you had all the hip lead parts and the third chair had all the jazz. I was playing second, which was known as "The Bermuda Triangle," where you got nothing. It was the lackluster position in the band, with no fun and no glory. I had no jazz to play except on the last set every night, when I had a couple of choruses of the blues in A-flat on "Woodchoppers Ball." Eventually I told Woody that it was ridiculous, because I had come on the band to blow, so I quit and I never did get my $300!

Around 1970 I had a call from Louie Bellson, who was rehearsing a band down at the union prior to going on the road with Pearl Bailey. He is the nicest man in the world, and I am still working with him thirty years later. Just before joining Louie, I had been working at a club owned by Fletcher Henderson's brother, Horace. He had known Pearl for years, and he gave me a note for her. She always did have an ego like a blowtorch, and when I gave it to her, she just exploded and started shouting at me about taking up her time with something she considered trivial. Louie told her to give me a break, and the next day, she bought me an expensive sweater as an apology. During the tour, every time we had a scene, she bought me another one, and I still have about twenty-five beautiful sweaters from getting beat-up by Pearl Bailey! One night I fell asleep onstage, and she hit me so hard that I fell over and took the rest of the sax section with me, music stands and all! The audience loved it and thought it was part of the act because it looked like the Keystone Cops. Louie told me that when Joe Louis was guesting with them in the fifties, she kept picking on Joe and throwing punches at him. Eventually he said to Louie, "Please tell your old lady to cut it out, because it really hurts when she hits, man. She's got a helluva punch!"

I made the first few rehearsals with Supersax, but I quit very soon because it was so arduous and repetitive. The concept of playing Charlie's solos was beautiful, and when I heard their first record, I was a little envious of the guys who stuck with it, because it took a long time to get it right. It needed a certain personality who would sit down and work hard, but I was not willing to spend that much time. If there had been opportunities to blow, I might have remained, but the guys were so tired from playing about 23,000 notes that, when it reached the point of someone taking a chorus, the saxes needed a rest. That's why Frank Rosolino or Conte Candoli were hired.

In the early seventies I met Warne Marsh for the first time at a rehearsal with Clare Fischer's big band. The tenors sat next to each other, and we shook hands as Clare counted off "Lennie's Pennies." Playing Tristano's line for the first time was like trying to change the fan belt on a car while it is still running. Afterwards, Warne told me that he was using an album of mine as a teaching device for one of his students, demonstrating which series of notes I used moving from chord to chord. He actually told me things about my playing I didn't know I was doing. He was totally unique, and you will never in your life hear anyone play with quite that same chromatic approach. The Tristano method could be tedious and involved, but Warne made it more palatable and less cumbersome by swinging a little harder. I learned different ways of improvising from him, especially with regard to economy and selectivity.[3]

I was on the *Tonight Show* from 1970 to 1990, and it was a great gig with steady money. We made scale, which was $175 per night, plus doubles, although everyone thought we made a lot more because they saw us on T.V. every night. These days, on the *Star Trek* show, for instance, I play clarinet, bass clarinet, flute, and a little tenor, and in one four-hour call, I take home what I used to make in an entire week on the *Tonight Show*. All through those years, I had regular offers to tour with people like Count Basie and Harry James, but I always sent one of my students. I kick myself now for turning down some good offers, but why go on the road when I had a steady gig in town?

I did get to play with Basie in 1983, when Eric Schneider telephoned and asked me to dep for him during the band's weeklong appearance at Disneyworld. Danny Turner and Eric Dixon were in the section, and the first tune every night was "Corner Pocket," featuring me. I had been listening to that arrangement for years, so I didn't have to read it; I just walked up to the microphone and blew the shit out of the solo. On the first night, after I sat down, Basie leaned over to me and said, "What did you say your name was?" I told him again, but he wasn't too good on long names, so he announced every number with, "Ladies and gentleman, Pete's on tenor" or "Now we are going to turn Pete loose on . . . ," etc., etc. He gave me features on everything and, man, I played high, fast, and loud all week and got to hang out with all those great guys. I have a tape of one of the shows, so now I can tell my grandchildren I played with Count Basie.

Over the years I worked a lot with Frank Rosolino, who had a real gift, and we had a wonderful relationship. He was a great trombone player and scat singer, and he swung so hard, it was like playing with another saxophone, because he had such facility. He was also extremely funny, and on the bandstand he could create total, hilarious bedlam. Sometimes the band couldn't play because we were too busy laughing. I knew nothing about his domestic problems, but they were enough to set him off, turning the whole thing into a tragic Italian opera, where everybody dies in the end, leaving everything in a minor key.

I had been working with Bob Florence, but when Bob Cooper passed away in 1993, I took his place on Bill Holman's band, and I have been there ever since. You know, people ask me about "free" jazz, which I have never liked, because there is enough freedom in the legitimate avenues of expression which hasn't been exhausted. Suppose you have eighteen guys together and, after the downbeat, you let them play free. It sounds like they are warming up. Someone has to come in and say, "Stop. Let's get down to business," and that someone would be Bill Holman, who is the leader of the intelligent big band movement. When Warne Marsh improvised, he could put a phrase anywhere between beats one and four and have it resolve twenty bars later in exactly the same place—displacement, in other words. As a writer, nobody can do that better than Bill Holman, and he is also a master of tension and release. He has a wonderful way of building tension and then more tension until you wonder if it is ever going to release, and when it does, the band is like a juggernaut coming out of the pipe with a momentum that is totally elevating. We have a lot of fun playing his music, but I don't know if every little detail is always right, because if concentration is lost for a second, you can slip out of the cog. I always tell anyone new who sits next to me that if he is playing with me, he is almost certainly lost; we all have our own part. There is nobody in the world who can shine Bill Holman's shoes when it comes to writing for a big band.

I have already mentioned some other influences, but Eddie "Lockjaw" Davis was also very important to me because he was so different to everyone else. Nobody could ever copy his incredibly ornate false fingerings, and he had about fifteen for any note you can think of. He was like a trombone with a plunger, only he was doing it on a saxophone. He could get the timbre, the slant, and the growl, swinging and ricocheting off this note and that note, and when he put it all together, he created a sense of excitement that had you on the edge of your seat. I had known him for years, and when we spoke before he died, I gave him a hug and a big kiss and told him how much I loved him and what his playing meant to me. I also listened a lot to the "Tasmanian Devil" of the tenor, the wonderful Johnny Griffin, who plays fast and furious. Sonny Rollins was important too, for his sound and tremendous command of the horn.

I have several tenors, but my favorite is an old 1949 Selmer with a balanced action, and I use a two and a half Rico plastic reed with a wide-open Berg Larsen mouthpiece, which gives me a lot of flexibility and lets me play. A closer lay with a three or four reed needs too much pressure, because it is like trying to get a diving board to vibrate. You have to blow so hard that you run out of air halfway between an idea and completing the phrase. Why work so hard? Phil Woods has a similar set-up to me, as did Al Cohn and Zoot Sims, but there are exceptions like that good old Washington boy, Corky Corcoran. He had a sound like a tree trunk because he used a five reed on his Link mouthpiece, which had a very narrow lay.

You know, you need other interests in life besides playing and rehearsing with bands every day, which is why I have been involved in drag racing for thirty years. They are the cars that do zero to two hundred miles an hour in seven seconds and need a parachute to stop. I used to drive, but now I just build them for my kids to race. Mechanically they need the same preventative maintenance program that an aircraft has, so with the cars and the music, I manage to keep pretty busy.

NOTES

1. Russ Cheaver can be heard on soprano with Frank Morgan, Buddy Collette, and Bob Gordon on a 1954 Lyle Murphy album called *Gene Norman Presents Four Saxophones in Twelve Tones*. Vogue VJD 570-2.

2. Nicolas Slonimsky was born in St. Petersburg, Russia, in 1894 and became an American citizen in 1931. He was the founder and conductor of the Boston Chamber Orchestra from 1927 to 1934. His book *Thesaurus of Scales and Melodic Patterns*, published in 1947, was also studied by John Coltrane and Gigi Gryce, among others.

3. On his Criss Cross release, *Conversations with Warne*, Pete ends his sleevenote essay with this tribute to the tenor man: "Forever his student." Criss 1043 CD.

Chapter Eight

Bill Crow

Bill Crow was born on December 27, 1927, in Othello, Washington. His auto-biography From Birdland to Broadway[1] *is a fascinating account of the life of a jazz musician, and when we met at the Local 802 AFM office on West 48th Street, New York, in 1995, it was soon clear that he has an apparently inexhaustible fund of stories about the jazz world. We talked mostly about his time playing bass with Stan Getz and Gerry Mulligan, but I began by asking him if he knew a lady named Gail Madden, who had been a pianist and a model in California before becoming active in New York jazz circles in the early fifties. She appeared on Mulligan's first album as a leader in September 1951, playing maracas on some numbers, and Gerry has credited her with suggesting the idea of a pianoless rhythm section to him before they left New York for California later that year.[2] When they arrived in Los Angeles, it was thanks to Gail and her previous relationship with Bob Graettinger that Mulligan was introduced to Stan Kenton, who very soon bought some of Gerry's arrangements. She also suggested hiring Chico Hamilton for Mulligan's first quartet, so Gail Madden was clearly a significant, if unseen, influence on his early career.*

I met Gail before I knew Gerry very well, thanks to a drummer friend of mine by the name of Buzzy Bridgford. He introduced us at an apartment in Greenwich Village owned by a lady named Margo, who was apparently a $100 a night hooker and was bankrolling Gail, who wanted to be a therapist and save all the junky jazz musicians in New York. Charlie Parker had agreed to go along with all this and was first on her list. Gail's plan was that, with Margo's money, she would buy a brownstone and start a clinic and all the guys would come and live there so she could straighten them out and get them off junk. Buzzy, who knew all the inside jazz gossip, claimed that Joe Albany, Serge Chaloff, J. J. Johnson, Stan Levey, and Gerry were also going to be involved, but unfortunately for Gail, she had an argument with Margo over money and the whole idea collapsed. Soon after, she and Gerry became a "couple," so we figured that if she couldn't save everyone on her list, she would concentrate on him. She started turning up on his gigs out at Queens, playing maracas, and I remember her being there when Gerry was rehearsing a band in Central Park on the shore of the 72nd Street lake.[3] Around that time they both disappeared from the New York scene, and the next thing we heard was that they were on the road, hitching to California, and we all laughed because that was exactly the sort of wild thing they would do. They made it, all right, and then those wonderful records that Gerry made with Chet Baker started coming out. I was with Stan Getz by then, and Johnny Mandel, who played trombone with us, transcribed some of Gerry's tunes, like "Walkin' Shoes" and "Line for Lyons," because Stan was so keen on the Mulligan quartet sound.

Looking back, I don't think there was any rivalry between Stan and Gerry, because they were both in a "star" position in the jazz world. Getz of course was more difficult than Gerry, and he was devious, which Gerry never was. Stan really was the "golden boy" who never had to make concessions to the commercial world, playing whatever he wanted in the clubs and recording anything he wanted in the studio. He was also a very good-looking guy, and I remember when I met him with his first wife Beverly, who was Buddy Stewart's younger sister, they looked like the beautiful young couple on a wedding cake. He never really did anything bad to me but he took advantage of my good nature as much as he could, although I was so thrilled to be playing with him that I didn't mind at all. I saw him do dumb, ugly things to other people who were his close friends, and I am sure that fooling around with junk exposed an unpleasant underlay in his personality that he managed to cover up most of the time.

I'll give you an example concerning the trumpeter Dick Sherman, and I can tell this story now that he and Stan are gone. Jimmy Raney had left the quintet after Stan had shown up high on a couple of jobs, so Stan hired Dick to come and play with us at Birdland.[4] Dick had been with me on the Thornhill band, and he was a wonderful player, but he was a junky, and everyone knew, including Stan, that he was trying to get clean and break his habit. Anyway, he came down to the club with us and played great all night, and at the end of the gig, Stan paid him off with a little bag of heroin. Duke Jordan and Kenny Clarke, who were in the group, and indeed everyone who knew Stan, had reservations about him as a result of that kind of behavior, because he really knew how to wound people. Everyone loved his fantastic musicianship and sunny disposition when sober, but the other side to his nature had come out too many times. I don't know what went on between him and Clark Terry because Clark would never say anything bad about anybody, but there were two names you could say to him that would ruin his day: one was Cat Anderson and the other was Stan Getz.

I'll tell you a funny story about Stan and Al Cohn, who was very fast and had a wonderful sense of humor. Al was with a crowd in Jim and Andy's, our musicians' bar, and somebody was telling us about the record Stan had just made with Joao and Astrud Gilberto.[5] Joao had been hired for the date because he was in town and he was "hot," and Astrud was with him as his interpreter. When they found out there were English lyrics to "The Girl from Ipanema" and that Astrud could sing a little bit, they thought it would be cute to have her sing a chorus in English. On the recording, Joao sang in Portuguese, followed by Astrud and Stan, but it was too long for a disc-jockey copy, so they cut out Joao's chorus. Apparently Stan telephoned the A and R man the next morning, who thought he wanted to make some sort of a deal for Astrud, who wasn't in on the royalties, but no, Stan was calling to make sure that everything stayed the same. He didn't want her to get any money out of his hit. When Al Cohn heard this, he just leaned back against the bar and with a big grin said, "Well, I'm glad to see that success hasn't changed Stanley!"

Tony Fruscella played with both Stan Getz and Gerry Mulligan for a short while in the fifties, but he didn't stay with anybody very long because he was so introverted that the commercial world, even at its most artistic, was too much for him to deal with. Having to show up at a job on time and be there for a set number of hours was something he found difficult. Red Mitchell was very friendly with him, and he used to say that he could see the poetry in Tony's playing. In the last few years before Red died, he would bring one of Tony's tapes with him if he was booked somewhere like Bradleys. He'd added lyrics to one of Tony's solos, and he would play along with it. He used to tell audiences that too few people knew him because he hadn't been recorded enough.[6]

Pianist Billy Triglia loved Tony and tried to use him on gigs when the job wasn't too heavy. In other words, Billy could cover for him if he didn't show up or was too stoned to play. We were in a club in New Jersey, and one customer in particular liked the way Tony was playing, so he called him over and offered to buy him a drink. Tony's response was, "Well, man, I'm already pretty stoned and the bread's kind of light on this gig, so would you mind just giving me the money?" The club owner overheard and was furious, but that was typical of Tony. Charlie Barnet once fired him because he couldn't hear him, although I don't know why he took the job, because he didn't like to play with big bands. If he couldn't be where he could play softly, he would just forget about it. I sometimes saw Tony or Don Joseph playing with Brew Moore at the Open Door on West 3rd Street. Now Don had worked with Jerry

Wald and a lot of other bands, and he was the same kind of poetic artist that Tony was, but he was very funny, with a wild sense of humor, whereas Tony was much more turned in on himself and tended to get depressed.[7]

Don was supposed to be in the sextet that Gerry Mulligan formed in 1955, because they were old friends from "the street," you know, scuffling around outside Charlie's Tavern or Hansen's drugstore like so many of the guys in the late forties did. All the young musicians would stand on the sidewalk talking in front of Charlie's when they didn't have enough money to buy anything if they went inside. They would be looking for some action, like word of a jam session or a job, because Charlie's had become a sort of clubroom established by musicians from the road bands. Hansen's was the turf of variety actors, comedians, straight men, and hoofers, but it was close to Charlie's, and we knew a lot of nightclub and theater comics because we worked in the same joints—that is when we worked at all. "The" alto player among the young "street" guys was Dave Schildkraut. Of course we knew Lee Konitz from his records, but he didn't hang around with us outside Charlie's, because the Tristano group moved in a separate world. I don't know what happened to Dave, but three or four years ago, Eddie Bert, who is famous for digging people out of the woodwork, arranged for him to come out and play with us. Davey sounded wonderful, but he is very spooky about seeing flying saucers all the time, and maybe he does, but he seems to see them more than anyone I have ever met. He used to live out at Brooklyn, but I have lost track of him.[8]

Getting back to the sextet, for some reason Don Joseph didn't show, so Gerry hired Idrees Sullieman, who knew Peck Morrison. Peck knew Dave Bailey, and I think that is how they all joined the band. Eventually Idrees and Peck had other fish to fry, so Gerry called me, and although I was happy with Marian McPartland's group, I couldn't pass up the opportunity of playing with him along with Bob and Zoot. I had played with Bob Brookmeyer when I was with Stan Getz, and he probably recommended me, since Gerry was looking for a rhythm section who were willing to take the role of accompanists; he didn't want fancy solo players. By now, Jon Eardley was with us and he was always complaining that he didn't get enough solos. Gerry used to say, "I understand how you feel but there isn't very much I can do about it. Being my band and wanting to play, I am going to solo a lot and I have Zoot and Bobby, who are two of my favorite soloists that I love to listen to, but I will give you as much of what is left as possible."

Jon was a wonderful player, but at that time he was messing around with junk, which didn't sit too well with Bobby, who thought he embarrassed us on our first European tour in 1956. We went over to Europe on the *Andrea Doria*, and we were very excited about seeing all these wonderful places and people, but Jon was in a terrible state. Most of the time, he hardly had his eyes open, and he would be sleeping by the window on the train, but Gerry understood, as long as he got himself together to make the job. We ran into places where we followed Chet Baker, whose group was leaving a trail of bad junky vibes around Europe.[9] As a result, we were not welcome in some hotels and we were searched quite seriously on the trains. Of course, the authorities nearly always picked on Dave Bailey to be the one they searched, and he is the straightest guy you can imagine, and always has been. When Jon finally got his act together and moved to Europe permanently, he was a brilliant player for many years. I recorded with him the last time he was in New York with Eddie Bert, Benny Aronov, and Mel Lewis, but Loren Schoenberg hasn't been able to sell the album yet.

After he broke up the sextet, Dave Bailey and I stayed with Mulligan when he reformed the quartet in 1958 with Art Farmer. I remember Gerry had a lot of unanswered mail from fans that nobody seemed to be bothering with, so for the next year until he disbanded again, I answered the letters and became the unofficial spokesman for the group. For our debut album he asked us all to contribute something, so I wrote "News from Blueport."[10] We rehearsed in the studio on the day of the recording, and I had to change it a little because I had written a continuous line without rests, which was very hard for Art to articulate. He asked if I would mind making some alterations, which of course I didn't, and I think that by removing some of the notes we improved the line. I know that Gerry liked the tune because, when he had the big band, he was always saying he wanted someone to do a chart on it.[11] We did a European tour with that group in 1959, and when Art and Gerry went back to the States, Dave Bailey and I stayed in Milan to record with Lars Gullin and George Gruntz on piano. The date came off very nicely and we were all paid, but for some reason the record never came out. I hadn't played with Lars before, but I liked his playing very much. I heard a little of Gerry in him and also a little of Serge Chaloff.

Bass solos in Gerry's pianoless groups could sometimes be a problem because the instrument was unamplified in those days and, in some of the rooms, the resonance of the bass didn't cut through as well as it might. It isn't that Gerry's accompaniment was more assertive than a pianist's would have been, but the timbre of the baritone was so close to the bass that it was sometimes hard for him to stay under my sound. It really depended on the club we were in, and occasionally he would just drop out because he couldn't play softly enough to keep from covering me up. In other locations he would be free to play anything he wanted behind me and I could still hear what I was doing. All the time I was with Gerry, I didn't consider myself much of a soloist, bearing in mind the exquisite company I was keeping, with people like Brookmeyer, Willie Dennis, Art Farmer, Gerry, Jim Hall, Thad Jones,

Zoot, Clark Terry, Gene Quill, etc., etc. When he gave me a solo, I felt as though I was out on the edge, and I didn't have sense enough to play within my capabilities. I was always going for it, and Gerry would hear the beginning of what I was trying to do and, if I missed a note, he would be able to finish my solo for me or complete it as an accompanist by playing a harmony line to what I should have played!

Once in a while, though, I could hear myself as clear as a bell, and I remember playing at a high school gymnasium in Oakland, California, where my solos were so coherent that Gerry and Bob were looking at me—like, where did you come from? It was terrific training because, until I joined Gerry, I never felt there was any restriction on what I did in a solo. Any note that sounded good to me was fair game. But without the piano, Gerry played his harmonies off my bass line, and sometimes he would say, "What are you doing playing my note?" I would ask how it became *his* note, and then I realized he was thinking structurally, as an arranger, expecting me to stay around roots, thirds, and fifths. If I was on a root, he would try to be on a tenth, and being a third an octave higher, he would imply all the notes of the chord in between. If I was playing around the sevenths and ninths, he would expect me to use those notes as passing tones, which meant I had to really start thinking about my solos in a different way that related to him. I would hear what he was doing in his backgrounds and try to turn my bass line in that same direction so that we could be together. It became an interesting game, and if you listen to the records, you can hear both of us listening carefully to each other when we solo. Of course, Gerry heard music from the point of view of a composer and arranger and improvised that way too, so that his solos sounded as though they could have been written.[12]

I came into Gerry's Concert Jazz Band after they completed their European tour in 1960. Some of the West Coast people, like Conte Candoli and Buddy Clark, wanted to go home, so he hired Clark Terry and me to join what was already a very well-broken-in band at the Village Vanguard. Bill Holman had already created a book from the old quartet and sextet arrangements, and all the other New York writers were very excited about the band. Gerry didn't write much original material, but Bobby and Al Cohn were contributing a lot, and Wayne Shorter wrote a chart called "Mama G," which was the one arrangement that wasn't in the style of the band. When Gary McFarland first started writing for us, he sounded very Dukish, but Gerry edited his work so that it sounded more like our band, and I remember Gary saying, "Oh, I see what you want." Johnny Mandel also expanded the music he had written for the film *I Want to Live*, and it was great to play. The *esprit de corps* of the band was so good because it really looked as though it was going somewhere. Gerry had some kind of understanding with Norman Granz where Norman would pick up the losses in the States if he, Norman, could have the recordings and European tours where he could make some money, and with that arrangement, we had a steady job. During that first week at the Vanguard, I couldn't believe how good the band sounded. During intermissions, we would jump off the stand and go in the kitchen to talk about the band until it was time to play again.

When Gerry first put the CJB together, I think he talked to everybody and said, "I have some money from the movies I made,[13] but to get the band started, we have to keep the overhead down as much as possible, so tell me what you can accept as your lowest figure." He paid the guys with families a little more, and speaking personally, I never had any problems with Gerry about money. He was always wonderfully fair, and in fact he used to give me raises without my asking for them.

What was so good about Gerry's band was having someone in each section who was a good riff-maker: Gerry in the saxes, Bobby in the trombones, and Clark in the trumpets. Also, because he didn't want to lose the inside parts, we never got too loud. We tried to keep our dynamic level from very soft to medium loud, rather than medium soft to very loud. He said you achieved the same dynamic effect when you changed volumes like that, and if you didn't get too loud, you saved everyone's chops, and Mel Lewis was the perfect drummer for a band like that.[14] On a job, if we were playing something that was not a structured ballad, we would begin with some kind of written figure for a chorus or two, and then we would start with the solos. If someone was playing well, we would never go to the next written section until we had the cue from Gerry, because he would start improvising backgrounds behind the solo, like he did with the quartet. If the background was simple enough and had a repeat, by the second time around the rest of the saxes would be playing in unison or harmonizing with Gerry; then Brookmeyer or Terry would think of a counter-line, and the brass section would join that. The band might stay behind a soloist for five or six choruses of improvised riffs and it would really get going, and only when it reached a certain level would Gerry give the signal to go into the next written section. For instance, that live version of "Blueport" from the Village Vanguard album was so long that Gerry didn't think he could put it on a record, so he took a big hunk out of it. Those fours and eights between Gerry and Clark went on forever, so he took out some of those, and there were other solos he removed when he found a spot where he could make an undetectable edit.[15]

Gene Allen was the baritone player in Gerry's band, and he was one of the pool of saxophone players, like Phil Woods, Gene Quill, Danny Bank, and Sol Schlinger, who did a lot of studio recordings in those days. He was a wonderful player who didn't get a big reputation outside of the musicians' world because he didn't have a strong ego, but his great skill was in blending with the rest of the section, who loved his playing because he made them feel so comfortable. He seemed to vanish off the scene when Gerry's band broke up, and I don't know what became of him, but a friend saw him on the Upper West Side a couple of years ago and apparently he isn't playing anymore. Gene Quill was our lead alto and clarinet player, and I had first met him on the Claude Thornhill band in 1953. He was a tough little Irishman who loved to drink and was always daring fate, but he was an excellent player, with a raucous approach to the alto. He had all of Bird's stuff down, except that belligerence was something that Bird never had. Bird was a *Pasha* of complete confidence, whereas Gene was a little street fighter. He played the lead clarinet book with Thornhill really well, and the part was written down in the section, not an octave higher like Glenn Miller. Occasionally he would get impatient with Claude if he thought we were playing too many dance tunes—"the go-to-sleep medleys." One night, instead of playing the dance medley on clarinet, he stood on his chair and played lead on alto as wild and loud as he could. Then, before he sat down, he turned round and gave Claude the finger! Claude just laughed, because he loved weirdness and he thought that was really funny.

After that I didn't work with Gene for a few years, although we would sometimes run into each other in Charley's Tavern or Junior's. Then I joined Gerry, and there was Gene again. Bobby Donovan was the second alto on the band, and he idolized Gene, trying to be exactly like him, including the self-destructive parts, and as a result ended up destroying himself with booze. Bobby was a good player, although not the stellar player that Gene was, but with a better role model he might have survived. Gene got on all right with Gerry, but once in a while he would have to calm Brookmeyer down, who used to get indignant when Gene didn't straighten up. Brookmeyer was a big drinker too, but he had a hollow leg. He could drink all day and you would hardly notice it because it didn't seem to be a problem. A lot of the older guys were like that. For instance, Charlie Shavers used to be drunk all the time but still played brilliantly. Our other trombone soloist was Willie Dennis, and we had met around town on a few record dates. I really got to know him on Gerry's band, and he was the perfect contrast to Bob Brookmeyer.

Nick Travis was our lead trumpeter, and he was also a very busy studio player. In New York at that time there was a large group of trumpeters like Bernie Glow, Joe Ferrante, Ernie Royal, Snooky Young, and Nick who knew how to phrase with whoever was on lead so that the section took on the character of that player's conception. For instance, Bernie Glow was a brilliant lead player who had distilled all the best standard phrasing from the Count Basie and Woody Herman bands, and he was very clear about reproducing those qualities. He knew how to telegraph his intentions to the rest of the section so that it sounded as though they had played together all year, even though they may have shaken hands on the stand that day and just seen the music for the first time.

Eventually Norman Granz sold Verve, and he and Gerry had some kind of disagreement. Faced with a summer with only one booking, Gerry couldn't afford to keep the band together, so he disbanded and went back to the quartet, and of course Judy Holliday was ill, but we were not aware of that until later. We worked with the small group unless he could get a couple of weeks in Birdland, when he would reform the CJB and usually do a recording date when it was broken-in again. After we realized that the band was only going to be a "sometime" thing, people started sending in deps when they had a conflict. Al Derisi came in for Nick Travis and Don Ferrara. If Clark Terry couldn't make it, he would send in Thad Jones, and Phil Woods used to sub for Gene Quill. Gerry didn't want to stay on the road all the time anyway, because he needed some personal life, and not having a manager who was out there drumming up business, there were a lot of holes in the schedule. Whenever there were two or three weeks free, Brookmeyer would grab Clark Terry, and they would do their thing at the Half Note with Dave Bailey, Hank Jones, and me. Hank was so busy, he nearly always sent a sub, and after three or four very good players, Roger Kellaway became our steady pianist, and he was wonderful.

Early in 1962 Gerry got some more work, and because Mel Lewis and Dave Bailey were busy, he was looking for a drummer. When he asked me who we should get, I suggested Gus Johnson, who had been one of my favorites ever since he'd sat in with the Terry Gibbs quartet at Birdland in 1954. There were a lot of good players around, but I knew Gus would be great, and I also knew he wasn't playing much, because he had been working as a bank guard.

Bob Brookmeyer has already placed on record that he was drinking heavily at that time, and for a while Gerry tried to keep up with him. He wasn't a good drinker, though, and there were periods on the road when he wasn't happy, because he was drinking too much and feeling lousy, but he wouldn't admit what the problem was. He preferred to blame the lack of support from the rest of the group, or club owners, or his reed—anything but the liquor. He did get over it, and whenever I talked to him over the years, he sounded very happy, and he was playing wonderfully—better than ever.

Dave Bailey seemed to drop out of the jazz scene at about the same time that Gerry finally broke up the quartet in 1965. He had been travelling first class with Mulligan, who had been his main connection to the jazz world, so I don't think he wanted to go back to playing those funky little clubs again. I had already left Gerry, after a disagreement that had nothing to do with music, and had come back to New York, where Kai Winding hired me to work at the Playboy Club. I played there with Walter Norris for the next five years, and whenever Bobby and Clark had a gig at the Half Note, I would take time out to play with them, and usually Dave would be the drummer. Eventually, when he got his flying license back, he started working for F. Lee Bailey, who liked the idea of having "Bailey and Bailey" at the controls of his Lear Jet. Dave became so busy he just stopped playing, and if someone asked him he would say, "I haven't played for so long, I don't want to come out and make a fool of myself."

Billy Taylor persuaded him to become a director of Jazzmobile, and Dave has been so successful that they now have their own building up in Harlem.[16] He has recently had open-heart surgery and is feeling better than ever, but he still won't play the drums. We tried to get him to the Oslo Festival a couple of years ago for a reunion of the Brookmeyer/Terry group, but he wouldn't do it, so we used Ben Riley. Al Grey replaced Brookmeyer, who had a writing commission that was approaching a deadline, and at the last minute Roger Kellaway had appendicitis. Norman Simmons played piano, leaving Clark and me as the only ones from the original group.

We concluded the interview when I asked Bill about that wonderfully evocative photograph on the cover of his book From Birdland to Broadway. *It looks as though he is going home at sunrise after a long night's playing.*

It was taken in the late fifties by Dennis Stock in connection with a book entitled *Jazz Street.* Nat Hentoff made the arrangements and asked if I would mind being photographed walking across Times Square with my bass. Just after dawn on a Sunday, I walked across the street a few times so Dennis could get his shot. I didn't even have a wheel for it in those days, so I carried it on my back, but it came out very nicely. I suppose that story might destroy the romance of the picture, but it does show what often happened—just like Joe Rosenthal's photo of the planting of the flag on Iwo Jima in World War II. The G.I.'s did plant it, but he had them do it again so he could get his picture.

NOTES

1. *From Birdland to Broadway* (Oxford University Press).

2. Gail Madden can be heard in the rhythm section on some titles from *Gerry Mulligan Complete Prestige Studio Recordings 1950–1952* (DRCD 11227). Writing the sleevenote for the quartet's initial Pacific Jazz album (PJLP-1), Mulligan had this to say about her: "I was first made aware of the possibilities of a pianoless rhythm section by Gail Madden, a person who possesses a most refreshing and revolutionary conception of the rhythm section and its function. I agreed with her wholeheartedly as to the misuse of the piano with the rhythm section. To have an instrument with the tremendous capabilities of the piano reduced to the role of crutch for the solo horn was unthinkable. Gail organized and rehearsed a pianoless rhythm section consisting of drums, bass and maracas which she played herself in a swinging, musical way . . . [they] were a breath of fresh air to jaded ears—jaded from overly aggressive drummers and non-listening piano players. I used this rhythm section successfully on many dates in Long Island and New Jersey. This was the birth of the pianoless band."

3. They were rehearsing in Central Park because Mulligan could not afford to hire a studio. Bill Crow took a picture of one of these rehearsals, showing Tommy Allison, Harry Bugin, Allen Eager, Jimmy Ford, Phil Leshin, Brew Moore, and Steve Perlow sitting on their instrument cases with the music spread out before them on the grass. It can be seen in the *Jazz Family Album* 2, published by East Stroudsburg University.

4. In his Stan Getz discography, Arne Astrup lists a Birdland broadcast on *Stars of Jazz*, January 15, 1953. Getz is accompanied by Dick Sherman, Duke Jordan, Bill Crow, and Kenny Clarke, but it does not seem to have been issued commercially. Sherman can be heard to advantage on an Al Cohn and Zoot Sims CD entitled *From A to Z* (RCA 74321), where his playing combines the fire of Jon Eardley with the lyricism of Don Fagerquist.

5. *Stan Getz/Joao Gilberto*. Verve 823 611-2.

6. Red put words to Tony Fruscella's solo on "I'll Be Seeing You" (Jazz Factory JFCD22808). In 1956 he told Leonard Feather that his favorite trumpeters were Donald Byrd, Dizzy Gillespie, and Tony Fruscella.

7. There is very little in print about either Tony Fruscella or Don Joseph, but while researching Bill Crow's career, I had many conversations with John Williams, who worked with Bill in Stan Getz's quintet. For a while Fruscella was part of the group, and John also knew Don Joseph well. This is what he had to say about them: "I loved Tony because he was one of the most gentle and loving little guys. I could sit at the old upright in my New York apartment when he would come by to play and he would absolutely kill you. I think he would have been happier on a flugelhorn because he always played in the lower register of the trumpet, but his lyrical creativity was unsurpassed. His problem was that he was totally out of it all the time, living in another world on the end of the flower stem, quite untouched by 'When does the gig begin?' 'Intermission is over; you are supposed to be up there ready to go,' 'What do you mean, you left your music under the bed at home?' etc., etc. He was not at his best onstage unless he was stoned enough to close it all out, and he couldn't perform on cue, as you can tell from the few records he is on. He always seemed to be stoned on a mixture of uppers and downers combined with alcohol, which made him appear so laid back that you wondered if he was really there at all, but at his best he could play so beautifully.

"One of my dearest memories of Tony is with another trumpeter called Don Joseph. During World War II, when many of the good musicians were in the service, guys that could really play like Don were in great demand, and he played with all the big bands that came to New York, at places like the Paramount Theater in Times Square. The joke became that the bands would change at the Paramount but Don Joseph would still be in the same chair, because he was such an excellent player all the bandleaders wanted him. Unfortunately he took some sort of downhill turn at the end of the forties, possibly through drugs, and he became the bad boy on the block, although he could still play beautifully. He would show up at jam sessions at places like Nola's, and he would be welcome, but he never had a dollar in his pocket. He always seemed to be down and out and on the take, and his reputation became so bad that he couldn't get any work with the bands. He wasn't even allowed in our musicians' bar, Charlie's Tavern, because he had abused the privileges there so much that Charlie would have one of the bartenders throw him out if he tried to get in. He used to come to the front door and shout, 'Hey, Charlie, it's me, Don Joseph. I'm banned from bars and I'm barred from bands!' He and Tony Fruscella were two of a kind, and needless to say they were close friends; they used to hang out and play duets together, and they would go to the same jam sessions. Anyway, the three of us were going to play at a session in Greenwich Village, so we jumped in a cab, and as I was the only one who had any money, and I didn't have much, I just knew that I was going to pick up the tab. But what I remember most is sitting there absolutely enthralled while these two lame-brained but incredibly talented musicians sang two-part Bach fugues all the way to the Village. That was Tony Fruscella and that was Don Joseph."

8. Dave Schildkraut died on January 1, 1998.

9. Chet Baker sat in and played eight numbers with the Mulligan sextet at the Air Force club, Landstuhl, Germany, on March 30, 1956.

10. Gerry Mulligan Quartet, *What Is There to Say?* Columbia CK 52978.

11. "News from Blueport" remained in Mulligan's repertoire until he finally disbanded the quartet in 1965.

12. Bill's modest view of his capabilities was certainly not shared by writers at the time. In a 1963 review of a Mulligan quartet concert in London, Ronald Atkins said in *Jazz Monthly*: "The role of the bassist has become distinctly freer due to Crow's development in the last few years. He gave an extremely striking performance, managing the orthodox time-keeping job with complete certainty and his own solos were just short of exceptional." When reviewing the CJB's performance at Birdland for *Down Beat* the following year, Ira Gitler said: "Bill Crow and Mel Lewis work as a real team and to say that they swing, would be an understatement. Crow's choice of notes is especially keen."

13. In the late fifties, Mulligan appeared and played in three Hollywood movies: *I Want to Live*, *The Subterraneans*, and *The Rat Race*. He also had a non-playing, acting role in the musical *Bells Are Ringing*, where he appeared in a comedy scene with the wonderful Judy Holliday, handling his part with considerable aplomb.

14. In *Jazz Masters of the 50s* by Joe Goldberg (Macmillan), Bill Crow is quoted as saying, "He knows exactly what he wants and he wants a quiet band. He can swing at about fifteen decibels lower than any other band."

15. Al Cohn's arrangement of "Blueport" actually lasts for eleven minutes, which by today's standards is anything but excessive. It is not known if the complete version still exists. On his time with Mulligan, Clark Terry is quoted in *Jazz Masters of the 50s* as saying, "Gerry's a real leader. He respects all the guys and knows how much they contribute, and you feel that you're part of things. He pays well too. He's not like one leader I worked for who used to say, 'I want you guys to remember it's me they're paying to see.'"

16. Jazzmobile is dedicated to jazz performances and education in New York, giving summer concerts in the Bronx, Brooklyn, and Harlem using a mobile stage.

Chapter Nine

Joe Dodge

Joe Morello of course was the longest serving drummer with the Dave Brubeck Quartet. However, it was while his predecessor, Joe Dodge, was in the drum chair that the group first achieved unprecedented success and popularity, overtaking the George Shearing Quintet as the highest-paid group on the jazz scene. Dodge remained with the quartet from 1953 to 1956, and in each of those years, the readers of *Down Beat* and *Metronome* magazines voted for the Dave Brubeck Quartet as the most popular small group in America. Somehow Joe became disillusioned with his playing, and by the end of 1956 he decided to leave the quartet, despite Brubeck's entreaties to stay. This decision has always intrigued me, and in 1992 I met Joe in San Francisco when he kindly visited my hotel to discuss his career. Joe, who is friendly and generous, came bearing gifts in the form of a cassette of an unissued 1955 performance of the Brubeck quartet, together with the latest release from his current group, Swingfever.

Joe Dodge was born on February 9, 1922, in Monroe, Wisconsin, but by 1926 the family had moved to San Francisco. Like many drummers of his generation, his first major influence was Gene Krupa, but he also listened to Jo Jones and Jimmy Crawford, and by the time he was with Dave Brubeck, his particular favorite was Shelly Manne, with whom he became very friendly. During World War II, he played drums in the Coast Artillery band, where he met tenor player Dave Van Kreidt, who introduced him to Brubeck and Paul Desmond. After demobilization in 1946, he worked in dance bands around the Bay area, including a stint with the Steve Sacco big band, which featured Paul Desmond. He followed this with two years in a quintet led by guitarist Nick Esposito, and he also worked in a Dixieland band led by trombonist Jack Sheedy.

Tiring of life on the road, he took a day job working in a bank but still kept in touch with his friend Desmond, who arranged for him to play an engagement with Brubeck's octet as a temporary replacement for Cal Tjader. The octet was playing at the San Francisco Opera House, where they opened the show for Nat "King" Cole and Woody Herman. A few years later, in 1953, when Lloyd Davis decided to leave the group, it was Paul again who recommended Joe to Dave Brubeck. At first he was skeptical about leaving the security of the bank, and as Ted Gioia says in his book *West Coast Jazz*, his first reaction on being offered the job was to say, "You're sure you work steady?" Brubeck apparently told him that they had to fight for a night off, and Joe was soon to see what he meant, because starting in February 1954, they did sixty one-nighters in a row, mostly in colleges.

Joe is intensely self-critical, and looking back on his recordings with Brubeck, he told me that he is only satisfied with his playing on the first two albums he made with the group, *Jazz at the College of the Pacific*[1] and the justly famous *Jazz Goes to College*.[2] Thereafter, he apparently became more aware of what he considered his shortcomings, although these were not apparent to either Brubeck or Desmond, both of whom have been lavish in their praise of Joe's playing.[3]

It was during the making of Paul Desmond's first album as a leader in October 1954 that Joe's doubts about his abilities began to surface. Dave Van Kreidt, who was playing on the date and was also responsible for the arrangements, was apparently quite a dominant personality, wanting Joe to play in a more aggressive, almost "Art Blakey" style. Creating mountains of rhythmic propulsion behind a soloist was totally alien to Joe's concept, because he saw his role primarily as a timekeeper and accompanist. He felt this recording was his "downfall," although on relistening to the album, it is difficult to see what upset him, because as usual his playing is tasteful and swinging. His desire to remain in the background and not interfere with the soloist's line extended to a reluctance to take drum solos. In this, of course, he was the opposite of the virtuoso Joe Morello, who replaced him in the group. Paul Desmond, who surely could have been a successful stand-up comedian, has said that asking Morello to play a drum solo "was like issuing an air travel card to a hijacker!" Joe Dodge's view of Morello's playing is typical of his generous spirit, because he told me that Joe Morello could play more with one hand than he could with two.

In 1956 Joe was in the studios again with Paul Desmond, this time in a pianoless group featuring Don Elliott on trumpet and mellophone. Comedian Mort Sahl, who wrote the sleevenote for the album, has been the innocent cause of confusion to some collectors over the years by humorously referring to the drummer as "Joe Chevrolet." The confusion has now spread to Fantasy

Records, who should know better: on their CD reissue, Joe Dodge is still "Joe Chevrolet."[4]

Joe was unlike many modern drummers, who are almost surrounded by their equipment. His kit was of minimal proportions while he was with Brubeck, being a bass and snare drum, two cymbals, and a hi-hat. A distinctive feature of his playing was the use of a fifteen-inch Chinese cymbal with rivets, which he used on medium and fast numbers. In a recent correspondence Dave Brubeck told me: "The main enjoyment I had from Joe's playing was when he got on that big Chinese cymbal with the rivets. In 1993 I did a telephone interview with one of New York's big disc-jockeys. I called the station because he had just played a 1950s track with Joe Dodge and Bob Bates on bass. He said on the air that this was his favorite of all the rhythm sections I had used in the quartet." The group definitely lost a certain indefinable quality when Joe Morello took over the drum duties. This is not intended as a criticism of Morello, who had a superb technique and an immediately recognizable sound on both brushes and sticks. However, while Dodge and, before that, Lloyd Davis were there, quietly concentrating on time-keeping, Brubeck and Desmond were free to indulge in improvised contrapuntal interplay, which was such a stimulating feature of their early work. Once Morello joined, this unusual neo-baroque approach was heard less and less. Indeed, as the years went on and the need to feature Joe Morello became more pressing, it seemed as though the great Paul Desmond was also heard less and less. He was obviously aware of this, because he once wittily observed, "You can tell which one is me because when I am not playing (which is surprisingly often), I'm leaning against the piano."

In an unpublished interview with Bill Schrickell, who is an expert on the music of Dave Brubeck, Joe said that he was aware of resentment from some East Coast musicians, because of the success of the quartet. However, he remembers a package tour with Duke Ellington, Stan Getz, and Gerry Mulligan in November 1954. One night, Ellington was standing in the wings, watching the Brubeck group at work. The next morning, as they were walking to the train, Quentin Jackson said to Joe, "Man, you really killed Duke last night. He looked out to the stage and said, 'That's the picture of jazz.'" Understandably, Joe has never forgotten just how good that remark made him feel.

In December 1956, unhappy with his own playing, Joe decided to leave the group and full-time jazz altogether. He had listened to the recording of the group's concert at the Newport Jazz Festival earlier that year,[5] and his reaction to his playing was apparently, "Oh God, that's terrible." Once again, Joe is his own severest critic, because the subtle and unobtrusive way he copes with several tempo changes in "Two Part Contention" and "I'm in a Dancing Mood" show him at his very best. He also felt that drummers in many jazz groups were becoming too dominant, and this was a direction he did not want to follow. He lacked sufficient confidence in his playing at the time to continue with the high-profile exposure he was getting with Brubeck, and although the pianist did his best to persuade him to stay, Joe returned home to his family and a day job in San Francisco. He told me that he would not have had the technique to cope with the many time signatures Brubeck featured after Joe Morello joined, although it should be pointed out that Dodge is heard on one of the earliest examples of the quartet playing in two simultaneous time signatures. "Lover" was recorded on *Jazz: Red Hot and Cool*, where the piano, alto, and bass are in 3/4 and the drums are in 4/4. Dodge successfully handles his part and makes a significant contribution to the success of the arrangement.[6]

In 1957 Joe had a chance to return to the jazz spotlight when Stan Kenton telephoned with the offer of a job. Stan needed a temporary replacement for Mel Lewis, but unfortunately Joe decided to turn him down. From 1958 until he retired in 1981, Joe combined working in the liquor business with musical engagements in the evenings. One of these performances was recorded when he played with the Ralph Sutton Quartet, which included trumpeter Ernie Figueroa and Vernon Alley on bass at Squaw Valley Lodge, Lake Tahoe, in December 1959.[7] For the past twelve years Joe has worked around the San Francisco area with a five-piece band called Swingfever, which includes the music of Ellington, Basie, Nat Cole, and Louis Jordan in its repertoire.[8] He kept in touch with Paul Desmond until the altoist's death in 1977, and he still sees his friend Dave Brubeck. He played at Dave's fiftieth wedding anniversary in 1992 at the Claremont Hotel, Oakland, with many of the pianist's former colleagues. On hand were Bob and Dick Collins, Bill Smith, Ron Crotty, Dave Van Kreidt, Wyatt "Bull" Ruther, Gene Wright, Norman Bates, Jack Six, Lloyd Davis, Randy Jones, and Gerry Mulligan, who organized a marathon jam session that carried on into the early hours. Because of problems with deteriorating sight, Joe Morello was unable to attend from his home in New Jersey.

On his time with the Brubeck quartet, Joe told me, "I admire Dave very much and am thankful to him for having me join his group when he did. It was a *great* experience. I can't say enough about Paul, except he was my good friend and I miss him."

The last word on this somewhat unsung percussionist should come from his longtime colleague, the poetic genius of the alto saxophone, Mr. Desmond himself: "Don't ever forget Joe Dodge. A marvelous drummer."

NOTES

1. *Jazz at the College of the Pacific*, recorded on December 14, 1953, was Joe's first concert with the Dave Brubeck Quartet. (Fantasy OJCCD-047-2. In 2002, the balance of this concert was issued by Fantasy on OJCCD-1076-2.) Asked for his initial reactions by Clark Coolidge for *Shuffle Boil*, an arts magazine, Joe said, "I couldn't get over the response, man, because I had been working casuals . . . weddings and things. But now people were asking for my autograph and I'm thinking, what the hell is this? It was a big change for me."

2. Dave Brubeck Quartet, *Jazz Goes to College*. CBS 465682 2. 1954.

3. In a 1976 *Down Beat* interview with Arnold Jay Smith, Dave Brubeck is quoted saying, "Joe Dodge would never get in your way. He was just a drummer that supported you. You never worried about what was coming from either side of you . . . just complete concentration on *you*, which is a very valid approach for a drummer to have. Hard to find a guy who is waiting to smile when the front line plays well. You'd see a grin on his face when he saw somebody start feeling free to play. For example, he would get on that Chinese cymbal and you knew he wasn't going to get off it and play some fill right in the middle of your idea."

4. Paul Desmond, *Quartet and Quintet*. Fantasy OJCCD 7122.

5. *Dave Brubeck and Jay and Kai at Newport*. Phillips BBL 7147.

6. Dave Brubeck Quartet, *Jazz: Red Hot and Cool*. Columbia CK61468.

7. *Ralph Sutton Quartet*. Omega OML/OSL 51.

8. In 1989, Swingfever recorded an album on Wistful Vista SF1.

Chapter Ten

Bob Enevoldsen

Bob Enevoldsen is well known as a member of an exclusive little group, including Bob Brookmeyer, Brad Gowans, Rob McConnell, and Juan Tizol, who have specialized in the valve trombone. What is not too well known is that Enevoldsen once played clarinet with the Utah Symphony Orchestra, and he has also recorded on tenor saxophone. Even more surprisingly, during the fifties when he was recording prolifically on his major instrument, the valve trombone, he was also working as a bass player in the Bobby Troup Trio. This interview took place in May 1998, when he replied on cassette tape to my written list of questions.

I was born on September 11, 1920, in Billings, Montana, but my family, who were all professional musicians, originally came from Denmark. My father and uncle were the first to emigrate around 1908, and on arrival in the States they were carrying a flute and violin, which they had to play for a suspicious government official who thought they were smuggling musical instruments into the country. Dad played the violin and conducted at a local silent movie theater, and there was always music at home, because my sisters were string players and my mother played the piano. I took up the violin when I was five, switching to the trumpet a few years later, with lessons from my uncle. I started playing clarinet and tenor during my second year at the University of Montana because my trumpet chops gave out, and of course my main influence was Lester Young. While I was at college, I also played some bass as a requirement for one of my courses.

I was drafted in 1942, joining the Air Force band in Utah, where I carried on playing clarinet and tenor along with Steve White's father, who also played tenor.[1] After my discharge in 1946, I joined a Kenton-style band in Salt Lake City, still on tenor, and this is when I started playing the valve trombone. The arranger, who was also a trombonist, loaned me one—and being a former trumpeter, the valve trombone came easy, as the fingering is the same. For two years, from 1949, I played clarinet with the Utah Symphony and, thanks to the G.I. Bill, I studied at the university there, where I did a graduate theory course with a tutor who had been a student of Paul Hindemith.

By 1951 I had run out of work, but luckily I met Gene Roland, who was playing in a small band with Vido Musso, and he told me to try my luck in L.A., where there was more happening. I moved there in May 1951 with my wife and two young daughters and, with Gene's encouragement, I started sitting in on the Monday evening jam sessions at some of the local clubs. This is when I met Herbie Harper, Harry Babasin, and Marty Paich, and I played bass, tenor, clarinet, or trombone, whatever was required. It was Gene who got me a job playing bass in Marty Paich's trio at a small bar on Sunset Boulevard called La Madelon Café. The drummer was Billy Wilson, who passed away several years ago.[2] I also played bass with Al Haig in Pomona, which is north of L.A., and when Bobby Troup needed a bassist, someone recommended me. Now I was not a schooled bass player, but I had a good ear for playing the right notes, and I stayed with him until 1959. Bobby was a poet and extremely talented, and he was married to Julie London, who was a really good vocalist. He was also a gentleman and a great guy to work with, and over the years Al Viola, Howard Roberts, and Don Heath all played with us at one time or another.

In 1953 I had a call for the Gerry Mulligan tentet date on valve trombone, and I remember we rehearsed at the Haig before the recordings. The only other occasion I worked with him was some time in the seventies at UCLA when Bob Brookmeyer wasn't available. Bill Perkins was in the band, and I remember Gerry's mother was in the audience. I jokingly said, "What's your mother doing after the show, Gerry?" but he didn't seem to see the funny side of it! The following year I made my first album as a leader with Howard Roberts and Marty Paich, and I played tenor sax and valve trombone.[3] In August 1955 I recorded on valve trombone with Tal Farlow, Bill Perkins, and Bob Gordon.[4] Later the same month, Bob was killed in a car accident while he was on his way to play with Pete Rugulo at a concert in San Diego. We had first met around 1951, when I subbed for Herbie Harper in a group featuring Alvino Rey in a small jazz club in L.A., and Bob was in the band. We had also worked together on an NBC show called *Musical Chairs* with Bobby Troup. He was probably my favorite baritone player, and he was also a fine singer, with a great personality. He was a very likeable guy, and I am sure he was destined for great things. Bob's widow wanted a band at his funeral, so Jack Sheldon, Joe Maini, Jack Montrose, and I played Montrose's arrangement of "Good-Bye," which under the circumstances was almost impossible to perform.

Throughout the fifties I worked a lot at Howard Rumsey's Lighthouse, sometimes subbing for Jimmy Giuffre on tenor but more often playing trombone. The drummer was usually Shelly Manne, although I also played there with Remo Belli, who makes drums now and is probably a millionaire.[5] As you know, I made a lot of records with Shorty Rogers, Bill Holman, Marty Paich, Art Pepper, and Buddy Rich, but I wouldn't say I was first call for those dates, because L.A. was, and still is, loaded with great trombonists. With a wife and now four children to support, I took all the work I could get, including some teaching, and over the years I played a lot with Mel Tormé, who was a good friend and a great talent. I remember after we recorded the 1988 Tokyo album,[6] he and I were backstage while I was waiting to go on with Tex Beneke. He started singing a scat line which I didn't recognize, but it turned out to be my solo on "Carioca" from the Tokyo CD!

In 1958 I appeared in a short film narrated by Bobby Troup called *The Form of Jazz* with the Allyn Ferguson Sextet, featuring Modesto Briseno, who was a fine baritone player.[7] A little later, in 1960, I was in *The Subterraneans* with Mulligan and Art Pepper, although I was having serious embouchure trouble at the time and really needed a dep. André Previn, though, who wrote the music, insisted that I do it. Soon after the film was completed, I moved to Las Vegas and played bass at the Stardust Hotel, until I got lucky when they fired me for swinging too much! My good friend Don Davidson was on baritone in the band, and he is still there in Vegas. He was in the Mulligan tentet with me, and he also worked and recorded with Kenton. After a few months I solved my embouchure problems by altering the mouthpiece, which is when I started playing with Billy Eckstine on both tenor and trombone, and he was a great guy—the best. I was doing some arranging at this time, including a couple of Bobby Troup songs for Kenton's Neophonic Orchestra, as well as a piece for Lionel Hampton. By 1962 I was back in L.A., doing the *Steve Allen Show* with people like Donn Trenner, Frank Rosolino, Jimmy Zito, Conte Candoli, Herb Ellis, and Bob Neel.

In recent years I have done a lot of T.V. work, including the *Woody Woodbury Show* and the *Donald O'Connor Show*. Don is a spokesman for Alcoholics Anonymous and is a really marvelous guy. He is still active, and I worked with him as recently as 1998. Since 1980 I have concentrated on the valve trombone exclusively, because I was not getting enough work on reeds to keep my chops up. I started studying the slide trombone about ten years ago, and the instrument I use is a Holton, which has a slide and valve attachment. It was designed for trumpet doublers, and Maynard Ferguson used to use one. I play a lot with the big bands of Bill Holman, Roger Neumann, and

Jack Sheldon, and of course Jack is a very funny guy, with lots of great gags. One of his opening lines is, "It's so long since I had sex, I can't remember who gets tied up!"

I asked Bob who some of his favorite instrumentalists were, but he preferred not to answer, saying, "There are too many good players. If I left somebody out, I would have to leave town!" He did say that when he relaxed at home, he liked to listen to Bach, Beethoven, Dvořák, and Mozart—an uncontroversial selection that should upset no one.

NOTES

1. The obscure Steve White *junior*, who played clarinet and all the saxes, is a legend within the L.A. jazz community. According to Bob Whitlock, who knew him well, he may have known more tunes than Jimmy Rowles. A good example of his "Stan Getz by way of Lester Young" approach can be heard on Nocturne Records OJCCD-1891-2. The album also features Herbie Harper, and Steve sings his own "My New Jet Plane," which was a minor hit for him.

2. Billy Wilson, who used to teach at Roy Harte's drum shop on Santa Monica Boulevard, is another forgotten figure. He can he heard with Dave Pell and Gerry Mulligan on a live date in 1952 at the Haig, with another equally obscure musician, trumpeter Ted Ottison. Jam Session Records JS 102-B.

3. *The Complete Nocturne Recordings*. Fresh Sound NR3CD-101. This album was given a four-star rating in *Down Beat*, and the reviewer said Bob had a "Pres-based command of the tenor."

4. *A Recital by Tal Farlow*. Verve MGV-8123.

5. Remo Belli married Art Pepper's ex-wife Patti Moore. In Pepper's autobiography *Straight Life* (Schirmer Books), he confirms Bob's estimate of Belli's financial status.

6. Mel Tormé, *A Concert in Tokyo*. Concord CCD 4382.

7. Allyn Ferguson studied with Nadia Boulanger in Paris and Aaron Copland at the Berkshire School. His 1958 sextet recording of *Pal Joey* with the amazingly talented Modesto Briseno on baritone, who was just nineteen years old at the time, is well worth tracking down. Candid Records CS 9030.

Chapter Eleven

Don Ferrara

What is really surprising about Don Ferrara, who worked with major figures like Georgie Auld, Woody Herman, Lee Konitz, Gerry Mulligan, and Lennie Tristano, is that he is not mentioned in any of the standard jazz reference books. Tristano once said that Ferrara had "absolutely everything," but in a long career, despite an earlier attempt by Leonard Feather, this is the first interview he has agreed to give. It took place in 1996, when he replied on cassette tape to my list of written questions.

I was born on March 10, 1928, in Brooklyn, New York. I started playing the trumpet when I was ten years old, and I was the only professional musician in my family. The radio was filled with music every night, broadcasting from clubs and hotels all over the city, and I would listen to Louis Armstrong, Roy Eldridge, Lionel Hampton, Glenn Miller, Harry James, Tommy Dorsey, Duke, Basie, and Woody. I was hungry to hear as much as I could, and I was knocked out by how well the trumpeters played and how different they all sounded.

Jerry Wald had a good commercial band, and it was the first big band I played with for four months in 1945, but he was more of a businessman than a musician and he didn't make much contact with the guys. I left to join Georgie Auld, and along with Diz and Woody, he had one of the best big bands in the country. Al Porcino, who was a great lead trumpeter, was there along with Al Cohn and Serge Chaloff. Al Cohn wrote most of the book, which was very loose and musical, and Georgie was a friendly guy who would hang out with the band. He was a wonderful musician, not at all competitive, and I stayed with him until May 1946, when I was inducted into the Army. That is where I met Red Mitchell, because we were both in the same Army band, and Howie Mann was there too. Howie was a friend of mine from high school, and he was a good drummer who later worked with Elliot Lawrence.

I first met Warne Marsh at this time, and we spent a lot of time playing together and listening to records, which is when I found out about Lennie Tristano. As soon as I was discharged in April 1947, I started studying with him, and right from the beginning he got me into chords, because I didn't know how any of that worked. It was thanks to Lennie that I was able to find my own direction, although I wasn't copying anyone's playing, so there wasn't anything to change. This was really when everything started for me, and I carried on studying with him for a total of fourteen years. 1947 was also the year I started teaching.

1950 was a very busy year for me because I was rehearsing with a band that Gene Roland put together for Charlie Parker. It was Al Porcino who recommended me to Gene, who was organizing an unusual big band with the idea of working and recording with Bird. A couple of weeks before rehearsals, Lee Konitz, Warne Marsh, and I went to hear him at a club out in Queens, and we all ended up on the bandstand with Miles and J.J., who were working with him that night. I really enjoyed it. I had never played in a band as big as Gene Roland's—eight trumpets, five trombones, eight saxes, and four rhythm—and it was unbelievable to hear Bird playing in an eight-man sax section. He was so strong and beautiful, playing lead the way he played everything else, and the feeling and looseness were just wonderful. One of the tunes was "Limehouse Blues," and even though he had thirteen brass in cup mutes behind him, his line and sound cut through everything. I did about two weeks' rehearsals, but I couldn't make the recording with Bird because, once again thanks to Al Porcino, I was called for a record date with Chubby Jackson.[1] Howard McGhee was in the trumpet section with Al and me, along with J. J. Johnson and Kai Winding in the trombones and a very hip sax section of Charlie Kennedy, Georgie Auld, Zoot Sims, and Gerry Mulligan, with Tony Aless on piano and Don Lamond on drums. There was talk of Chubby taking the band out to a new club in Texas, but I didn't go because Red Mitchell had recommended me to Woody Herman, so I started working with the Third Herd in April 1950.

Our first job was a month at Bop City in New York, and we had some wonderful soloists like Milt Jackson and Bill Harris that I really enjoyed listening to. The trumpet section was very strong, and Bernie Glow played most of the lead, although the way the book was written, some of the tunes had the lead split three ways. Being a "Four Brothers" type band, the saxes had most of the solos, but once in a while the trumpets got a chance. On "Route 66" for instance, Woody asked me to write a chorus for the section to play in unison in harmon mutes, which was followed by a solo for Doug Mettome. I arranged for Jeff Morton to take Sonny Igoe's place on the band for three weeks when Sonny got married, and the rhythm section sounded wonderful. Woody was nice to work for and I stayed with the band for fifty weeks, but eventually I left and went back home to Brooklyn to study with Lennie again, and I think that Don Fagerquist took my place.[2]

Over the next few years I was teaching and studying as well as playing at lots of jam sessions around town. Then, in 1955, Lee Konitz asked me to join his group with Sal Mosca, Peter Ind, and either Dick Scott, Ed Levisen, or Shadow Wilson on drums. Billy Bauer sometimes worked with us, and the repertoire consisted of originals by Lee and me, pieces by Lennie, together with some of Bird's lines. It was a great band. I loved the way Lee, Peter, and Sal played, and we had a wonderful time for a couple of years, playing at clubs like Birdland, Café Bohemia, and the Half Note.

The first time we worked opposite Mulligan and Brookmeyer, Gerry said he was so knocked out with my playing that he called me to record with his sextet. I rehearsed with the group in the afternoon of September 26, 1956, and after we took a break and went out for something to eat, we recorded the album later that night.[3] That was the only time I played with the sextet, but a few days later Bill Crow called and said that Gerry wanted me to join the band. I didn't because I was still working with Lee, although I really liked the sextet. The writing was very good, the blend and intonation of the four horns was perfect, and everyone could really blow. The following year I recorded again with Gerry, only this time in a big band, and just about everyone had a short solo.[4] That same year Lee and I were in the studio for Norman Granz, and on "Billie's Bounce" we played Bird's four choruses from memory, because most of the people studying with Lennie were memorizing solos by Lester, Bird, and Roy Eldridge.[5]

One of my students was a good friend of Mulligan's, and Gerry told him to get me to call because he wanted me to join the Concert Jazz Band, which he was organizing. After three months of auditions and rehearsals we played our first gig in January 1960 at Basin Street East. The club was filled every night, and I couldn't believe how many musicians were coming to hear us, as well as film and stage people who were friends of Judy Holliday. I had already met her at the rehearsals, and she was there at the band's first night, sitting next to Dora, my wife, and they were having as much fun listening as we were playing. I remember one night later on at the Village Vanguard, someone was whistling loudly after solos and at the end of every tune, generally having one hell of a time. When we came off the stand I asked Dora who was making all the noise, and she said it was Judy!

Nick Travis played all the lead, and he had good chops and excellent time. He was a fine consistent player with a relaxed feeling, but when we were in Europe he had a loose tooth on the top, right under the mouthpiece. He really had a problem for the last part of the tour, but it wasn't apparent to anyone, and as you can hear on the records, he sounds as full and consistent as always. Gerry already had Brookmeyer, but he wanted another strong soloist in the trombone section, so a couple of months before we left for Europe, Willie Dennis joined us, and he was perfect. I had first met Willie when he was with Elliot Lawrence in 1948, and he was a very good friend of mine. When he left Elliot's band, he moved to New York and started studying with Lennie, and his playing was just beautiful. He had very good chops and great time, with a soft texture to his sound, and despite what you may think, he was not slurring all the time but tonguing very lightly. He was very spontaneous, immediately reacting to what was happening. He was also a very good cook, and if you ate at his house, you ate well. Unfortunately Willie was killed in a car accident in Central Park; Dora and I went to his funeral, which had a closed casket. His wife, Morgana King, told us that on the night of the accident, it had been raining, and the road turned but the driver didn't. He hit a tree, sending Willie through the windscreen.

Gene Quill was a great character, and one of his features in the band was "18 Carrots for Rabbit," which was nearly all alto followed by a short solo from Gerry. One night after Gene finished and Gerry took over, the audience exploded because Gene had played so well. He took an extravagant bow, turned round to the band, giving us a real dirty look, and kissed himself on the shoulder. We just broke up and couldn't play anything, missing a whole bunch of phrases to be played behind Gerry's solo. At the end of the piece, Gerry asked us what had happened. We told him what Gene had been doing and Gerry, shaking his head, said, "I don't want to play after him anymore. Who the hell can play after him!" Which is when we all started laughing again. It was great having Zoot Sims on tour with us because he was so musical. He had great time and a sound that projected a wonderful feeling every time he played. On the subject of sounds, Gerry had the best of any baritone player, and he was extremely melodic. Bob Brookmeyer, too, had a superb sound and time, and they both played piano very well.

It was very easy working with Gerry. He was definite and consistent, so you knew exactly how he wanted his things played, and he always listened intently to the soloists, letting them know how much he dug their playing. We were all friends, and it was a happy band, in fact the best big band I ever played with. Gerry also had a good sense of humor. I remember one night he became angry with some of the audience for keeping time with the band by tapping on their glasses. He walked to the mike and told them he didn't like it and it was costing everyone in the room a lot of money to hear us. Those people got up to leave, and Gerry announced that it would be a good time to play "Walkin' Shoes."

I started working with Lennie at the Half Note in November 1962, and it was the best time I ever had playing. For about a year and a half we did three weeks there every two or three months, and Lennie was just unbelievable; his surprises were endless. I had been listening to him for years at lessons and jam sessions, but to be on a gig with him was something else, because he totally followed through on everything he told his students. He had great time and he was the most melodic player I ever heard. His chords and lines were extremely rich and intense, and I couldn't believe what a great sound he got out of those terrible nightclub pianos. Lennie would ask what tune I wanted to play and at what tempo. He would tap off, and we would just start improvising.

In 1964 Dora and I were busy with the first home that we had bought in New Jersey, and for the rest of the sixties I carried on teaching and making sessions. In 1972 we moved to Pasadena, California, which is where Warne Marsh introduced me to Gary Foster. I started teaching at Gary's studio and did some playing with Gary, Alan Broadbent, and Putter Smith, who are all excellent musicians.

Lennie Tristano was very important to me, as well as being one of my best friends, and I kept in touch with him until he died in 1978. Jeff Morton was a great drummer, and we played together as often as we could until his death in 1996. We have now moved to southern California, just north of San Diego, and because I teach by cassette, we can live anywhere in the country and still keep all my students.

No interview with Don Ferrara would be complete without discussing Roy Eldridge, who had an enormous influence on his playing, and his comments in a 1956 series of articles he wrote for Metronome *magazine are particularly succinct: "Every note Roy played had meaning and life . . . his feelings pushed the valves down, not his fingers." In a recent telephone conversation Don told me, "Roy was the most important trumpeter for me. His time and sound were great. His line was always melodic, and the feeling was always very intense. He had the best chops of all the trumpeters, sounding loose and strong, and it didn't matter what tempo or in what range he played; it was all meaningful."*

I concluded the interview by asking Don to list some of his favorite instrumentalists, singers, arrangers, and bands. His selections are as follows:

Trumpet—Roy Eldridge. Trombone—Bob Brookmeyer, Willie Dennis, and Bill Harris. Alto—Lee Konitz and Charlie Parker. Tenor—Lester Young, Warne Marsh, and Zoot Sims. Baritone—Gerry Mulligan and Lars Gullin. Clarinet—Artie Shaw and Lester Young. Vibes—Milt Jackson. Piano—Lennie Tristano, Sal Mosca, and Bud Powell. Guitar—Charlie Christian, Jim Hall, and Billy Bauer. Bass—Peter Ind and Red Mitchell. Drums—Jeff Morton, Max Roach, and Roy Haynes. Singers—Billie Holiday and Frank Sinatra. Arrangers—Ralph Burns, Neal Hefti, Gerry Mulligan, Bob Brookmeyer, and Bill Holman. Big Band—Gerry Mulligan and Woody Herman. Small Group—Lennie Tristano, Lee Konitz, and Dizzy Gillespie/Charlie Parker.

Don Ferrara's solo abilities are well represented on the albums he made with Mulligan's sextet and the CJB. In 2000 Peter Ind released previously unissued tapes of a 1957 Lee Konitz engagement at the Midway Lounge, Pittsburgh, Pennsylvania, containing four numbers featuring the trumpeter.[6] A particularly good example of Don's work in a small group situation is the L.P. he mentions in the interview, where he and Konitz play Parker's famous solo on "Billie's Bounce." The album allows him to stretch out and really develop his highly individual ideas, and it has the additional advantage of including two of his distinctive compositions, "Sunflower" based on "Yesterdays," and "Movin' Around" based on Tristano's "Pennies in Minor." It is a recording that is long overdue for reissue on CD.

NOTES

1. *Chubby Jackson Big Band.* Fantasy OJCCD-711-2.

2. In Bill Clancy's book on Woody Herman, *Chronicles of the Herds* (Schirmer Books), a June 1950 photograph shows Don Ferrara playing with the band at the Capitol Theater in New York.

3. Gerry Mulligan Sextet. Emarcy Jap 826993-2.

4. Gerry Mulligan, *Mullenium.* Columbia/Legacy CK 65678. In addition to some examples of Gene Krupa and Elliot Lawrence playing Mulligan charts from the late forties, this CD also features six titles recorded by a Mulligan big band in April 1957. It includes a restored Ferrara solo on "Thruway" that had been removed on the original L.P. The CD booklet has some excellent and previously unpublished photographs from the session.

5. Lee Konitz, *Very Cool.* MGV 8209. May 1957. Talking about Ferrara on the sleevenote to Nat Hentoff, Konitz says, "Don is a real improviser and a very complete player—sound, ideas, time. He possesses very cohesive intuition." More recently he told me: "Don was a powerful player and one of the few trumpeters to have some of Roy Eldridge's heat."

6. *Peter Ind Presents Lee Konitz in Jazz from the Fifties.* Wave CD 39. February 1957.

Chapter Twelve

Herb Geller

Herb Geller, who was born on November 2, 1928, is a regular visitor to the United Kingdom, and this interview took place in March 1994 prior to an evening's engagement at the Bull's Head in Barnes. Geller wittily reminisced about a career that has spanned more than forty years, and he had fresh and original observations on people as diverse as Clifford Brown, Art Pepper, Ornette Coleman, Billie Holiday, Benny Goodman, and Stan Getz.

The first well-known bandleader I worked for was Joe Venuti in 1946, when I was seventeen years old and on vacation from Dorsey High School in L.A. We did two weeks at a theater in San Diego, and of course I found him to be a marvelous musician and a real character. Eric Dolphy and I were fellow students at Dorsey High, and we were very good friends, but the best saxophone player at the school was Vi Redd, who played better than either of us. She sounded very soulful and could play Benny Carter and Johnny Hodges solos, note for note, with a nice sound.

I also played with a band run by trumpeter Jimmy Zito off and on for about a year. He was a fine player and a good friend of mine whose claim to fame was that he had been married to June Haver, a big movie star at the time. I remember when the band was playing at a dance hall in San Francisco and every night, after work, we would go to the Filmore district to jam in after-hours clubs. One night we were packing up to go home and a little boy, no more than twelve years old, asked me if I wanted to buy a saxophone and a clarinet. I looked at them and they were both better than mine, and although I was a little wary, I took a chance and paid him the $75 he was asking. The next day I met Bob Kesterton, who was a friend of Charlie Parker's and had played on the 1947 "Lover Man" session with Howard McGhee. I told him that I had bought a sax and clarinet early that morning and he said, "I'm working with a guy who lost

88

his last night!" We both realized what had happened and he said, "If you like, I won't say anything," but I couldn't do that, so Bob gave me the guy's telephone number and it turned out to be Paul Desmond, who confirmed they were his instruments. He came to my hotel to collect them, and this was the first time we had ever met. I mentioned the $75 I had paid, which I would like to get back, and he promised to talk to his insurance company. When he phoned me he said, "They say I shouldn't pay you, but instead I should lodge a police complaint against you!" Luckily he didn't, but a few years later I saw him in New York when he was with Dave Brubeck and I didn't have too much money. He said, "I never did give you that $75," and he paid me, which was nice. I really needed it because I was working out my union card and had very little work.

After meeting him about this stolen saxophone business, I returned to L.A., where Jack Fina was organizing a band to go to New York. I was hired after auditioning, and on the drive to the first engagement in Salt Lake City, I asked who else was joining the band, and someone said, "An alto player from San Francisco called Paul Desmond." I said, "Oh no. I've just had a big experience with him!" Anyway Paul and I were roommates on the tour and became very good friends, and over the years I often saw him. He was a wonderful player—very original, with excellent melodic phrases and a very good harmonic sense. He was also a fine piano player.

In the late forties, Joe Maini and Jimmy Knepper lived in an apartment in New York which became famous for all-night jam sessions. We were all friends from L.A., and Jimmy and I had grown up together, as we were both born there. Joe was born in Rhode Island but moved out with his family when he was about fourteen years old. About a year or two after the Jack Fina trip, I had returned to New York and they had an apartment on the corner of 136th Street and Broadway. It was like a twenty-four-hour jam session, where you could visit at any time and there was always music being played, together with all kinds of nefarious activities going on. The music was wild, and as I could play a little piano, at least I knew the right chords, I would very often end up as the pianist. Once, though, I remember playing "Out of Nowhere" on the saxophone when Charlie Parker walked in, and of course I froze. I turned to the guys and said, "I can't think of anything interesting to play!" Everybody used to go there—Dizzy, Joe Albany, Max Roach, Miles, Warne Marsh, Gerry Mulligan. In fact, if you went to Joe's, you would meet the entire "who's who" of jazz. They had two beds in the middle of the room, and sometimes you would be blowing, and Joe or Jimmy would say, "I've been up for about four days now. I'm going to bed." They would go to sleep and snore and everybody else would still be playing.

I was with Claude Thornhill for about nine months in 1950. I recorded with him in Chicago, and we also made a "Band Short" in L.A. for Universal. These were fillers between movies and usually lasted about fifteen minutes. Med Flory was in the band, and a legendary character by the name of Red Kelly was on bass. What I really wanted to do at that time was to get my union card in New York, but during the six months it took to get it, I was not allowed to work. I did some playing illegally in clubs in Nyack, New York, with people like Tony Fruscella, Red Mitchell, Phil Urso, Bill Triglia, Bill Crow, and Ed Shaughnessy, and we once did a rehearsal which was taped. Years later it was issued on Xanadu Records under Tony's name, but I never did get paid for it.[1]

Anyway, six months to the day after applying, I got my union card and was offered three jobs. I took the one with Jerry Wald because he had a good library of Al Cohn arrangements and Al was to rehearse the band. Jerry played clarinet like Artie Shaw, though not nearly as well, and he wanted me to replace Gene Quill on lead alto, because they didn't get along and Gene didn't have a union card. The band was playing at the Arcadia Ballroom, where there was a strict Local 802 policy for tax reasons. Of course at first there was some resentment, because Gene was very popular with the guys and he was an excellent player, but quite soon I was accepted and everything was fine. Gene, though, was angry at me for taking his job. A couple of years later I had another unfortunate incident with him concerning a studio date with Nat Pierce. I was having dinner with Nat at his apartment, and he had to leave early for the recording. I had my alto with me, as I was going to a jam session, and about a half hour after he left, Nat telephoned to say Quill hadn't shown up and could I get down to the studio straight away. I took a cab, and as I arrived, another cab pulled up and Gene came running in. Nat was waiting and said, "Listen, Gene. Herb is going to do the date because whenever I use you, you're either late or you don't show up at all." Gene of course flipped out and said, "You can't do this" and told me that I was always taking his jobs. I felt bad and told Nat to use Gene, but he wouldn't change his mind, and naturally Gene was very bitter towards me and I can understand why. Many years later, after I moved to Germany, I heard that he was very ill. He had been badly beaten up, could never play again, and desperately needed money for his family. I sent him $100 and received a well-typed letter, signed in barely legible handwriting, "Thank you, Gene Quill." He was a wonderful player.[2]

Another fine altoist from that period was Dave Schildkraut, who was quite superb and was one of the greatest. I don't know what happened, but he just seemed to stop playing and started working for his father, who had a grocery store and didn't like jazz musicians. It was a sad situation because there was no drug or alcohol problem; he was just a nice Jewish boy from Brooklyn who played great alto and fantastic clarinet. He was very creative and original with his own sound, and he had made a recording with Miles. I never heard of him again, but he was one of the best saxophone players I knew, just sensational.[3]

Early in 1952 I married Lorraine Walsh, who was an excellent jazz pianist. She could play every tune in any key, tempo, or style, and she had a very rhythmic feel, so of course she was much in demand as an accompanist. I was with Jerry Wald at the time, but quite soon I had an offer to join Billy May, who was coming to the New York Paramount Theatre, which was very well paid. Willie Smith was the other alto, and to sit next to him was a great thrill for me. I was with Billy May for about five months, and when the band went back to L.A., I took Lorraine with me to meet my parents. We decided to stay, because suddenly L.A. was very promising. There was a lot of jazz going on and general recording activity, as this was the beginning of what the critics were calling West Coast Jazz.

When I first arrived there, I sometimes worked in striptease clubs, because I knew "Night Train" and "Harlem Nocturne," which I suppose qualified me! Lenny Bruce was the comic at several clubs, and we got to know each other real well. He loved jazz music and jazz musicians, so we would hang out together, and sometimes Joe Maini and I would split a job. If I had a jazz gig, he would cover for me at the strip club, and *vice versa*. It was a wild scene, and all three of us were very close. Later on I worked with Lenny at an infamous burlesque club called Duffy's Gaiety near Santa Monica Boulevard. He was the M.C., his wife Honey Harlow was stripping, and I was the bandleader, with Lorraine on piano. We also had different drummers at various times, like Philly Joe Jones and Lawrence Marable. Philly Joe became very tight with Lenny, who taught him his Dracula routine, which Philly Joe recorded as "Blues for Dracula." During the drum solo, he did a monologue imitating Lenny imitating Bela Lugosi. Jack Sheldon was there every night, because Lenny was really infamous then, not quite a star yet, but "in" to the real hip people. Bob Hope, Hedy Lamarr, Ernie Kovacs, and a lot of movie people came, and I remember Bing Crosby's son Gary used to date the girls. Someone should write the story of Duffy's Gaiety, because every night was an adventure.[4]

I played a lot with Chet Baker, and we got along real well. We made an album together in 1953 with Bob Gordon and Jack Montrose, and despite what you hear, Chet could read music, although he was not a sight-reader. After playing the part through slowly a few times, he could play it perfectly. In fact, nobody could play it better. Early in 1953, when he and Gerry Mulligan were at the Haig, Gerry eloped with a waitress from the club and Chet asked for me, because he needed another horn in the quartet to keep working. We played for about three weeks, until Gerry got back from his honeymoon, by which time he was probably divorced already!

Bob Gordon was a wonderful baritone player who was just establishing himself when he was killed in an automobile accident. In 1988, when I was in New York for a recording session with Benny Carter, I met a young man who said, "You knew my stepfather, Bob Gordon." The youngster played alto, and he played very well. I saw Jack Montrose as recently as 1992 in Las Vegas, where he and his wife, who is a violinist, work in the shows. He is a dear friend and I like him very much personally, but jazz-wise, I don't know what happened. He is semi-retired now, but for a long time he was writing classical music. He studied the twelve-tone system and has written lots of twelve-tone music that will never be played, and he knows it will never be played. But he owns his own house, has a lovely wife, and they are O.K. in Vegas.

In the mid fifties, Lorraine and I would often play Tuesday nights at Zardi's. Tuesday was the off-night for the main visiting attraction who would play the rest of the week there. Of course the management left the star's name outside all week, and people would come up to me thinking I was Dave Brubeck. One time, I swear to God someone said, "You are Miles Davis, aren't you?" He was there for the other six nights, and they mistook a white saxophone player for Miles Davis. That's how much they knew about jazz.

In 1954 I recorded with Clifford Brown and Dinah Washington.[5] We were all under contract to Mercury, who wanted to use several of their artists in a jam-session setting with a live audience, rather like "Jazz at the Philharmonic." The highlight for me was playing with Clifford, who was a marvelous, extraordinary human being and musician. He was one of the nicest people you could meet, and a complete "natural" who could play anything. Rather like Chet, he could pick up any instrument and fool around for a while, and then play it real well. I remember once when Max Roach, who had been playing at the Lighthouse with Lorraine, decided to have a party. A lot of jazz people were there, and everyone was smoking and drinking except Brownie, who didn't smoke or drink at all. He never swore and was just a lovely person: clean-cut, unassuming, and modest. Anyway, Max had been carrying a set of vibes with him everywhere he went, but he never touched them, just set them in a corner. Clifford started fooling around with them, and in about an hour or so he was playing with four mallets. Max was furious. He'd had them for years and couldn't even play a scale, but Clifford learnt to play them while everyone was getting drunk. He was such a loss, because there is nobody today to match him. I mean Freddie Hubbard is wonderful, Wynton Marsalis can play, but I don't hear in anyone what I heard in Brownie. His sound was so beautiful and soulful, with such a sparkling way of playing.

One of the records Lorraine and I made together was with Ziggy Vines, who is probably almost forgotten today. He was even obscure at the time, and

Leonard Feather, who did the sleevenote for the album, thought he was actually a pseudonym for Georgie Auld, but he really did exist. He came from a very rich family in Philadelphia and had a natural, unbelievable talent. He was a legend in New York when I first met him, although he never seemed to have a horn, but he sure could play. One day in 1955, out of a clear blue sky he telephoned, saying, "It's me, Ziggy Vines. I'm in L.A., and I need some money. Have you got any work for me?" Lorraine and I were just about to do a quintet album with Conte Candoli, and I thought it would be a good idea to rewrite it for a sextet using Ziggy.[6] Two days before the date, he phoned again and said, "I need a horn, a mouthpiece, some reeds, and a place to stay." I lent him my tenor, bought him some reeds and a mouthpiece, and arranged for him to move in with Lorraine and me. Anyway, he came to the date, and although he hadn't touched a saxophone for quite a time, he played just great because he was a natural, swinging musician. I don't know what happened to him after that, but there is a rumor that he was taped playing with Clifford Brown the night before Brownie was killed in Philadelphia.

In the late fifties Don Cherry stayed at my house for a while, when he and his wife were evicted from their apartment, but I never really cared for his music. He was playing in a "free" way even then, because he couldn't play normally. People said that he and Ornette Coleman could play changes, but I don't believe it, man. I heard Ornette's recording of "Embraceable You," and it's a laugh. I'm sorry, but that's not "Embraceable You." I mean, put him to the test—the Emperor has no clothes. They both played some nice, folksy, rather primitive, naïve-sounding things that had a certain charm, but I couldn't take their approach seriously, even to this day. Ornette came to my house once because he wanted to have his music corrected. He showed me his tunes, and they were a catastrophe, because the bar lines were in the wrong place and there were no chord symbols. He took his saxophone out, and I notated what he played. I asked him what chord he was using, and he blew the arpeggio of a G chord thinking it was a B minor. He just didn't know anything about chords. Years later he was talking about George Russell's Lydian Concept, so I asked him if he had found out the difference between B minor and G yet! I liked Ornette as a person, and he did a sweet thing after my wife died. He wrote a piece which I think he called "Lorraine," and I was very touched by that.[7] Some of his tunes have haunting melodies, but I don't really care for that type of playing. I can play "free," but it's just a lot of meandering about, and anyone can meander; you buy an instrument and make a record in two weeks!

Charlie Mariano and Art Pepper were very active in California during the fifties. Charlie and I were always friends, and I took his place with Shelly Manne's group when he wanted to go home to Boston. I have always liked the way he plays, and among my contemporaries, I would say that he is my favorite. He is very original and plays with a lot of soul in a completely different style to me, which is great. I don't bother him, and he doesn't bother me! Regarding Art Pepper, I have to say that there was never any love lost between us, or between Art and Joe Maini, or Art and anyone else for that matter, because nobody liked him personally. Musically it's a matter of taste, but I was never much of a fan, to tell you the truth. He played well, but I don't think there was any great content, and Joe was of the same opinion.

I'll tell you a funny story concerning the three of us. Both Art and Joe had been to jail, and there had been rumors that Art had named names. You get arrested and the police say, "Just give us some names and we'll let you off." The word for that is a "fink" and that's what people were calling Art. Anyway, there was an after-hours club in the fifties on Hollywood Boulevard where Bill Holman had the group, along with Lorraine, Mel Lewis, and a bass player whose name I have forgotten, and musicians would go there after their gigs to jam. Joe Maini and I would usually go together, and one night we met Art in the parking lot, getting ready to go in, and it's, "Hi, Art," "Hi, Herb, Hi, Joe," bla, bla, bla. Art's wife, Diane, who was a pretty out-front woman, said, "How can you be so friendly, when you know that you all hate each other?" Art said to Joe, "Yeah, you've been going around telling everyone that I'm a fink and that's not true." Joe said, "Listen, I was in the joint too, and I would never call anyone a fink, unless I really knew for sure. I didn't call you a fink; all I said was that you couldn't blow shit, man. I've been telling everyone that!" They were going to start fighting, and Joe whispered quietly to me, "Hold me back." I grabbed him real tight while he shouted out loudly, for Art's benefit, "Let me go, let me at him!" Diane did the same thing with Art, saying, "Don't do it, don't do it." Luckily they were being held by two strong people so nothing happened, but it was a wild incident.

I joined Benny Goodman's band thanks to André Previn, who was a good friend of mine. Benny, who idolized André, had asked him for a lead alto player and he recommended me. I did three tours with the band, but the first one in November 1958 was a big event in my life because, after I was rehearsing all day, my mother called to say that Lorraine had died. I left the band in New York for the funeral and to make arrangements for my one-year-old daughter to be adopted by my sister. Later I telephoned Benny and asked if I could come back, and he said, "Great. We miss you." He was so nice, and I know you hear many bad stories about him, but he was just wonderful to me at a very trying time, really taking care of me. He paid very well, and whenever he was interviewed, he would mention me and praise me a lot. I also recorded with him when he wanted to re-record some of his original classics in stereo, which was a great thrill.

Of course I was emotionally distraught with the death of my wife and the adoption of my daughter because I couldn't provide a proper home for her, but I kept busy. One night I had a call from a lady who said that a friend of mine was in town and wanted to surprise me at the club where I was playing, and would I give her the address? I was working in a burlesque club on Santa Monica Boulevard called the Pink Pussycat. Later that night, I was playing "Night Train" or some boogie-woogie thing with my eyes closed, and I felt a hand on my shoulder. It was Stan Getz, a very old and dear friend who I loved very much. Just like Benny Goodman, I've heard a lot of terrible stories of what he did to other people, but to me, he was just a great human being. During the intermission we talked, and he suggested that I go to Europe for a while. I had already given some thought to that, because L.A. had too many memories, and Stan said he would contact the owner of the Montmarte club in Copenhagen to get me some work while I decided what to do, and that's how I came to leave the U.S.A.

One of the first people I met in Europe was Brew Moore, who I was very fond of. I remember during the Berlin Jazz Festival they had a theme called "The History of the Tenor Sax," and Brew represented the Lester Young school. All the guys got completely drunk after the concert, and the next morning he called me over to his hotel in a panic. Apparently he had been so drunk that he had left his horn, coat, and wallet in a taxicab and had thrown up all over his clothes. He had sent his suit out to be cleaned, and when I arrived, he was sitting in his underwear. He said, "Herb, I can't speak German and nobody here speaks any English. I've lost my horn; I don't have my passport, and I can't get out of Berlin without it. What am I going to do?" Luckily the story had a happy ending because he sobered up, recovered everything, and got out of Berlin alive! Do you know the sad story of how he died? He inherited a lot of money from his grandfather I think, gave a huge party to celebrate and, in the middle of everything, fell down some stairs and died of a broken neck. It could only happen to a jazz musician. He was a wonderful, natural player, like Zoot. It was strictly talent and intuition with both of them.

Getting back to Stan Getz, we first met in L.A. in 1946 or '47. He had left Benny Goodman in New York, and he was waiting to get his union card, so he didn't have too much work or money, and of course he had his first wife, Beverly, and a child to support. We were both playing tenor in a band led by Dick Pierce. Stan played lead and I was on second, although I never really was a tenor player, but I was so fascinated by the way he played, I asked him for a lesson to show me some of the things he was doing. I had never heard a style like that because at that time, when I played tenor, I had Ben Webster and Don Byas in mind, but Stan had a different approach. I spent several hours at his house, and he showed me many things to practice, and at the end of the lesson, he gave me a mouthpiece, saying, "That will help you get the sound you want." Now Stan didn't have any money, and I wanted to pay him for the lesson, because I had learned a lot, but he wouldn't take anything; he was just great.

There's very little in jazz today that I enjoy. When I get depressed or need a mood change, I put on some old Billie Holiday and she does it every time for me, because immediately I'm touched. Of course I listen to Charlie Parker, Duke Ellington, Bill Evans, Art Tatum, and Clifford Brown. I have exotic tastes; I also listen to Mildred Bailey and Stephen Sondheim musicals, as you know, but I don't listen to my own records because it makes me nervous and I never like what I play. I like Don Byas, who is almost ignored now, but nobody plays that good. He had such a beautiful, musical sound, which tenor players don't have today. Everybody thinks that "baagh!" is the sound, and that's not for me. [*Here, Herb imitated a high-pitched whine, so popular with many post-Coltrane tenor players.*] Two more of my favorites are Zoot Sims and George Coleman. One of the greatest jazz musicians of all time was Artie Shaw; his records still sound great. The two biggest disappointments in my life were that I never played with Artie Shaw or the Duke Ellington Orchestra. Once in Las Vegas, when I was with Louis Bellson and Pearl Bailey, I played with Basie's band because Frank Wess was sick. That was exciting, but nothing like playing with Shaw or Duke.

At this stage of the interview, I showed Herb a copy of Leonard Feather's 1956 Encyclopedia of Jazz, *where one hundred and twenty leading players were asked to name their favorite instrumentalists. He was one of those canvassed, and I asked him who his choices would be now.*

As I made clear earlier, it would be Clifford Brown and Chet Baker on trumpet, along with Roy Eldridge, Dizzy, and Fats Navarro. On trombone, I like Teagarden, J.J., Jimmy Knepper, Bob Brookmeyer, and Slide Hampton. On alto, my favorites haven't really changed; they're still Parker, Sonny Stitt, Johnny Hodges, Benny Carter, Willie Smith, and Charlie Mariano. Tenors are Al Cohn, Zoot Sims, Don Byas, George Coleman, and Stan Getz. On baritone, I like Gerry Mulligan very, very much. Pepper Adams was a wonderful player, as is Nick Brignola, but the most musical of all has to be Gerry, because he doesn't just play a lot of bebop hot licks. He is composing when he plays, and that's what I like.[8] On clarinet, it's Goodman, Artie Shaw, Ken Peplowski, and Eddie Daniels. And on flute, I think Hubert Laws is marvelous. Milt Jackson is terrific, but my all-time favorite on vibes is Victor Feldman. Pianists are Tatum, Bud Powell, Horace Silver, Bill Evans, and Joe Albany. And bass has to be Jimmy Blanton, Ray Brown, Niels-Henning Ørsted Pedersen, and Red Mitchell. Red was a one-man rhythm section. I could play all night in a duo with him, and it would be terrific. Drummers I like are Kenny

Clarke, Philly Joe Jones, and Sid Catlett. And Mel Tormé and Tony Bennett are my favorite male vocalists. I saw Tony Bennett recently and he is singing better than ever, and he has such taste. I'm not really a fan of Frank Sinatra, although in the old days he sang well, and "Only the Lonely" was nice. But for me, Bennett is far superior. Girl singers I like are Carmen McRae, Helen Merrill, Ella, and Peggy Lee, but Billie is my all-time champion. She is the only one who can make me cry or laugh within eight bars; she reaches that much of a spectrum of emotion. The best arrangers are people like Gil Evans, John Lewis, Billy May, George Russell, Al Cohn, Bob Brookmeyer, and Gerry Mulligan. Kenny Napper is also a fine writer.

Charlie Parker's music is very important to Herb, so I asked him what he thought of Med Flory and Supersax.

Med is an excellent musician, and we are old friends. He is a man of many talents, because he plays the saxophone, sings, arranges, acts, and he does everything well. All I can say is that I heard Charlie Parker's recording of "Parker's Mood" on the radio recently, and immediately after, they played the Supersax version. Bird's record moves me to tears, and Supersax left me cold. It's a tribute and a work of love, showing great dexterity and hard work transcribing, but I would much rather hear the genuine article. Also, I don't like the way they voice the saxes, with the baritone doubling the lead. As a result, the inner voices are very dull, because they don't move well.

I liked Clint Eastwood's film *Bird*, and I have it on video. Lennie Niehaus and I have been friends for years, and I think the way he recreated the string parts on "April in Paris" was masterful. The whole film was a work of love, and my hat is off to Lennie. I still remember his first arrangement on "Seems Like Old Times" for a non-union Latin band that we worked for in the early fifties in L.A.

I have just retired after twenty-eight years playing for the North German Radio Orchestra, but I like to keep busy, because I'm a workaholic. I teach a lot, and I'm a professor at two universities, and I have also been involved in two musicals. The first one concerns all these stories I have been telling you. About five years ago, a friend told me that I should write my memoirs, and I said that if I ever did, it would be in the form of a musical. Soon afterwards I read that Joe Albany had died, and he was a very important figure in my life. He was the first *avant-garde* jazz pianist, if you like, playing across bar lines, ignoring strict tempo, and playing wild chords. He was very emotional and sometimes played poorly, but when he was "on," it was just fantastic. The *Herald Tribune*, however, gave him about three lines. Soon afterwards Chet Baker and Al Cohn died, and I was very touched. I wrote songs with lyrics for all three, and I thought, "What am I going to do with these songs?" That was when I decided to turn my memoirs into a musical, and I put words to an older original of mine called "Playing Jazz," which has become the title of the show. I came up with a story, writing twenty songs in all, and recorded it for the N.D.R., but I am not too happy with the results, as it needs more work.

I was also asked to write the music for a show based on Josephine Baker, called *Josephine for a Day*, which opened in Frankfurt in February, and I have just heard that it is a hit. One of the reviews called it "A show that nobody should miss." I hope that with the success of *Josephine* I will be able to have my own show, *Playing Jazz*, staged.[9]

NOTES

1. Tony Fruscella, *Complete Studio Recordings*. JFCD 22808.

2. Gene Quill obviously did not bear a grudge, because when Leonard Feather once asked who his favorite alto players were, he named Charlie Parker, Phil Woods, Charlie Mariano, and Herb Geller.

3. Many contemporaries of Dave Schildkraut shared Herb's enthusiasm, among them Stan Getz. In the fifties he was quoted saying that after Charlie Parker, Schildkraut was the best on alto. Schildkraut appeared on the first recording of Miles Davis's composition "Solar," which is recommended as an excellent example of his work (Miles Davis Quintet. Original Jazz Classics OJC 213). It is probably his best, and certainly most famous, solo on record.

4. Readers should not be surprised at major jazz figures working in strip clubs. Zoot Sims, who was no stranger to the burlesque scene, once said: "I was twenty-one before I saw a naked woman from the front!"

5. Clifford Brown, *The Complete Emarcy Recordings*. 838 306-2.

6. Herb Geller Sextet. JapEJD-3074CD.

7. Lorraine Geller died on November 11, 1958, and two months later Ornette Coleman recorded "Lorraine" for his second studio album, *Tomorrow Is the Question*. OJC 342 CD.

8. Gerry Mulligan died on January 20, 1996, and Nick Brignola on February 8, 2002.

9. In October 1994, a few months after this interview, *Playing Jazz* was successfully premiered at a West Coast Jazz festival in Redondo Beach. Three months later, producer Dick Bank recorded it in Hollywood for Fresh Sound Records (FSR 5011). The structure of the show is somewhat similar to *Side by Side by Sondheim*, where a narrator links events in Herb's life and adds historical footnotes. It is a brilliantly conceived and executed *tour de force* for Geller, who has written music and lyrics of the very highest quality. At least one ballad, the haunting "Midnight Memories," deserves to become an instant standard.

Chapter Thirteen

Corky Hale

There can be very few performers who list Billie Holiday and Liberace on the same résumé, but Merrilyn Cecilia Hecht, aka Mrs. Mike Stoller,[1] aka Corky Hale, has worked with both, as well as with many other top jazz and popular music stars. Nevertheless, as writer John S. Wilson once said, "Corky Hale is virtually unknown to the public although she is a legend among musicians." Corky was born on July 3, 1931, in Freeport, Illinois. When we met at her London hotel in October 1996, I told her that I first became aware of her singular abilities as a jazz harpist on an album she made with the Herbie Harper Septet in 1953.[2]

I can't believe you have that record I made with Herbie. I thought he and I were the only ones in the world who had it! He is a lovely player and a charming fellow, and Jimmy Rowles was on the date, too, may he rest in peace. At the time I was working with Liberace, who was the nicest, dearest man, and although everyone made fun of him, he was an excellent pianist. The only other jazz musician in the orchestra was the French horn player John Graas, who was a good friend of mine, but unfortunately he died very young. Touring with Liberace was first class all the way: totally glamorous, and every night was champagne and caviar.

I first went to Hollywood in the early fifties, and the man who ran the Harp Studio in L.A. took me to Harpo Marx's house to play for him. After one number Harpo said, "Young lady, I'm going to make you a star." I couldn't believe people actually talked like that, and I told him I didn't want to be a star, I just wanted to play in a big orchestra, like David Rose's. He told me that I was a very ungrateful young lady, and I never saw Harpo Marx again. Soon afterwards, in 1953, I landed a job at the Coconut Grove in the Ambassador Hotel, playing with Freddy Martin. Right across the street was the Haig, where Gerry Mulligan, Chet Baker, Russ Freeman, and all the other great jazz stars played, and I went to listen every night. Howard Roberts, who was my first boyfriend, was in the Coconut Grove Orchestra with me, but he also played with those guys, so he introduced me to everyone and we all used to hang out together.[3] Many years later, after I married Mike Stoller, he told me that he had also been at the Haig every night when Gerry was there, but we had never met. In 1954, when I was dating Johnny Mandel, we had been invited to Richard Bock's wedding. Strangely enough, Mike was there, and he remembers spending the night talking to Johnny, but we still didn't meet.

While I was at the Ambassador Hotel, we did a lot of remotes: "And now from the beautiful Coconut Grove in Hollywood, California, we bring you the music of Freddy Martin." I had already acquired the nickname "Corky" as a child, so I was known as Corky Hecht at the time and singing the occasional number. But really, "Vocals by the lovely Corky Hecht"? No, I don't think so. The first name I thought of that began with an "H" was Hale, and that is how I became Corky Hale. While I was there, we accompanied all the top acts, like Tony Bennett, Martin and Lewis, Lena Horne, Peggy Lee, and Frank Sinatra.

In 1954 I played harp on a Leonard Feather date called, "Cats v. Chicks."[4] The other "Chicks" were Terry Pollard on vibes, Norma Carson on trumpet (she was married to tenor player Bob Newman), Beryl Booker on piano, who was Dinah Washington's accompanist, Mary Osborne on guitar, Bonnie Wetzel (married to trumpeter Ray) on bass, and Elaine Leighton on drums. The "Cats" included Clark Terry, Lucky Thompson, Urbie Green, Horace Silver, and Kenny Clarke. About this time I was also recording with Chet Baker, Bud Shank, Anita O'Day, and June Christy, as well as doing practically every T.V. and radio show in town. I took whatever work was offered, like the Red Skelton show with David Rose, the Dinah Shore show with Frank DeVol, and the Spike Jones show, together with movies like *The Benny Goodman Story* and *The Ten Commandments*. I did find time, though, to date James Dean, who turned out to be quite obnoxious.

During all this studio activity, mostly on harp, I was playing piano for Ray Anthony and Harry James, and I wound up, as I usually did, doing the vocals and a little number on the flute as well. Harry was business-like and pretty cold, but he could be very nice, too. "Corky" Corcoran was in the band, and that could be confusing, and so was Willie Smith, who was like my father, because he was always looking out for me. I always worked with men, as I was usually the only girl in the band, although I always tried to be one of the "guys." Occasionally someone would offer to leave me their room key, and I would say something like, "Get lost, jerk," but nobody really bothered me. I wouldn't have lasted a day in the business if I'd had the same attitude as today's women's-libbers.[5]

I played on Mel Tormé's album *It's a Blue World*,[6] and in 1957 I was his pianist off and on for about a year in the clubs. It was usually just a trio, and we worked in L.A., Detroit, and New York. He was probably the most talented of all the singers, and the only reason he didn't make it as big as Sinatra is that he was somewhat difficult to get along with. I could excuse him anything, though, because of his fantastic talents: marvelous pianist and drummer, and of course the greatest singer. I knew Frank Sinatra very well at that time, and for a while in 1956, although we didn't have a real romance, whenever he was invited to a party he would usually take me instead of one of the showgirls, and we would talk music all night. He changed politically after the Kennedy assassination, but when I knew him well, he was a left-wing Democrat, very charitable, and just a wonderful person. I played on some of those Nelson Riddle albums, and I am on *Songs for Swinging Lovers*, with the famous Milt Bernhart trombone solo on "I've Got You Under My Skin." Unfortunately, Milt runs a travel agency now and doesn't play anymore.[7]

During the summer of 1956 I got a call from Jerry Gray to play piano with his band at the Dunes in Las Vegas. We were rehearsing on the afternoon of opening night when he told us that there had been a last-minute change and Billie Holiday would be on the bill with us. At that moment she walked in, saw me at the piano, looking pretty young with peroxide blonde hair (because Liberace liked blondes), and gave me a look that said, "This is the pianist? Are you kidding?" Anyway, at the end of the rehearsal she just said, "Corky, you is my little girl." I did three weeks with her at the Dunes, and then we went to L.A. to play Jazz City, with Bob Neel on drums, but I can't remember who the bass player was. Red Mitchell's wife, Doe, who was Billie's very close friend, used to come into the dressing room every night to help fix her hair, and I would help her get dressed. By then, she was in really bad shape because she was drinking gin all day, and she was so screwed up, I had to help her on and off the stage, but I never saw any drugs. I would have run a mile if I had. After Jazz City she wanted me to go on a tour of the Philippines with her, but I turned her down because she was married to Louis McKay, who was violent and scared me to death. He once threw a telephone at Billie and split her head open; he was a terrible person, and I think he died in prison. That film *Lady Sings the Blues*, which was supposed to be about Billie, had as much to do with her life as it had to do with yours, because Louis was still alive when they made it, so he was portrayed as this loving person. In the movie they showed Billie looking for her long-lost son, which was quite untrue, because although she always wanted a baby, she never had one. When I knew her, she was carrying a Mexican chihuahua around that she fed with a bottle.

A few years later in 1961, I divorced my English husband and moved to Italy for three years, where I appeared weekly on a Rome television show *Tempo Di Jazz* opposite Romano Mussolini. I went back to the States in the mid sixties and worked for Tony Martin as his pianist, until I settled in New York. Joining the union there was difficult, because they wanted me to join under the name on my birth certificate, and I said, "How many people are going to hire Merrilyn Hecht?" I had to legalize my name, which is now Corky Hale Stoller. In 1966 I played with Clark Terry, who I love, in his big band at the Riverboat at the Empire State Building, and for the rest of the sixties and seventies I worked with people like Tony Bennett, Barbra Streisand, Nina Simone, James Brown, and Peggy Lee. I have also worked as a musical director for songwriters like Hal David and Marilyn and Alan Bergman. Currently Hal David, Freda Payne, and I do an act built around the Bachrach and David songs, which Hal narrates.

A couple of years ago I had an unfortunate experience with Anita O'Day when I was booked by her manager to play in a big band backing her at Vine Street in L.A. I had recorded with her just prior to the booking, and in the afternoon rehearsal with the band, under her musical director Gordon Brisker, everything had been fine. When she saw me setting up that evening, just before showtime, she said, "I don't want no damn harps with me." Unfortunately, that was that and I am still out several hundred dollars for harp transportation. Anita is seventy-six years old, but she still looks unbelievably great, really fantastic. She lives in a trailer in the desert in a town called Hemet, California.

In 1996 I played at the Playboy Jazz Festival in Beverly Hills, with the Don Bagley Orchestra. Don had played with Stan Kenton, and I had often worked with him, so I knew he was an excellent bass player. What I didn't know was that he is a fine arranger, with a wonderful sixteen-piece string orchestra, although some of them double on woodwinds.[8]

As far as favorite instrumentalists are concerned, I love Billy Taylor's playing, but without question, my number one pianist is Gene Harris; I could listen to Gene all day and all night. Hubert Laws is the very best on flute, and of course he plays with the New York City Opera, and he is also a darling, wonderful person. Dorothy Ashby is my favorite harpist. She was a true jazz player and a magnificent singer, just fabulous.[9]

It is seven years since Corky Hale played in the United Kingdom, when she appeared at Ronnie Scott's club in London opposite Marian Montgomery. It is high time that some enterprising promoter brought her back, because she really has something quite different to offer from the standard jazz-club fare. Leonard Feather, one of her biggest fans, said it best: "Corky has long been one of the most underrated artists on the entire music scene, largely because she chooses to work so infrequently. She is a treat not to be missed.

NOTES

1. Mike Stoller, with his partner Jerry Leiber, wrote a large number of rock 'n' roll hits, including "Hound Dog," "Jailhouse Rock," Poison Ivy," "Charlie Brown," "Yakety Yak," and "Love Potion No. 9." They did the lyrics for "Bernie's Tune," and they also wrote "I'm a Woman" and the classic "Is That All There Is?" for Peggy Lee. The latter has a haunting arrangement by Randy Newman that is worthy of Gary McFarland.

2. Herbie Harper Septet (with Jimmy Giuffre and Charlie Mariano). Bethlehem BCP 1025.

3. Howard Roberts was on Corky's first album as a leader, with Buddy Collette, Red Mitchell, Chico Hamilton, and Larry Bunker on vibes. The album title was *Modern Harp*. GNP 17.

4. Leonard Feather, *Cats v. Chicks*. MGM E225.

5. Although never officially a member, Corky also played in the all-girl bands of Ada Leonard and Ina Ray Hutton as a guest when they worked on television. However, in a 1952 Hal Holly *Down Beat* article entitled "Corky: The All-Girl Harpist," she said, "If a girl is a good musician she doesn't want to work in an all-girl band since it implies that she is working in it because she is a girl. A girl doesn't feel successful as a musician unless she can work with guys. She wants to feel she has been hired not because she's a girl but because she can play the job."

6. Mel Tormé, *It's a Blue World*. Bethlehem BCP 34.

7. Since this interview, Milt Bernhardt passed away, on January 22, 2004.

8. Corky played a set of superior standards, like "Nobody Else but Me," "Here's That Rainy Day," "Yesterdays," and "My Romance." She had a rave review from Mel Sands of the *L.A. Jazz Scene*, who called her "An American original who is in a league, class, and category all by herself. See her once and you'll know why."

9. On the subject of playing jazz on the harp, Corky said on her first album: "The harp is not technically constructed to swing, since the harmonic changes are accomplished by the use of seven pedals at the base. Even the quick footwork of Fred Astaire could not change pedals fast enough for a chromatic scale or sudden change of key."

Chapter Fourteen

Peter Ind

Peter Ind was born on July 20, 1928, in Uxbridge, England, and we met at his Twickenham home early in 1996. In an ideal world he would still be running the Bass Clef in London and playing with guests like Nick Brignola, Kenny Barron, Eddie Henderson, Bob Dorough, and Tal Farlow.[1] As we all know, it is not an ideal world, and Peter has now lost his club and is facing the very real possibility of bankruptcy. Despite his problems, and with no trace of bitterness, the man that Lee Konitz called "one of the great bass players," and Charles Mingus acknowledged as an influence, happily looked back on his career in New York during the fifties.

In 1949 I auditioned with Geraldo as a bass player on the *Queen Mary*, and although the money was terrible, I worked on the boats for the next eighteen months, travelling back and forth to New York. I played with Bruce Turner, Bill Le Sage, Ronnie Ball, and Dill Jones, and all of us eventually studied with either Lennie Tristano or Lee Konitz. Whenever we docked in New York, we visited as many jazz clubs as possible, and in 1949 that meant going to 52nd Street, with its legendary venues like the Three Deuces, the Onyx, and the Orchid Room. It was at the Orchid Room that I first saw the Lennie Tristano Sextet, with Lee, Warne Marsh, Billy Bauer, Arnold Fishkin, and Jeff Morton, and quite frankly I had never heard anything like Lennie's music before. It is one of my regrets that this aspect of jazz has been ignored, because it is great music. The first time I played with them was in 1950. Arnold Fishkin couldn't make the gig at Birdland one night, and although strictly speaking it was illegal, Lennie asked me to take his place. Fortunately I knew the music and felt quite at ease, despite my excitement. Eventually I obtained a visa, which was fairly easy in those days, unless you happened to be a Communist, and in April

1951 I arrived in New York and, with the help of Warne Marsh, found somewhere to live.

Lennie Tristano, who had been blinded at six years of age after a severe bout of measles, was a deep thinker and very much his own man. As time went on he played less and less in public, because he found clubs too noisy, and concert venues lacked the closeness and immediacy that seemed essential for improvised jazz. Over the years he concentrated on teaching and recording in his own private studio and, if I am critical of him, it all became a little inward-looking, because you need that give-and-take from an audience and the input from other musicians. There were some great things, though, and those 1949 sextet recordings like "Wow" and "Crosscurrent" were marvelous, because the music jumps out at you with its enthusiasm and joy. I hope that one day someone looks back at them and says, "Hang on. What's happening here?" I would like to live long enough, and for my sins, I probably will.

Lee was playing so well at that time, and some of the things he did with Kenton and Mulligan were absolutely divine. When I first heard him with Warne Marsh, they were both only twenty-one years old, but they were playing these incredibly beautiful lines. We really owe it to Lennie, who saw that direction and developed it. I remember him saying in 1951 that he had worked out what to do and then "Lee went out there and did it before I did!" Looking back, there seemed to be an intensity of playing and commitment, with Lennie at the center and including Lee, Warne, Don Ferrara, Willie Dennis, Sal Mosca, Ted Brown, Ronnie Ball, Jeff Morton, Al Levitt, Billy Bauer, and of course the wonderful jazz vocalist Sheila Jordan.

Many others came and studied with Lennie at his studio on East 32nd Street, and some, like Red Mitchell, Bud Freeman, and Zoot Sims, were already established players. We used to have all-night sessions there on Wednesdays and Saturdays, depending on the gig situation. I remember, once, Stan Getz was completely intimidated by Warne Marsh, who was so far ahead of him harmonically—but then, Warne was ahead off nearly everyone, ideas-wise. His father, Oliver Marsh, had been a cameraman in Hollywood and, when he died in 1941, had left the family very well off financially.[2] Lee Konitz didn't have a rich family to fall back on, and he used to rib him, because if things got too tough in New York, Warne could always go back to live with his mother in California. Warne always seemed spaced-out, rather like an absent-minded professor. Once, after playing all night at Lennie's studio, Willie Dennis, Warne, Lennie, and I shared a cab to Penn Station so that Lennie could catch the train to Flushing, Long Island, where he lived. Willie and I waited while Warne put Lennie on the train, and the next time we saw him he said, "You put me on the wrong train Sunday morning." Warne replied in his usual vague way, "Come to think of it, so I did."

Lennie was an inspiration to everyone in that circle because he was such a brilliant guy with a lot of insight, but I don't think I am being unfair when I say he traded on it as well. Bird was taken with him, as was Mingus, who was in awe of him. They had never met a white musician on that level, because he could really play and not just copy what had been done before. He was on the same level of creativity as Bird, and we all felt—Willie, Don, Sal, and I—that we were part of something significant. We were close, being a strata of society that lived apart from middle-class America, the *avant-garde* if you like, but one day I woke up and found myself "old hat." As time went on, it was clear that the world was going to go its own way and what we were doing just didn't count.

It was then that the bitterness crept in for people like Willie Dennis, who was such an incredible trombonist and was married to the singer Morgana King.[3] He came from a large, poor family in Philadelphia and knew what it was like to scuffle, and because of his background, he felt he had to make a success in music. I think that produced a conflict in him, unlike Warne, who said that you mustn't compromise, but Warne had that family safety net. Willie often felt he was compromising, and although he worked a lot in Mingus's bands, he still felt ill at ease in the work situation. Don Ferrara, too, expressed his dissatisfaction and seemed to be waiting for the time when he could really play the way he wanted, although he could play beautiful music. I don't want to misjudge him, but he didn't seem to know just how good he was. I suppose we were all reaching for the sky, which blinded us to the nature of the world out there, where you really had to make it. So many jazz musicians were in love with their art that the reality of the music *business* didn't dawn on them until it was too late.

Lennie was doing things that were beyond the bop vocabulary, and he found that many drummers were not sensitive enough for his music, because they played all kinds of fills that got in the way. He would develop a phrase that had a melodic rhythm of, say, seven and superimpose a rhythmic accent of three. This recurring pattern would be played with an underlying pulse of 4/4, so it was no wonder that drummers became anxious! Bird and Prez played phrases that crossed bar lines, but Lennie had taken that several steps further, and unless the drummer really knew what he was doing, playing fills in the usual way led to some pretty weird clashes. Lennie would tell them to "Just keep the pulse going. Whatever you do, don't interrupt the pulse." He often said that his ideal rhythm section was Jeff Morton and I, which is why we made those rhythm tapes for him when we went on the road with Lee Konitz and Ronnie Ball. We taped some tracks with just bass and drums for Lennie to play with while we were away, and we really claim a "first" for that, because recording jazz rhythm tracks hadn't been done before. Much later, of course, this concept became popular in the "Music Minus One" series. In 1955 Lennie released an album on Atlantic, which included his piano overdubs on two of those prerecorded titles, and "Line Up," with "East 32nd Street," is jazz still unsurpassed forty years on.[4] It wasn't easy improvising a swinging bass line without the support of a chordal instrument or horn, and later, on my first album, I did bass overdubs against a prerecorded bass line, which also hadn't been done before.[5]

Like his brother, Michael Tristano, who later became a psychologist, Lennie also played tenor sax, and he insisted that we learn tunes in every key, which is par for the course now but was very unusual in those days. Warne, for instance, would play "Cherokee" in B, and that would faze most of us at the time, but being familiar with all the keys is essential if you want real freedom. Lennie would encourage us to learn other instrumentalists' solos, so that our fingers had to obey the logic of the solo, whereas too many players today develop a style where the instrument dictates the path they take. This was partly what made Bird so great, because he learnt other solos apart from alto solos.

When I first lived in New York, Lee Konitz was not having an easy time of it, even with his records and reputation. He was finding it difficult to support his family, because nobody was getting rich from jazz, and work was pretty thin on the ground. We both found employment in the British Information Service at the Rockefeller Center, which was probably Lee's first contact with English civil servants. We worked in the mailroom, and he used to say, "I can't understand these people. They seem to spend half the day saying, 'Good morning' to each other." Later on he went on the road with Kenton, which Lennie obviously thought of as a compromise, but I think that some of Lee's greatest playing is on those Kenton records; in jazz, you can sometimes put the most unlikely people together and something clicks.

By the end of 1951 I was getting offers to go with all sorts of people, like Woody Herman, Dave Brubeck, and Red Norvo, but I turned everything down to work with Lennie and Lee. I was so taken with their music that everything else seemed to be a shadow in comparison. Looking back, it would have done me a lot of good to have played with Woody, for instance, and I would have certainly gained more by being less choosy and open to other offers. I did work with the Red Norvo Trio at the Embers for a while, thanks to a recommendation from Charles Mingus, who had just left, but I didn't stay because I wanted to keep playing with Lennie. I had first met Mingus in 1949 at Noah Wulfe's bass shop on West 49th Street. At that time very few bass players had a classical technique, and even though I felt myself to be a comparative greenhorn as far as jazz was concerned, I did have classical training and had learned to play, simultaneously, both parts of a Bach Two-Part Invention. So I was in Noah's shop, trying out a bass and playing my party piece, when Mingus walked in. That is how we met, and we remained friends for the rest of his life, and in a funny kind of way, I became a *guru* to him. I know he felt me to be a positive influence, and I was one of the few people he didn't pick a fight with. The last time we met was at the Bim-huis in Amsterdam, shortly before he died, and he said in that staccato way of his, "You know this and I know this, that you were the first cat to do all that high-shit on the bass."

In 1954 I went on the road with Lee Konitz, Ronnie Ball, and Jeff Morton. We were managed by George Wein, and all through that year we travelled around the United States, until eventually in 1955 he booked us into his Storyville club in Boston for a two-month engagement. Towards the end of the gig he arranged for Charlie Parker to play with us, because he wanted to present the two leading altoists together in a quintet. When Bird didn't show, we thought he didn't want to play with us, but quite soon we found out that he had died. Years later I heard that virtually his last words were, "I've got to get to the gig, man." Another memorable job was when Joe Glaser booked Lee's group opposite Louis Armstrong's All Stars at Basin Street West in New York City. His idea was to have both ends of the spectrum, Lee's quartet for the modernists and Louis's band for the traditionalists, and it worked, because the house was packed every night. Nineteen fifty-four was also the year I did my only gig with the Dave Brubeck Quartet, when they were playing at the Blue Note in Philadelphia. His bass player, Ron Crotty, was ill and, as I was due to open with Lennie the following night, I took his place with Dave, Paul Desmond, and Joe Dodge. It's funny because, a couple of years ago, a party was given for Dave at the Ambassador's residence in Regents Park, London, and I was invited. When he saw me, he remembered straight away and said, "You played with me at the Blue Note." We talked for a while, but there was a queue behind me, so I had to move on. Incidentally, Paul Desmond always said how much he respected Lee.

In 1956 Ed Thigpen and I worked for about a year with the talented German pianist Jutta Hipp at the Hickory House on 52nd Street. We recorded two albums for Blue Note, and Zoot Sims joined the group for a while.[6] She eventually dropped out of the jazz scene, because it was very hard for a woman then, especially someone like Jutta, who had more of a retiring personality than, say, Marian McPartland. Later on, the Hickory House became Marian's residency, and I sat in with her there many times. Shortly after that I played with Charlie Ventura at the Colonial Tavern, Toronto, and Charlie was easygoing and very pleasant. Like most of the guys from that earlier generation, he was less demanding and very appreciative.[7]

In 1957 I did a winter season in Miami Beach with Buddy Rich, when he had a quartet with Flip Phillips and Ronnie Ball. Flip was a good guy, and I have warm memories of him because he was fun to be with, but it is no secret that Buddy could be difficult. He was a fantastic drummer and we played well together, but we didn't get along. That and the fact that I had some new recording equipment being delivered to me in New York caused me to quit before the season was over. When I got back to the city, I started working again with Lee Konitz at the Half Note. The following year, guitarist Al Schackman, who later played for and managed Nina Simone, called me for a trio gig at a basement club on Madison Avenue called the Den. Ronnie Ball was with us, and later Sal Mosca took his place, and that was where I met Lenny Bruce, who made his New York debut at the Den in 1959. The club was packed every night, and we became very friendly during long conversations about all manner of esoteric subjects between sets. His reputation as a "jazz" comic from the West Coast was already legendary, and there is no doubt that he really changed the course of American humor.

In 1960 I worked in a trio backing Chris Connor with Ronnie Ball and Dave Bailey, playing around New York, Chicago, Atlantic City, and sometimes down South. Later that year I played a lot with Coleman Hawkins and Roy Eldridge at the Metropole on Seventh Avenue, and although they were great friends, they always seemed to be fighting. Roy would arrive at the club sometimes and say, "I'm not talking to Bean tonight," and I of course would not investigate! Tommy Flanagan was the pianist, and Hawk always had big ears for whatever changes Tommy was playing, because he could immediately follow him and have those changes down, just like that. Roy did his own thing, and his great strength was in that marvelous sound, something that was not matched by any other trumpeter before or since, and he could always make it happen much more than Hawk. [*Here, Peter clicked his fingers rhythmically.*] Eddie Locke was the drummer and we got along well, because he was a good friend.

I was the only white guy in the group, and they used to say, "Get that man some sunshine!" In the late fifties and early sixties, reverse prejudice began to creep into the New York scene, what was called "Crow Jim," but the older guys like Roy and Bean were not like that at all. They were like elder statesman; they just did their thing and that was that. They had a heart, and that's what made the playing. Even though they are both gone, it's as if they're still around, because the experiences are so vivid, and of course we have the recordings, which makes this century unique. From a personal point of view, I was very close to Roy. We just hit it off, because the chemistry was there, and we always remained good friends.

Nineteen sixty was also the year I moved into a loft and studio in Lower Manhattan, in an area that became known as the East Village, which was a center for jazz, poetry, writing, and art. Allen Ginsberg lived across the street, and Jake Hanna, Ronnie Ball, and Jackie McLean were just some of the musicians I had as neighbors. The local jazz club was the Five Spot, which was very much alive in those days. We recorded many great sessions in that studio, like Al and Zoot with the blues singer "Kid" Haffey. He reputedly taught Jimmy Rushing, and was paralyzed down one side, but that didn't stop him from being the bouncer at the Blue Note in Philadelphia. We did an album with Lee Konitz and Don Ferrara, playing some free things, and it was beautiful, but Verve bought the tapes, which were lost in a fire at MGM. As far as free music is concerned, musicians have to really listen to each other, and they must be very skilled on changes, otherwise nothing is going to happen and it ends up being self-indulgent. Booker Little's last album was recorded at my studio, and some of the other musicians who recorded there were Bill Evans, Yusef Lateef, McCoy Tyner, Howard McGhee, Tommy Flanagan, and Cannonball Adderley. I still have the tapes somewhere of Gerry Mulligan rehearsing his Concert Jazz Band there, and of course Judy Holliday was with him, although nobody realized that she was soon to depart the earth. It was the same with Billie Holiday when I played with her at the Cork 'n' Bib on Long Island in 1956. The Lee Konitz quartet accompanied her that night, and it was a magic evening. She had such a strong personality, and nobody had an inkling that, three years later, she would be gone.

There were lofts all over town where musicians would gather to play, and Sheila and Duke Jordan had one on West 18th Street, where they often had all-night sessions. I remember visiting one lunchtime when Duke came in very excitedly and said, "Do you want to hear my new tune?" And he sat down and played "Jordu." These are all treasured memories. After the Jordans split up, Sheila had a difficult time for many years, working as a secretary during the day and singing at the Page Three at night in Greenwich Village, which is where Barbra Streisand started.

Living the bachelor life in a New York loft is O.K., but by 1963 I was married and the father of a little girl, and lofts are not places to raise a family. With the advent of the Twist and the growing popularity of rhythm and blues, jazz gigs were becoming scarce, and many musicians were finding it hard to survive, so we decided to move out to California. Bob Dorough had telephoned a friend of his called Eduardo Terrella, who knew everybody and was a wheeler-dealer out there, to ask him to find a place for us in Big Sur. Later on Al Schackman came out, and we used to play at Eduardo's parties, where there were a lot of movie people, and that is how we met Kim Novak. Kim is a jazz fan and a good painter, and she and Al had an intense romance for a while. Eventually, Lee Konitz and Warne Marsh came West, and we used to jam at Kim's house in Carmel Highlands every Sunday, and I think she still has the tapes.

In 1965 a movie mogul commissioned Dalton Trumbo to write a film called *The Sandpiper*, about a wayward lady artist and the Big Sur artist colony where she lived. The part was tailor-made for Kim Novak, but she turned it down. In a fit of pique, the movie mogul hired two of the most expensive stars in the business, Elizabeth Taylor and Richard Burton, and set up filming right in front of Kim's house. A number of locals, including Al and me, were hired as extras, and we also played the music for one of the beach scenes. One night Johnny Mandel, who was writing the film music, gave Al and me something he had just written. He asked us to play it, as he was thinking of using it as the theme for the film. We played it through a few times, and Johnny was anxious to know what we thought. I said, "It's good, although it reminds me of Hoagy Carmichael's 'New Orleans'—but it will probably make it." Of course it does sound a little like "New Orleans" at the start, but we know it better now as "The Shadow of Your Smile."

Looking back, I played with a lot of great people, but I took it all in my stride. I was able to contribute, and I had my own voice in the music, but I think it might have been wiser to have taken care of business a little more. As far as my favorite instrumentalists are concerned, there are so many, but today, Kenny Barron stands out. I also loved Roy Eldridge, Clifford Brown, Dizzy, Lester Young with Basie, Charlie Parker, Lee Konitz, Warne Marsh, Lennie Tristano, and Al and Zoot for their down-home beauty. Thinking of home territory, I am always moved by Matthew Ross's playing. I have known him for fifty-three years, and he has always inspired me. Finally, I must mention Martin Taylor, who, like a number of English jazz musicians, is better known and appreciated abroad than here in the U.K.

Most of the anecdotes in this interview will be expanded in Peter Ind's forthcoming autobiography Jazz Émigré, *and the events surrounding the closure of his club, the Bass Clef, will be the subject of another work,* Financially Disabled. *When time permits, he is also working on a third book,* Cosmic Metabolism.

NOTES

1. Since this interview, Nick Brignola passed away, on February 8, 2002, and Tal Farlow passed away, on July 25, 1998.

2. Among Oliver Marsh's many screen credits are *David Copperfield* (1935), *A Tale of Two Cities* (1935), and *The Great Ziegfeld* (1936).

3. Morgana King, who had previously been married to Tony Fruscella, was also an actress; one of her more celebrated roles was as Mrs. Don Corleone in *The Godfather* and *The Godfather, Part II.*

4. Lennie Tristano, *Requiem*. Atlantic SD 2.7003.

5. Peter Ind, *Looking Out*. Wave LP No. 1.

6. *Jutta Hipp Trio*. Blue Note 1515 and 1516.

7. Peter obviously impressed Charlie Ventura, because when Leonard Feather asked him who his favorite bass players were, he named Red Mitchell and Peter Ind.

Chapter Fifteen

Frank Isola

For a time during the early and middle fifties, Frank Isola's subtly understated approach to the drums was very much in demand from a variety of high-profile leaders. He worked and recorded with Stan Getz off and on from 1952 to 1957 and spent the whole of 1954 with Gerry Mulligan, which included a visit to the Paris Jazz Fair in June of that year. He played with Bob Brookmeyer and John Williams and appeared on Mose Allison's famous *Back Country Suite* in 1957, but after that it seemed as though Frank disappeared from the jazz scene entirely. It wasn't until 1992 that I was able to find out what had happened to him, when his good friend pianist John Williams was staying at the Hilton Hotel in London. John told me that although he had worked with Max Roach, Kenny Clarke, Mel Lewis, and Gus Johnson, Frank Isola was his favorite drummer. Over the course of the next two years, as a result of several long, long-distance telephone calls to Frank and numerous letters from John, I was able to find out more about Frank's career in the fifties, a period that could be called jazz music's last golden age.

Frank Isola, who was the youngest of seven children, was born on February 20, 1925, in Detroit. He was eleven years old when he was taken to the Fox Theater to see Gene Krupa play with Benny Goodman. After the show, he went home and told his parents that he wanted to be a drummer. Mr. and Mrs. Isola had both immigrated from Italy, and his father certainly preferred opera to American popular music, but they were obviously understanding people because, quite soon, Frank was catching the trolley car every Saturday for his drum lesson in the old Wurlitzer Building in downtown Detroit.

He played in his high school band, and his first success occurred in 1942, when he won the Detroit section of a national Gene Krupa contest. Many of the major cities in the United States had a competition to send the best young drummer to the final, which was held in New York, and one of the tasks was to play along to Krupa's famous recording of "Drum Boogie." Unfortunately, the thrill of winning was swiftly followed by the disappointment of disqualification on a technicality. Frank had joined the union just before taking part, which was enough for the judges to decide that he was a professional and therefore ineligible. The runner-up was sent to New York, where the national contest was won by a youngster called Louie Bellson.

During World War II, Frank served in the Army Air Force as a musician, doing his basic training with Louie Bellson, with whom he formed a lifelong friendship. He was stationed initially at Columbus, Georgia, transferring later to Fort Wayne, Indiana, and on discharge in February 1946 he traveled to California. With the help of the G.I. Bill, he enrolled at the Los Angeles Conservatory, but after two semesters transferred to the more modern music college at Westlake, where Dick Kenny and Conrad Gozzo were fellow students. In January 1947 he took time off to go home to Detroit to marry his high school sweetheart, Pat Sheahan. Later that year, having now left college, he went on the road with the Earle Spencer big band touring the West, and it was during an engagement in Kansas City with the band that Frank first met the nineteen-year-old Bob Brookmeyer. Big bands were finding it hard to survive in the late 1940s, and faced with limited bookings, Spencer disbanded after a gig in Dallas.

By 1948, after an invitation from Dick Kenny, Frank had joined Johnny Bothwell's big band, which had John Williams on piano. Many other fine jazzmen played with Bothwell in the forties, and Don Lanphere, Jimmy Knepper, Allen Eager, Teddy Kotick, and Joe Maini were all with the band at various times. The leader had played alto with Gene Krupa, Tommy Dorsey, Woody Herman, and Boyd Raeburn, but unfortunately his band didn't fare any better than Earle Spencer's. Business became so bad that, towards the end of 1948, Frank, Joe Maini, and John Williams left the band in Ohio and drove to New York, determined to secure a change of fortune.

It is difficult to put all of Frank's activities into strict chronological order in the years from 1949 to 1952, when he first played with Stan Getz, but there are some events that can be determined with accuracy during this period. In January 1949, along with Don Lanphere, John Williams, and Teddy Kotick, he accompanied Babs Gonzales in an audition for Capitol Records. The audition was successful, because Babs got his contract, but a different instrumental group was used when the singer came to record. Don Lanphere told writer Alun Morgan that, at about the same time, he recorded several unreleased octet sides, possibly for a company called Motif, with, among others, Tony Fruscella, Milt Gold, Herb and Lorraine Geller, and Frank Isola. In June 1950 Frank was recorded at a private session with Charlie Parker, and on

Gene Allen (far left) with the Tommy and Jimmy Dorsey Band at the Statler Hotel in New York City, 1956. Courtesy Gene Allen.

Mose Allison in London, 1994.

Dave Bailey in New York City, 1998. Courtesy Dave Bailey.

Chuck Berghofer in Los Angeles, circa 2000. Courtesy Stan Levey.

Eddie Bert in London, 1998.

Larry Bunker in Los Angeles, circa 2000. Courtesy Larry Bunker.

Bob Brookmeyer (left) with John Williams in Santa Monica, 1953. Courtesy John Williams.

Pete Christlieb in London, 1999. Courtesy Don Jordan.

Bill Crow in New York City, 2000. Courtesy Judy Kirtley.

From left to right, Paul Desmond, Joe Dodge, Norman Bates, and Dave Brubeck at the Blackhawk in San Francisco, 1956. Courtesy Joe Dodge.

Bob Enevoldsen (right) with Herbie Harper in Los Angeles, 1998. Courtesy Bob Enevoldsen.

Don Ferrara (center) with Nick Travis (left) and Conte Candoli (right) in Paris, 1960.
Courtesy Don Ferrara.

Herb Geller (left) with Gordon Jack in London, 1994.

Corky Hale at the piano, with Billie Holiday and Bob Neel at Jazz City in Los Angeles, 1956. Courtesy Corky Hale.

Chico Hamilton, circa 1995. Courtesy Anthony Barboza.

Peter Ind in London, 2001. Courtesy Susan Jones.

From left to right, John Williams, Tony Fruscella, Bill Anthony, and Frank Isola at Birdland in New York City, 1955. Courtesy John Williams.

Lee Konitz in London, 1996.

Drummer Stan Levey trying to earn a few extra dollars! New York City, 1948. Courtesy Stan Levey.

Jack Montrose in Las Vegas, 2001. Courtesy Jack Montrose.

From left to right, Gil Barios, Bob Whitlock, Art Pepper, Alvin Stoller, and Gerry Mulligan at The Haig in Los Angeles, 1953. Courtesy Bob Whitlock.

Lennie Niehaus in Los Angeles, 1989. Courtesy Stan Levey.

Jack Nimitz in Los Angeles, circa 2000. Courtesy Jack Nimitz.

Hod O'Brien, circa 2000, location unknown. Courtesy Hod O'Brien.

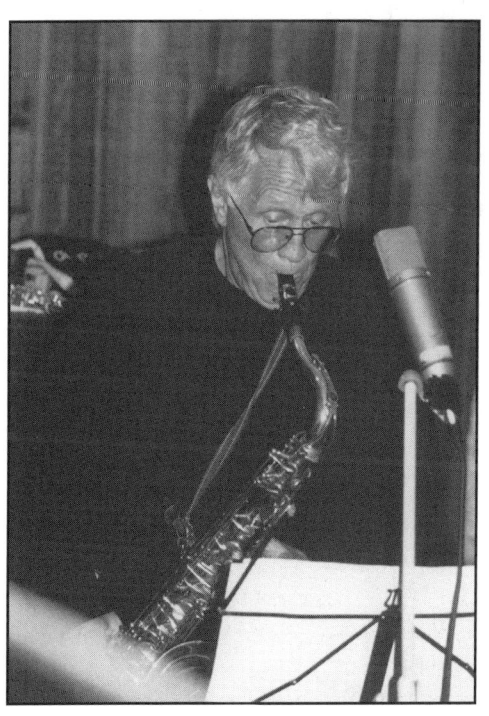

Bill Perkins in London, 1999. Courtesy Don Jordan.

Bud Shank in London, 1995.

Carson Smith (left) with Charlie Parker and Chet Baker at the University of Oregon, 1953. Courtesy Shirley Smith.

Phil Urso with the Chet Baker Quintet at the Loop Lounge in Cleveland, 1954. From left to right: Bob Neel, Phil Urso, Bob Whitlock, Al Haig (hidden), and Chet Baker. Courtesy Bob Whitlock.

Phil Woods, circa 1982. Courtesy Russ Chase.

Bob Whitlock in the late 1950s, location unknown. Courtesy Bob Whitlock.

March 19, 1952, he made his first studio recording with Eddie Bert on the trombonist's debut as a leader.[1]

The story behind the Parker recording is quite fascinating. It took place at an apartment rented by Joe Maini, Jimmy Knepper, and a tenor player named Gerson Yowell. Regular jam sessions took place there, and the list of musicians who attended reads like a "who's who" of the new music. Charlie Parker, Herb Geller, Gene Quill, Joe Albany, Dave Lambert, Gerry Mulligan, Zoot Sims, Warne Marsh, Lee Konitz, Jon Eardley, and John Williams all came to visit and sat in at various times. Comedian Lenny Bruce was often there, socializing with the musicians. Frank Isola was one of the regulars, and he was recorded on four separate occasions as part of the rhythm section with John Williams and Buddy Jones that backed Charlie Parker. Don Lanphere made the recordings, and the tapes, which had circulated among musicians for years, were finally released commercially in 1977.[2] In an interview with A. C. Stone for *The Mississippi Rag*, Frank said, "Warming up before a session, I asked Bird what tempo he wanted for a number we were recording. He just looked at me and said, 'Whoosh,' and made a motion with his hand like a jet taking off." One of the titles was a super-fast "Donna Lee," which of course is based on "Indiana." Gerson Yowell's sleevenote for the album says: "The ensemble went into 'Indiana' by bus, while Bird flew!"

It is impossible to be quite as specific about Frank's other activities at this time, but these were certainly busy years, as he worked mostly in and around New York City. A few random examples, though, will give an indication of the musical company he was keeping between 1949 and 1952. He did a few months in Atlantic City with Gene Quill, and John Williams remembers taking a bus to State College, Pennsylvania, with Jon Eardley, Buddy Jones, and Frank for a jazz gig after a big football game there. He played with Louis Prima's big band in New Jersey and was often involved in jam sessions at a studio called Don José's, which was situated on West 49th Street between Broadway and Eighth Avenue and was a favorite venue for Lester Young, Zoot Sims, and Gerry Mulligan. Frank also did a short tour from New York to Chicago in 1951 with a trio backing Peggy Lee. He is quite sure of the year because on October 3, 1951, Bobby Thomson hit his famous home run for the New York Giants in the final game of the National League Pennant against the Brooklyn Dodgers. This became known as "The Shot Heard Round the World," and the two events have remained connected in his memory ever since. In explaining to a non-American the significance of that phrase, writer Jerome Klinkowitz told me that it came from "the American Revolution, pertaining to the gunfire from the militiamen ('minute men' available for duty at a minute's notice) at Lexington, Massachusetts, that started the fray. Journalists transposed it to sports for Thomson's hit."

For ten months from 1951 to 1952, Frank worked with the Claude Thorn-hill Orchestra, and some of the sidemen who played with him at various times included Dick Sherman, Sonny Rich, Gene Quill, Phil Sunkel, and Bob Brookmeyer. Thanks to Bill Crow's book *Jazz Anecdotes*,[3] we know that there was definitely one leader Frank did not work for during this period, and that was Tommy Dorsey, "The Sentimental Gentleman of Swing." Dorsey's manager apparently telephoned Frank and asked him to come to the Pennsyl-vania Hotel in New York, because Tommy was auditioning drummers and wanted to hear him play. Knowing that Dorsey would only be happy with an-other Buddy Rich, Frank thought for a minute and said, "Aaah, thanks but tell Tommy I'm not in a sentimental mood." He has always regretted not playing with Tommy Dorsey, because he really admired the band. Bill Crow, who played with Frank at this period, has told me: "I met Frank at jam sessions in New York in 1950 and had the pleasure of working with him when we were both with Stan Getz, as well as on a few casual gigs. He played quietly but with a wonderful swing, and sometimes his hi-hat closing on the afterbeat was the loudest part of his playing."

In 1952 Stan Getz had the problem of replacing the great Tiny Kahn, who was leaving the quintet, so Frank's friend Teddy Kotick arranged for him to play with Stan at an engagement at the Savoy Ballroom in Harlem. Al Haig and Jimmy Raney were in the group, and Joe Newman and Kai Winding also sat in that night. At the end of the set, Getz was so impressed with his play-ing he simply said, "Step into my office," and Frank remained with the tenor-man off and on for the next five years.

In Arne Astrup's revised Stan Getz discography,[4] he lists Frank on a broad-cast at the Tiffany club in Los Angeles on September 14, 1952, but Frank told me that he did not play on this date. He thought that Stan probably used a West Coast rhythm section, with possibly Donn Trenner on piano. Frank's first booking as a member of the group was at a club in Providence, Rhode Island, and Teddy Kotick and Jimmy Raney were still there, but Jerry Kamin-sky had taken Al Haig's place. Frank remembers that the club had a policy of booking guest stars at weekends, and on one such occasion he had the plea-sure of playing with Billie Holiday. On November 14, 1952, the Stan Getz Quintet, with Frank on drums, appeared at Carnegie Hall as part of a musical celebration to mark Duke Ellington's twenty-fifth anniversary as a band-leader.[5] Also on the bill that night were Charlie Parker with Strings, Billie Holiday, Ahmad Jamal, Dizzy Gillespie, and Frank's good friend Louie Bell-son, who was on drums with Ellington.

In December, Isola made his first studio recordings with Stan Getz, which have been reissued with a fine sleevenote by Bill Crow.[6] It was while this al-bum was being recorded that Jimmy Raney decided to leave the quintet and gave Stan his notice. Frank recommended Bob Brookmeyer as a replacement, because they had been playing in jam sessions around New York together and he knew the trombonist would fit in perfectly. In a recent letter, Bob said he considered Frank one of his favorite drummers, and that from 1952 to 1954, he was his first choice for recording and club work. Brookmeyer was not immediately available to join Stan Getz, but he did manage to play one engagement with the group at the Hi-Hat in Boston, although there is some confusion over the date and the drummer. Bob remembers playing at the Hi-Hat in December 1952 with Getz and Frank Isola, but Fresh Sound Records have issued two CDs from this booking, quoting March 8, 1953, with Al Levitt on drums.[7] Astrup's discography goes for December 8, 1953, and says that the drummer is Roy Haynes. The exact date may never be known, although December 1952 may be the most likely, but when I sent Frank a copy of the CD, he confirmed that he was playing the drums, not Levitt or Haynes.

Bill Crow's notes for the Getz and Jimmy Raney recordings are enlightening about the apparent "revolving-door" policy the tenor-man applied to his drummers at this time. "We had come back to New York in January for a week off after a week in Boston, then Stan called and said that he had filled in the open week at Birdland. When I got to work on Tuesday, I found Kenny Clarke setting up his drums. I didn't know what had happened to Frank but assumed he had already booked another gig. Tuesdays at Birdland included a live broadcast of an early set to help publicize the attraction of the week. During the second set, Frank Isola walked in and sat listening beside the bandstand. When we finished playing, I went down to say hello and asked what had happened. 'I don't know,' he said. 'I turned on the radio and discovered I was fired.'"

In May 1953, Teddy Kotick, John Williams, and Stan Getz drove across country from Washington, D.C., to spend the summer playing in Los Angeles. Bob Brookmeyer, who was now with the quintet on a permanent basis, joined them from Kansas City, and Frank flew out a few weeks later. Their first engagement was at the Tiffany club, where Stan used local drummer Richie Frost, who was a friend of Brookmeyer's. After a week's break, the group, this time with Frank Isola, took up residency at Zardi's, where they remained for the next four months. Zardi's was situated on the corner of Hollywood Boulevard and Vine Street and was the premier jazz club in Los Angeles at the time. During that summer the quintet visited the Hollywood studios on three occasions to record fourteen titles for Norman Granz,[8] but in September, Getz disbanded to go on the road with a package tour called "A Festival of Modern American Music," with Erroll Garner, June Christy, and the Stan Kenton Orchestra.

The rest of the group went back to New York to freelance, and around Christmas 1953, Brookmeyer received a telephone call from Gerry Mulligan, inviting him to join the quartet he was reforming in Los Angeles. As he intended to go back to the East to work, Mulligan did not want California-based players, so he asked Bob to bring a New York rhythm section to Los Angeles with him. Frank and Bill Anthony were selected, and while the new quartet was rehearsing in January, they played a concert as part of Gerry's tentet at the Embassy Theater, Los Angeles. This had been a short-lived project of Mulligan's, but luckily the tentet had made one album for posterity, recorded the year before, in 1953.

Initial rehearsals over, the new Gerry Mulligan Quartet made its debut at the Blackhawk, San Francisco, late in January 1954. Their next engagement was at the Storyville club in Boston, so Mulligan bought two cars for the long trip back East. Bill Anthony and Frank traveled together, while Brookmeyer and Mulligan were in the second car with Gerry's wife Arlyne, who was also his personal manager. After Boston, they went to Toronto and then New York, arriving there in April, where they appeared at Basin Street opposite Frank's original inspiration, Gene Krupa, who was there with Eddie Shu and Dave McKenna. By this time, a significant change had occurred in the rhythm section, as the superb Red Mitchell had taken over from Bill Anthony on bass.

It was during a booking at the Blue Note in Philadelphia that Henri Renaud invited Mulligan's group to appear at the Third Salon du Jazz in Paris, France, where they were a huge success. Luckily, Vogue Records was on hand to record the concerts, and thirty-one titles were eventually released, representing a fine example of Frank's stay with Mulligan.[9] He follows the tradition established by Chico Hamilton and Larry Bunker in playing brushes almost exclusively with the quartet, and one might be forgiven for thinking this was at the request of the leader. Frank told me, though, that this decision had been his. In fact, when Gerry originally hired him, he said that he particularly liked his stick work. Compere Charles Delauney, whose introductions are on the L.P. (but not on the CD), has said, "Contrary to many modern musicians, whose attitude seems to be one of utter boredom, the members of the Mulligan quartet showed their evident pleasure in what they were playing." During the group's weeklong stay in Paris, where they were featured at five concerts, the drummer became very friendly with Thelonious Monk, who was also appearing at the festival. They had sat next to each other on the flight from America, and in the evenings they walked back to the hotel together after the concerts. When they returned to America, Mulligan had the problem of replacing Brookmeyer, who had decided to leave the group. He selected Tony Fruscella, who had established a reputation in New York circles as a sensitive and lyrical trumpeter.

On July 17, 1954, the Mulligan quartet with Fruscella, Mitchell, and Isola played at the first ever Jazz Festival at Newport, Rhode Island. They followed the Oscar Peterson Trio onstage and were introduced to an enthusiastic audience by Stan Kenton, who was the master of ceremonies that year. Kenton called Frank "A veteran of a number of outstanding jazz units and a percussionist of skill, control, and imagination." As for Tony Fruscella, a tape exists of part of the program the group played that day, and his approach sounds extremely tentative and lacking in confidence. John Williams has said that in the right setting, and the Newport Jazz Festival was probably anything *but* the right setting, Fruscella's lyrical creativity was unsurpassed. Almost immediately after Newport, Mulligan decided to replace him, and at Frank's suggestion he chose Jon Eardley. Apparently Jon was playing at the Open Door in Greenwich Village with Fruscella and Don Joseph, and Frank was in the rhythm section. Gerry and Arlyne Mulligan were in the audience, and it was Arlyne who made the introductions, when she asked Eardley how many white shirts he had. On being told that he had three or four, she took him over to Gerry's table, where Gerry said, "Would you like to come and work for me?" The new quartet opened in Baltimore three days later, and Jon's ebullient sound and striking ideas were to remain a feature of Mulligan's groups for the next two years. It is a source of regret that the group with Eardley, Mitchell, and Isola never recorded. The only permanent memento that seems to exist is a photograph in *Time Magazine* dated November 8, 1954, the issue that had Dave Brubeck on the cover.

In September 1954, John Williams made his first album as a leader[10] with Bill Anthony and Frank Isola, and towards the end of the year, they were all involved in a seven-week, nationwide tour organized by Norman Granz. John and Bill Anthony were part of the Stan Getz Quintet with Bob Brookmeyer, and Frank was still with Mulligan. The Dave Brubeck Quartet and the Duke Ellington Orchestra were also featured, and the tour started in New York's Carnegie Hall, moving on to Boston, Philadelphia, Milwaukee, Detroit (where Frank's family, including his sixty-year-old mother, sat in the front seats of the Lafayette Theater), Chicago, Cincinnati, Cleveland, Denver, and San Francisco before concluding at the Shrine Auditorium, Los Angeles. This represented the end of Frank's career with Gerry Mulligan. The day after the Shrine concert, Stan Getz recorded six titles for Norman Granz,[11] using Frank instead of Art Mardigan, who had been his drummer on the tour. Frank told me that "Jeru could be pretty stubborn and was upset that I had made the L.P. with Stan. He said it was unfair to Art Mardigan." The baritonist still had commitments on the West Coast, so Frank, who was anxious to return to his family in New York, took the opportunity of rejoining Stan Getz. After their argument, Gerry had driven off with Frank's drums in his station wagon, which necessitated Getz hiring drum kits for Frank while they worked their way back East. Bob Brookmeyer also stayed in California for a while, so Stan added Tony Fruscella to the group for a Birdland engagement, although by March 1955 Brookmeyer was back again.

Isola continued to freelance around New York, and in 1956 he recorded with Dick Garcia in a group that included Gene Quill, and Terry Pollard.[12] He played with the German pianist Jutta Hipp in a trio with Jack Six at Basin Street East, and he worked in Cleveland for a while with Helen Merrill. During this time his wife, Pat, was contributing to the family income by holding down a job as a receptionist/secretary at the William Morris Booking Agency. He also played in jam sessions with Al Cohn, and at one such session in a loft on 34th Street, he met Mose Allison. By early 1957, the pianist had joined Frank in the Stan Getz Quartet, and it was around that time that he was rehearsing his famous *Back Country Suite*. When it was recorded,[13] the drummer showed himself to be perfectly able to adapt to Allison's charming and idiosyncratic compositions. The *Suite* was Mose Allison's first recording, and it proved to be Frank's last for thirty-seven years.

In the 1959 *Metronome* yearbook, Frank, together with six other leading drummers, was asked to select some of his favorite artists. His selections make interesting reading, because he chose Charlie Parker, Miles Davis, Red Norvo, David Allyn, Milt Jackson, Ray Charles, Gerry Mulligan, Artie Shaw, and Count Basie with Joe Williams. By the time this entry appeared, Frank and his family had returned to Detroit, and his days of playing with major jazz figures were over. The sixties was not a good decade for Frank, or for jazz in general, although the music survived, unlike Frank's career, which never recovered the high profile that it enjoyed in New York during the fifties.

In 1961 he played in a trio that opened Hugh Hefner's Playboy Club in Chicago, but for most of that decade and into the seventies, he stayed close to home, playing casuals with local musicians. He did return to New York in the mid seventies, working with tenor player Victor Lesser at the West End. But jazz gigs were still very scarce in the city, so he went back to Detroit, where to some extent his life has come around full circle. Until 1992 he lived downtown in an apartment at the Lenox Madison Hotel, close to the old Wurlitzer Building, where he used to have his weekly drum lesson. As a result of the Urban Renewal Program, the Lenox Madison has been demolished, so Frank has moved to another apartment, near to the Fox Theater, which of course is where he was inspired to become a drummer at a Gene Krupa performance. He was recently a victim of what has become a regular feature of inner-city life; his car was stolen, and worse, his drum kit was inside. Somehow, Louie Bellson heard of Frank's loss, and he immediately arranged for his old friend to receive a new kit.

In October 1994 he was reunited with John Williams when they recorded a quartet CD down in North Miami, Florida. Also involved were Spike Robinson and Jeff Grubbs, a bass player from the Florida Symphony.[14] Earlier that year, he was heard with Franz Jackson and Marcus Belgrave at a Jazz Festival in Windsor, Ontario, where a live recording was produced,[15] and in November 1994, at the same venue, he was the guest of honor at a concert billed as "A Tribute to Legendary Detroit Drummer Frank Isola."

Other than "Bark for Barksdale" with the Mulligan quartet in Paris, there are no recorded examples of Frank taking extended drum solos, but his four- and eight-bar breaks are models of taste and restraint, with no over-elaborate displays of technique. Within the ensemble, he never imposed himself in the way that perhaps Art Blakey might have done. Excellent though Art's more aggressive and dynamic approach was, Frank Isola's relaxed and gently swinging style was just as valid for the contexts in which he worked.

NOTES

1. Eddie Bert Quintet. Vogue EPV 1097.
2. Charlie Parker, *Apartment Sessions*. Spotlight SPJ 146.
3. Bill Crow, *Jazz Anecdotes* (Oxford University Press).
4. Arne Astrup, *The New Revised Stan Getz Discography* (Per Meistrup Productions).
5. Stan Getz Quintet. Fresh Sound FSCD 1003.
6. Stan Getz Quintet. Mosaic MD3 1003.
7. Stan Getz, *In Boston*, vols. 1 and 2. Fresh Sound FSCD 1014 and1015.
8. Stan Getz Quintet. MGN 1000/1087/1088.
9. Gerry Mulligan, *Pleyel Concerts 1954*, vols. 1 and 2. Vogue 74321134112 and 74321134122.
10. John Williams Trio. Emarcy MG 26047.
11. Stan Getz Quintet. Norgran MGN 1029/2000-2/Verve MGV 8200.
12. Dick Garcia, *A Message from Garcia*. Dawn DCD 108.
13. Mose Allison, *Back Country Suite*. Original Jazz Classics OJC 075.
14. John Williams, *Welcome Back John Williams*. Marshmallow Records MYCJ 30061.
15. Franz Jackson and Marcus Belgrave, *Live at Windsor Jazz Festival*. Parkwood Records PWCD 117.

Chapter Sixteen

Lee Konitz

Lee Konitz, who was born on October 13, 1927, in Chicago, was one of the very few alto saxophone players of his generation not to fall under the spell of Charlie Parker. Throughout a long career, his unique sound and approach to improvisation have shown him to be one of the great individualists of the music. This interview took place in May 1996, when he was visiting London to play at Ronnie Scott's club.

It was thanks to Milt Bernhart that I got my first job with Teddy Powell's band in 1945 when I replaced Charlie Ventura, which meant I had all the hot solos on tenor. Unfortunately, the chords were written in concert, which was difficult for me, as I was just beginning to understand how all that worked. When I stood up to play on my first gig, I was told that Teddy walked off the stage and started banging his head against a wall. He wasn't an instrumentalist, but he had a fine jazz/dance band, with good musicians like Boots Mussulli, who was very encouraging but mystified by my lack of knowledge. Boots was a lovely guy, and he wasn't only a very fine saxophone player but he was also the best poker player in the band; he never lost. A month after I joined, Teddy Powell had to disband because of tax problems with the IRS. A little later, I went with Jerry Wald for a while, and he could certainly play the high notes on the clarinet, but he didn't let me play any solos.

In 1947 I joined Claude Thornhill, who had a lovely "ballad" band, as you know, and I did my first recording with him. He had excellent arrangements by Gil Evans and Gerry Mulligan, and Gerry of course was mainly a writer then. His charts were great, and I also played his music with Stan Kenton, and those pieces were some of my favorites, because he really knew how to write for saxophones.

Moving on to the Miles Davis "Birth of the Cool" group, Miles was the titular leader because he had more of a name, and I suppose he could get the gigs; big deal, so he got one week at the Royal Roost. It has been said that we did two weeks there, but the way I remember it, the band did the first week, and for some reason Miles and I did the second week as a quintet with John Lewis, Al McKibbon, and Max Roach. I appreciated that Miles asked me, but we were basically playing bebop and I was not all that comfortable. The nonet was an arranger's band, because they rehearsed the music. Miles made some suggestions, but very few that I recall; I thought of it as Gerry's band really. What really concerns me is the way the band has been called "The Birth of the Cool," which I think is a little off. The nonet was a chamber ensemble where the solos were incidental to the writing, which was the most important aspect. The real "Birth of the Cool" for me was Lennie Tristano's music.[1]

I wrote "Subconscious-Lee" for my first recording session as a leader in 1949,[2] but the title is not mine; I would never call a tune "Subconscious-Lee." I think it was my colleague Arnold Fishkin who came up with that name, and all the other "Lee" titles over the years have been suggested by other people as well. Tony Fruscella was supposed to be on the date, but when he came to my room to rehearse, I apparently offended him in some way with a couple of suggestions, so he pulled out. He was a sad guy, and I didn't play with him again. I had real trouble relating to him because that whole junky mentality was always a big turnoff for me. I could never identify with it and hated that aspect of my environment.

During the late forties I rehearsed with a band Benny Goodman was forming with Wardell Gray, Gerry Mulligan, Doug Mettome, and Buddy Greco. I was playing lead alto, and I remember Benny sitting in a chair right in front of me as we ran down one of Eddie Sauter's arrangements. I was able to read alright, but I had no lead alto experience to speak of, and Benny said, "O.K., Pops, can you do something with it?" In other words, he wanted some "Hymie Schertzer"-like vibrato. He asked me to go on the road with the band, but I turned him down, as I was studying with Lennie Tristano. I remember him saying, "You're studying with Tristano? Why don't you study with Paul Hindemith?" Looking back, I wish that I had gone on the road with him, because I am sure I would have enjoyed the experience. Something else I remember from those rehearsals is that Benny and Gerry didn't get along at all.

Lennie Tristano played very little in public, because the club pianos were so bad. It was also difficult for him to get around, and he didn't like depending on others for that. We didn't work much, except at the Half Note once in a while, and I could probably count the gigs there on a couple of hands and maybe a foot. Audience reaction to him, though, was always great. Leonard Bernstein was very interested in Lennie's ideas and music, and they were very good friends. He once brought Aaron Copland to Lennie's studio to find out what Lennie was doing currently, and they both liked "Intuition," our free improvisation piece.[3] They wanted to know if there was a score to look at, but Lennie pointed out that it was fully improvised. Bernstein was always curious about jazz.

Neither Tristano or Warne Marsh, who was one of the great improvisers of this music, have been fully acknowledged, and I think they were both resentful about that. Two other Tristano students, Sal Mosca and Don Ferrara, have since retired from the active scene. Sal has followed in Lennie's footsteps and become a teacher, and Don, who was a very capable player, seemed to drop out just as he was becoming known for his work with Mulligan's CJB in the sixties. Apparently he started to change his embouchure, and the next I heard was that he was teaching but not playing, in California. Willie Dennis was another of Lennie's students, who unfortunately died in the mid sixties. He was a wonderful trombonist and a lovely guy, but I didn't know him that well because he used to drink and hang out at places like Jim 'n' Andy's. Being a family man, I didn't hang out there, and as a result I didn't work that much. Things have changed—I still don't hang out, but I work a lot now.

In 1952 Stan Kenton was trying to get more of a jazz band with charts by Bill Russo, Bill Holman, and Gerry Mulligan, so I joined playing the jazz alto chair, with Vinnie Dean on lead. Stan was a heavy drinker and I wasn't, which meant that I didn't hang out with the guys in the back of the bus, but a certain reputation had preceded me, and I just quietly tried to do my job. I appreciated him very much because he was great to everyone in the band, although he used to tell them not to smoke pot on the road, so there wouldn't be any legal problems. Some time after Vinnie left, Davey Schildkraut joined, and he was a very musical guy. He played really well, and I remember when Warne Marsh heard his recording of "Solar" with Miles, he thought it was Bird playing.

Charlie Parker of course was the major influence on alto, but it wasn't difficult for me to avoid, since temperamentally that music didn't really get to me. It was more intense than I was able to identify with at the time, but eventually I decided that was all ego and I was missing the greatest alto player who had ever lived. I started to learn his music without adopting his whole vocabulary, because it is such a temptation to play all those nice melodies like everyone else did, but I had other stimuli.

When the Kenton band was at the Palladium in Los Angeles, Gerry asked me to come and sit in with his quartet at the Haig on our nights off. I loved the pianoless concept, and I have worked in many similar groups over the years. I had heard stories about Chet not reading, but I was never in a situation to check that out. I had also heard that he didn't know chord changes, but I remember seeing him at a piano, playing changes to tunes, so that wasn't true. On my recordings with the quartet, I actually rejected "Too Marvelous for Words" because it didn't seem to fit into Gerry's context.[4] Later on, in 1957, I played on another Mulligan album called *The Sax Section*, with Al Cohn, Zoot Sims, and Allen Eager, and that was a fun date. What impressed me most was how nice Zoot sounded on alto—Allen Eager, too.[5] Looking back, Gerry and I didn't play that much together, but he was very encouraging to me in the early days, and I always felt he was an ally. We even got high together for the first time because we had that kind of close relationship.

A few years later, in 1959, I came to England with a group called "Jazz from Carnegie Hall," with Zoot Sims, J. J. Johnson, Kai Winding, Phineas Newborn, Oscar Pettiford, and Kenny Clarke, but I don't have happy memories of that tour. Oscar, rest his soul, was a beautiful musician but a terrible drinker. He became very hostile when he drank, and I got some bad vibrations from him. Before the tour, he had asked me to play with a little band in New York, so we already had a relationship. In Europe, though, he became really mean, which intimidated me, and if I get uncomfortable I can't play. Every night he and Kenny Clarke would be arguing back and forth, accusing each other of rushing the tempo, but eventually they would hug and kiss. Kenny of course was a lovely guy and a great drummer, and I used to sit behind the curtain, playing time with some sticks when he was on with Jay and Kai. Zoot didn't have trouble with anyone, as he was pretty stoned most of the time anyway.

Another time when I was uncomfortable in a playing situation was fairly recently at Carnegie Hall, just before Red Rodney died in 1994. We were both with Gerry Mulligan, John Lewis, Paul West, and Roy Haynes, and I just didn't feel that I was fitting in, but I never heard Red play so brilliantly—wow! When I play, I try to improvise from the first note, and if the acoustics are right I can do it. If they are wrong I'm messed up, because I don't have all that ready vocabulary, like a real professional should, I guess. All those clichés and hot licks carry you through sometimes.

I moved to California in 1962 because my wife and I felt there was a need to separate from Lennie Tristano, who was a very strong father-figure to me. We had been living at his house, but she encouraged me to move away to see what was happening elsewhere, and we stayed on the West Coast for a couple of years. I wasn't working much, but Warne and I used to play at Kim Novak's house in Big Sur on Sundays. Kim was not only a lovely woman but she was really nice, and she was quite a jazz fan. I wasn't soliciting for work, and it was nice forgetting about all that for a while, but I remember around 1963 going to see Miles with Frank Strozier at the Jazz Workshop in San Francisco. He asked me to sit in, which I didn't want to do, because that is the type of situation I am uncomfortable with, especially when another sax player is there. It was almost as though Miles was checking out a replacement, and I could never do that. I did sit in with Miles at the Village Vanguard when Herbie Hancock was with him, but again, I wasn't happy just jumping into an organized band and trying to find a voice.

During the seventies I did some work with my own nine-piece group. Dave Berger, who is a very fine writer, suggested the instrumentation, which was two trumpets, two trombones, alto, baritone, with three rhythm, and although I couldn't afford to pay for arrangements, there were a lot of people who were eager to write for it without a fee. Kenny Berger was with us for a time, and he is a fine baritone player, but he had to take a night off. Someone suggested Ronnie Cuber, who I didn't know, but he turned out to be very impressive. Kenny had been taking long solos with the band, and even though I wanted to give everyone a chance to play, I had suggested to him that we shorten the solos a little. For instance, I would start off with a couple of choruses, then the next guy would play four, someone else would take six, and suddenly you say, "Hey, wait a minute!" Not being a leader as such, I found I was sitting there listening to all the guys blow, which is fine up to a point, but eventually I decided that I wanted to do the playing myself. Getting back to the baritone chair, because Ronnie was so good, I hired him, and Kenny didn't forgive me for a long time, but sometimes these decisions have to be made.

In 1980 the band was booked to play some concerts in Washington, D.C., and we were asked to recreate some of the "Birth of the Cool" arrangements. I called Miles to see if he still had the charts, but he wasn't interested in helping, so I started transcribing from the records. In the end, I had to call Gerry Mulligan, because there were ensemble passages that I couldn't decipher. I went to his house in Connecticut, and he rewrote "Godchild," "Jeru," and "Rocker" in four hours. It was great to see him work.[6]

In 1992 Gerry asked me to join the "Rebirth of the Cool" band, and I stayed with him until the end of the European tour, when Jerry Dodgion took my place for some concerts in South America. After the initial novelty of playing those arrangements again, it became a little much for me. It was Gerry's show, and he did it very well, God rest his soul, but I was just sitting there interpreting the parts, and I felt I wasn't playing enough. The very last time we worked together was in Marciac, France, when Bob Brookmeyer and I were guests with his quartet in 1993. At Gerry's memorial concert I played "Alone

Together," which had been my feature on the "Rebirth" tour, and I asked everyone to hum a D concert, which is common to all the chords of the tune. I often do that so audiences and I are doing something together. While I played, there was a beautiful photo image on the wall of Gerry.

I travel six or seven months of the year, and I often do workshops for students. I sometimes ask myself what I can tell these young people, who probably play three times faster than I do and know every pentatonic scale created by man. In Austria last year I did a workshop with a difference, because I wanted to focus very directly on the music, so I just used hand signals and didn't say a word. Communicating these concepts in English can be difficult, but a translator creates even more problems. I got through two of the allotted three hours in that way in total silence, and humming was the main point. They warmed up their musical instrument with a hum and placed that hum in different parts of the body. I then played an interval and a chord and the students had to hum them both, and it really worked. They all seemed pleased to be doing something and not just listening to a bunch of concepts, but then I started to talk and spoilt everything!

Leonard Feather, who got a lot of things wrong, once claimed that I had turned down the chance of playing with some of the "name" bands, but that wasn't true. I would have loved to play with Duke Ellington or a real jazz band like Woody Herman, but they never asked me. I keep busy, though, by recording, and since December 1995 I have appeared on about twelve CDs. I'm just making them left and right, and I think these little boxes will be the only things left after it is all over!

NOTES

1. In Ira Gitler's *Jazz Masters of the '40s* (Da Capo), Gerry Mulligan is quoted agreeing with Lee: "As far as the 'Birth of the Cool' is concerned, I think Lennie is much more responsible than the Miles dates. It's hard to say unemotional because it's not exactly that, but there was a coolness about his whole approach in terms of the dynamic level. Lennie always had his own thing going. He never came out in the big world."

2. Lee Konitz Quintet. PRLP 7004.

3. Lennie Tristano Sextet. EAP 1-491.

4. Gerry Mulligan Quartet with Lee Konitz. Mosaic MR5-102. We must be thankful that Konitz did not get his way in rejecting "Too Marvelous for Words," because the title sums up his playing both on this track and on an inspired "Loverman." Mulligan and Baker, however, were not at their best, and for this reason Gerry initially felt that the material should not be released. He changed his mind because of the brilliance of Lee's playing.

5. Gerry Mulligan and "The Sax Section." Pacific Jazz 7243 8 3357520.

6. Whitney Balliett reports in *American Musicians: 56 Portraits in Jazz* (Oxford) that after Miles Davis had refused to help and Mulligan had transcribed some of the charts, Konitz called Davis again, telling the trumpeter that the arrangements had now been rewritten, and Miles apparently replied, "Man, you should have asked me. They're all in my basement." Konitz told Gil Evans about the conversation, who said, "Miles wouldn't have told you he had everything in the basement if you hadn't first told him you'd gone to the trouble to transcribe the records." Lee told Balliett that "Miles is a bona-fide eccentric."

Chapter Seventeen

Stan Levey

Stan Levey was one of the first drummers to apply the new rhythms introduced by Charlie Parker and Dizzy Gillespie in the early forties. At the same time, though, he was fighting professionally as a heavyweight boxer, once on the same bill as the great Joe Louis. Burt Korall accurately described him as a "Bop Pioneer," but in 1973 he stopped playing to become a highly successful commercial photographer. This interview took place in 1998, when he replied on cassette tape to my written list of questions.

I was born in Philadelphia, and my actual birth date is April 5, 1926. The mistake in the jazz reference books, which quote 1925, occurred many years ago, but I never bothered to correct it. I was completely self-taught because we couldn't afford a teacher, and that's why I play left-handed although I am right-handed; it just felt easier that way. I didn't learn to read really well until I joined Kenton's band in 1952, once again teaching myself. By the time I was doing studio work in the sixties and playing all the mallet instruments, I had become an accomplished reader. My first big influence was Chick Webb,[1] who I saw with Ella when my father took me to the Earle Theater when I was about ten years old.

School didn't have anything for me, so by the time I was fourteen I was on the street. A little later, in 1943, I started playing piano in the Downbeat club, which was close to the Earle Theater, although looking back it seems more like 1843! Anyway, I played by ear because I knew all the tunes, and guys like Coltrane, Jimmy Heath, Mulligan, and Ziggy Vines used to play there, too. Ziggy and I grew up together, and he was a great tenor player, but he was insane—mentally deficient for real. They had to put him away several times, but it didn't affect his talent because he could really play. I knew Gerry pretty well, but in those days he was a cocky little kid with a bad attitude. Around this time I was playing drums with Dizzy Gillespie. I was one of his first drummers, and he taught me a lot, because he was a carload of information which he was happy to share. As you know, he could play a little drums, and if you didn't understand something, he would sit down and demonstrate. He was a great guy, and "it" for me, and race was never a problem, because Dizzy was musically color-blind. Black musicians would sometimes ask him why he had a white drummer, and he would just tell them that if they could find a black drummer as good to let him know.

Another one of my early jobs was with Oscar Pettiford at the Tick Tock club in Boston, and he was a sweetheart—the best—as long as you could do the work, and if you couldn't, you would not be in the band. He liked to drink, and being a Native American he could get pretty rough, but with me he was always great, just a beautiful guy.

By 1944 Levey had made the move to New York, and he told Burt Korall about the first time he heard Max Roach with Gillespie at the Onyx club on 52nd Street: "The ferocity of the playing was new to me. I had never heard time split up like that. Max's playing had music within it . . . he changed the course of drumming." During World War II, Stan worked a lot in the clubs along 52nd Street, often opposite his friend Max Roach, but as he told writer John Tynan, "At the time, the street was a sideshow for most people. Not many dug what we were trying to do and most of them came by the Deuces, the Onyx, or the Spotlite because they heard there was some weird music being played. It was like a freak show I guess, and the musicians were the freaks."

I worked with Allen Eager at the Three Deuces, and he was another guy with an attitude—really sold on himself. He was a pretty good swing player, rather like a hard-edged Lester Young, though not as laid back, and of course he stole from Prez, but they all stole from Prez; everybody steals from somebody. I also worked with Charlie Parker on his first date as a leader at the Spotlite club, with Hank Jones or sometimes Joe Albany on piano. We played there on Mondays as a trio, because we couldn't afford a bass player, and Joe of course was an incomplete player and he was the first to admit it. He loved the music but he couldn't play it the way he wanted to. Around that time, Charlie and I were hired by Ben Webster because Ben wanted to upgrade his sound, but after about three nights he said, "You two—get out of here." Ben was a great guy and a wonderful player, and much later we became friends, but we were not playing his type of music.

In 1945 I made the trip to Billy Berg's in Hollywood with Dizzy and Bird. Dizzy decided to add Lucky Thompson to the group because Bird could be unreliable, so Lucky was hired as an "off the bench hitter." He was there to fill in if Bird was late or didn't show, which happened a lot. Nineteen forty-five was also the year I played with Woody Herman's First Herd, probably the greatest band he ever had. I took Davey Tough's place, and the band was so fantastic, it didn't really need a drummer. I was with him for about six months, and he had the Candoli brothers, Flip Phillips, and Bill Harris. It was just unbelievable. I wasn't too good with big bands in those days, and eventually Don Lamond took over.

A little earlier, before I left Philly, I had been with Benny Goodman on the road for a couple of months. I must have been about sixteen or maybe seventeen, so I was a little green for the band, and anyway, Benny was weird; he never looked at me or talked to me while I was with him, and when he got rid of me, his brother Irving came over and said, "Benny says you should go home," and that was it. Another big band I worked with in the forties was Charlie Ventura's at the Spotlite club. Charlie was straight down the middle and a nice guy, but over the years he got taken for a ride and ended up broke. I wasn't too crazy about his approach, but he played his horn pretty well. He just wanted to blow, so you didn't really connect with him, because he wasn't a talker, just a lot of "Yeah, man, that's great"; one of those sort of guys.

In those early years around 1943 and 1944, I was boxing professionally as a heavyweight to earn a few extra dollars. I fought at Madison Square Garden, and I was one of the preliminary bouts at the Polo Grounds in the Bronx when Joe Louis was the headliner. I carried on fighting until 1949, and I boxed a lot of very good fighters who beat the crap out of me! The story Ira Gitler mentions in his book[2] about Max Roach, Art Mardigan, and me sharing an apartment near 52nd Street in 1946 is something I don't remember, unless my memory has gone, which it might have done. Art was a very private person and a middle of the road player who had some good points but didn't do anything outstanding. He didn't have a lot of drive, but he was a swinger and a nice guy. I liked him very much, and we got along fine. I also played with George Shearing when he first came to the States and had just got off the boat, but this wasn't the Shearing you know from his famous quintet. He was a very rigid player in those days, and his time was very up and down, rushing like crazy; he was just not terrific. Of course later on, George developed into more of an act, and he played some damn good music. I worked with Dizzy at the Spotlite when he had Leo Parker on baritone, who was a very good player. He got all over the horn and had all of Bird's licks down, but he died much too young. In 1947 I worked at a Long Island restaurant called the Happy Monster with Lennie Tristano and Chubby Jackson. Tristano was another very private guy whose style was a little brutal, but it was different harmonically and advanced for the time. He was interesting to listen to, and I enjoyed playing with him.

By 1951 I had decided to return to Philadelphia. Apparently David Allyn once said that he and I worked with Art Mooney's band around this time,[3] but I was *never* in Art Mooney's band unless I was drunk; they're not going to pin that on me, man! Anyway, I formed a little quartet in Philly with Richie Kamuca, Red Garland, and Nelson Boyd, and it was a great little group. All the singers that came to town, like Ella and Sarah Vaughan, would ask for us to accompany them, and it was a lot of fun.

In 1952 Stan Kenton was playing in Philadelphia, and this is when he asked me to join the band, thanks to recommendations from Conte Candoli and Buddy Childers. I took Frank Capp's place, who was an excellent drummer, but in those days he was not strong enough to handle the band. Gerry Mulligan, who was a wonderful arranger, was writing for the band, although I think he felt we were too loud most of the time. Personality-wise, he had mellowed a little since I had first known him when we were kids, and he had become a premier baritone player, having really brought that instrument to the forefront. I loved the group he had with Chet at the Haig, because they created a new sound, and when that happens you have really achieved something. Those guys were great. Bob Graettinger was another one of the writers, and we roomed together for a while. His charts were really out there and not my cup of tea. But what did I know; I was only the drummer! I was on "City of Glass," and he knew what he was writing but I didn't. With the soloists, Stan would allow the guys to play to the limit of their ability but no further, and if someone got too far out and it was getting a little nuts, he would put the brakes on. When I was with him, the rhythm section was not the greatest, because a couple of players, whose names I won't mention, had an agenda of their own. In other words, they were not good team players, which made it difficult, because it put most of the work on my back. It was a hard job, but we got it done. Kenton was about forty when I was in the band, and we were all in our mid twenties, so he was something of a father-figure. He was a great guy, and we all miss him.

In 1954 Max Roach wanted to get out of his contract at the Lighthouse, and he called me to see if I would take over. I was ready to leave Kenton, so I joined Howard Rumsey and the All-Stars and stayed for the next five years. Howard was very innovative as far as putting groups together, and he was a good, honest guy, but I was at the Lighthouse too long. It started to get to me, because you can't do the same thing over and over. How long can you stay in one place? While I was there, I did some recordings with Oscar Peterson and Stan Getz, and there is nobody better than Oscar in his style; he is just wonderful. Stan, of course, could stand up with the best of them, like Parker and Gillespie, and it was a big loss when he died. He could be tough, especially with money, where he would screw you pretty good, but he didn't try it with me, so we didn't have any trouble at all. We got along just fine, and I did some of my best work with him, like the album *For Musicians Only*.[4] The date also featured Sonny Stitt and Dizzy, and although there was no real leader, Gillespie chose the material, and it was his idea to play most of the tunes at such a breakneck tempo. It was a bebop album, and there was some competitiveness between the three of them, because they were the front-runners of that music. Having said that, there were no real egos, and Stan and Sonny got on well together, but it was strictly work; no fooling around. I think Stan stole the whole thing, because he was the most creative player on the album, outblowing everybody, and his solo on "Wee" was just fantastic. Sonny Stitt, for me, was just a clone of Charlie Parker, droning out chorus after chorus of licks and then more licks. He just would not stop playing, and he rushed like crazy. Parker once said that if you played more than four choruses, you were only practicing, but it took Sonny four choruses just to get going! I liked him better on tenor, believe it or not.

I recorded a lot in the fifties with Shorty Rogers, who was an innovator in the West Coast sound, whatever that is. He was a great little guy who never gave anybody any trouble in his life. One of the best trumpeters of all time is Conte Candoli, who is still underrated.[5] He is a terrific player, and I would like to see more things happen for him. Another one who falls into that category is Jack Sheldon, who has become more well known for his comedy act, but he can really play, and he is also a fine singer. One of my favorite tenor players was Zoot Sims, who was one of the top three who ever lived. I always enjoyed him, because he was a great guy, and I'm sorry he had to leave. Dexter Gordon, like Zoot, was another one of the real swingers who used the Lester Young approach, but with a more modern sound and swing. He played on one of my best albums, and he was a helluva guy and a wonderful player.[6]

In the early sixties I worked with Victor Feldman, Dennis Budimir, and Max Bennett, backing Peggy Lee, who was a very nice lady, a great musician, and a terrific singer. She was always fair about the money, which was never a big problem, but sometimes she added a bongo drummer to the group, and that was a drag. I also toured all over the world with Ella Fitzgerald, along with Paul Smith and Wilfred Middlebrooks. She was another wonderful musician, just fantastic, and although she was shy, she could be very tough when it was necessary. Like Peggy, Ella was very fair with the money, and she always mentioned the guys' names when we played. In 1964 I toured Japan with Pat Boone, and I would like to forget that! Actually Pat was alright, because he was a nice guy and he treated us O.K., but he wasn't a musical icon, and once again Paul Smith was the musical director. I also worked on an ABC television show for Frank Sinatra with a whole bunch of jazz guys like Bud Shank and Plas Johnson. We didn't talk to Frank, and we never saw him until showtime, when he would come in, do his shtick, and get off. But if things weren't going well, he would be real tough. Bill Miller, who was a lovely guy as well as being a good pianist and writer, used to rehearse the band without Frank, and he was with him until the end. One of the pianists who accompanied Peggy, Ella, and Frank was Lou Levy. I have known him for about fifty years, and he is a wonderful guy and a mainstay of the piano. He is still working and looking good.[7]

As far as some of my contemporary drummers are concerned, Shelly Manne was an innovator, because he did many different things that had never been done before. He was a good swinger who had everything. Technique-wise, Art Blakey was like a diamond in the rough, but he had that hard swing that could swing you right off the bandstand. Joe Morello, of course, was a good technician. I remember one time in Washington, when I was with Ella and he was with Brubeck, we were hanging out the way drummers do. Now Joe has very bad eyesight, maybe as bad as legally blind. Anyway, I asked him what his hobbies were and he said, "Target practice," and I remember saying, "Not with me, Joe!" There is nothing to say about Buddy Rich that has not been said before. You can't add anything because he is just the top, the cream of the cream. Kenny Clarke was another swinger and one of the originators of bebop music, and Jo Jones created the hi-hat sound that you hear today. Boy, was he something. He had that floating rhythm, and he was a nice guy.

In a 1961 interview with Alun Morgan,[8] Stan said that he was going to carry on "Hitting those drums until the drums start hitting back at me," but by 1973 he had stopped playing completely. "I already had my photography business, so I cut out the drumming and I don't miss it at all. I never played again because the music business changed and I went on to other things." As a coda to the interview, he mentioned some of his all-time favorite musicians:

Trumpet—Dizzy Gillespie. Trombone—Frank Rosolino, Carl Fontana. Alto—Charlie Parker. Tenor—Sonny Rollins, Stan Getz. Baritone—Gerry Mulligan. Clarinet—Benny Goodman. Flute—Frank Wess, Bud Shank. Vibes—Victor Feldman, Milt Jackson. Piano—Bud Powell. Guitar—Charlie Christian. Bass—Oscar Pettiford. Drums—Max Roach. Singers—Nat Cole, Frank Sinatra, Ella Fitzgerald. Arranger—Bill Holman. Big band—Count Basie. Small group—Dizzy Gillespie/Charlie Parker.

NOTES

1. Stan once told Burt Korall, "Most drummers were just time-keepers but Chick brought much more to the music. He was so inventive and always enhanced what the band played" (*Modern Drummer*).
2. Ira Gitler, *Jazz Masters of the '40s* (Macmillan).
3. Ira Gitler, *Swing to Bop* (Oxford University Press).
4. Dizzy Gillespie, Stan Getz, Sonny Stitt, *For Musicians Only*. Verve MGV-8198.
5. Conte Candoli died on December 14, 2001.
6. Stan Levey, *Stanley the Steamer*. Affinity AFF 766 CD.
7. Lou Levy died on January 23, 2001.
8. Alun Morgan, "Stan Levey," *Jazz Monthly* (September 1961).

Chapter Eighteen

Jack Montrose

During the fifties, when the jazz media spotlight shone brightly on Los Angeles, Jack Montrose's writing and playing were very important ingredients in what became known as West Coast Jazz. In April 2000 he replied on cassette tape to my list of questions about some of his career highlights, which included recording with Chet Baker, Shelly Manne, Bob Gordon, Art Pepper, and Joe Maini.

I was born in Detroit on December 30, 1928, which of course was during the Depression, and although we were very poor, I was never unhappy. I thought that everybody was like us and all kids had one pair of pants per semester. To escape the poverty, we moved to Chattanooga when I was about five years old, where we lived in a black ghetto called Onion Bottom. Thanks to a relative who financed my Dad in a grocery store which had a jukebox, I heard my first records by people like Lionel Hampton, Johnny Hodges, Benny Goodman, and Duke Ellington, and I was thrilled by it all.

Nobody in my family was musical, but I acquired a metal clarinet when I was about twelve, and a couple of years later, I worked a whole summer in a pawnshop to buy a C melody sax for $20. I was completely self-taught because we couldn't afford a teacher, and by the time I was fourteen, I had joined the union and played my first professional job on alto. Although I didn't really know what I was doing, I had also begun writing arrangements by ear—and right away discovered the bottom line: whatever sounds right is the truth. I switched to tenor when I heard Don Byas and Joe Thomas, and for the next couple of years I played with bands down South. By 1946 I moved with my family to Los Angeles and started doing one-nighters around town with people like Lennie Niehaus, Jack Sheldon, and Russ Freeman. Russ always knew more tunes than anyone else and was very generous with his harmonic knowledge. He helped us all and influenced my progress to a great degree, and I have always loved him for that. He lives in Las Vegas now, and it never ends, because he still knows tunes that I don't.[1] The only other person who may know as many tunes as Russ is Herb Geller.

It was around 1948 that I first met Bob Gordon. He was with Alvino Rey's band, and we used to play together whenever he was in town. I never knew him to play anything except the baritone, which was the perfect instrument for him because he played it so well, with an absolutely beautiful sound. I have heard some guys play very effectively, but nobody sounded like Bob; he was unique. He and Gerry Mulligan both played Conns, because they made the best baritones, and although Gerry had a great sound, Bob's was even better. He had a natural mind-to-hand coordination that gave him fast fingers, which was unusual on the baritone at that time. Incidentally, Paul Desmond was also in Rey's band, and I enjoyed his playing very much, even though it was a little one-dimensional. He was very poetic and melodic, but his intensity never seemed to change. He actually sounded better on recordings than in person, because he didn't have a big sound, so he was hard to hear in clubs. The only time I ever worked with him was when we played with Jack Fina for about a month. Jack had been Freddy Martin's pianist, and he had a band at the Coconut Grove in the Ambassador Hotel with three tenors: me, Paul, and Herb Geller.

For a lot of us growing up in the late forties in Los Angeles, Herbie Harper's jam sessions at the Showtime on West Ventura Boulevard were an important part of our musical education. They were like a postgraduate study in jazz for guys like Bill Perkins, Shorty Rogers, Chet Baker, Art Pepper, and myself. Art of course was always one of my heroes, and I was unashamedly influenced by him and Chet Baker. One of the first things I notice about a player is his sound, and I think that Art had the loveliest sound on alto, outside of Johnny Hodges. He admired Zoot Sims very much, and he even sounded like Zoot to me. I adored his playing, and still do, but I think he lost it for a while when he became too influenced by John Coltrane towards the end of his life. He lost what was valuable, because a great artist should search within *himself* without copying, and Art fell into that hole. As Lennie Niehaus told you, Art lost his honesty and played in a style that didn't suit him; he was just not playing "Art" anymore.

Chet was always an outstanding player. He immediately grabbed your attention, and just like a comet blazing through the sky, he wouldn't be denied. Gerry Mulligan in his wisdom really nailed it when he said that Chet knew everything about chords except their names, because he had the best ears of anyone I have ever encountered. The other myth about Chet not reading music is quite untrue. He played my charts, which were far from easy, as well as anyone.

In 1949 I played in Tom Talbert's Jazz Orchestra, which included Art Pepper and Claude Williamson. I loved that band and, funnily enough, four or five years ago Sea Breeze reissued one of our albums and Tom sent me a check for $41.25, which was scale for a record session at that time. There were a lot of very talented players in the band who were never heard of again, like Steve White, who was a marvelous tenor player. He was one of the greatest white Prez-influenced players I have ever heard and could have been one of the "Four Brothers" without any trouble. His ears were so good that he could play anything, and he had all the makings of becoming a legend.[2]

I also did a lot of playing with Shorty Rogers, and around 1952 Bob Gordon and I worked in John Kirby's last group at the 5-4 Ballroom, on 54th and Broadway. It was a sextet that played for dancers, and that is where I first met Gerry Mulligan. His girlfriend, Gail Madden, was a photographer at the ballroom, and he used to sit in with us every night when he came to pick her up. I had already become aware of him from the "Birth of the Cool" sessions, which was the only jazz writing that influenced me at that time. Those charts were wonderful, and the arrangers seemed to be affected by something that was quite unearthly. Gerry was a genius, and when he and Chet were at the Haig, I used to visit two or three nights a week. It was an unbelievably stimulating experience, hearing them play together, and the rest is history, because that is one of the best jazz groups *ever*. This was around the time I had a seven-piece rehearsal band, which included at different times Bob Gordon, Bill Perkins, Stu Williamson, and Dave Madden, and for a while we worked the off-nights opposite Gerry's group. Dave isn't too well known, but he was a very talented tenor player and one of my best friends.[3] When Chet left Gerry, Dick Bock wanted to do something different with him, so he recorded him with my band on an album called *The Chet Baker Ensemble* in December 1953.[4]

By this time I was studying for my degree in music and composition at L.A. State College, and one day between classes, I went down to CBS on Sunset Boulevard to audition for Jerry Gray's band. I got the gig, which was the jazz tenor chair, and I stayed with Jerry off and on for about five years. We were resident on the Bob Crosby radio show, and we played at the Ambassador Hotel on Wilshire Boulevard. Bob Gordon also had a steady gig, working around town with George Redman, who was the drummer with the Harry Zimmerman orchestra on the Dinah Shore T.V. show. George had a great following, and it was a very hip little group, usually one horn and rhythm, so there was a lot of jazz. Whenever I was free, I used to sit in with them at places like the Bombay club, and later on, Bud Shank and Maynard Ferguson were with the band. One way to keep busy when things were slow in the music business was to work in one of the many strip joints around L.A., so I started playing at the Body Shop on Sunset Boulevard. Herb Geller was the first real jazz player I knew to work those clubs, and it kept his head above water when times were hard. I used to sub for him there if he had other work.

In May 1954 I arranged and played on Bob Gordon's only date as a leader, and we used his friend Billy Schneider from St. Louis on drums.[5] We had been working in clubs like the Purple Onion, Peacock Lane, and Peacock Alley, and at the time of the recording, one of my original ballads was untitled. Bob asked if I would dedicate it to his wife, which I was happy to do, and I think "For Sue" came out very nicely. Another title, "Onion Bottom," was a reference to the area that my family had lived in when we first moved to Chattanooga.

I was also playing a lot with Art Pepper at the Angel Room on South Crenshaw Boulevard and Esther's on Hermosa Beach, and that summer our quintet appeared opposite Max Roach and Clifford Brown at the Tiffany club. Dick Bock wanted to record them with some West Coast musicians, and I was booked to write the arrangements, but I didn't play, despite what Ira Gitler has written, although I would have loved to.[6] Dick decided the instrumentation and personnel, and it was his choice to do "Blueberry Hill" and "Gone with the Wind," not Brownie's. Clifford had an old studio upright at his motel in the West Adams district, and I used to visit him every day to work on the music, which was written with Max in mind, because he was supposed to be on the session. Unfortunately he got into a money hassle with Dick and bowed out at the last minute, so Shelly Manne was called, and he played just beautifully, bless his heart. I spent about two months writing the charts, and we rehearsed the band three or four times over at my place. As you can hear on the record, everyone jelled immediately and it was a very friendly date.[7]

I have already said that Chet Baker was an unsurpassed "ear" player with no theoretical knowledge. Clifford Brown on the other hand had Chet's ears, but he was also a thoroughly schooled musician who would have practiced all day if he could. He was an absolute giant, very advanced in theory and totally immersed in music. He was also a sweet person, without a drink or drug problem, living a perfectly clean lifestyle. Along with Stu Williamson and Bob Gordon, Zoot Sims was the other horn on the Brownie date, and for a while he caused me the same problem that Pepper had with Coltrane. I loved his playing so much that I couldn't imagine it any other way, and I had a rough time until I discovered myself again. Zoot was a marvel, and *still* is. He may no longer be with us, but as John O'Hara said about Gershwin's death, "I don't have to believe it if I don't want to."

While I was working with Clifford, Art Pepper and I recorded an album with our own group which we used to refer to as Art's "Spice Suite."[8] This was because it featured a number of his originals like "Nutmeg," "Cinnamon," "Thyme Time," and "Art's Oregano." I don't know the significance of the other titles, but nutmeg was something inmates in confinement used to get high on. After the record release we planned to go East with our quintet, but as so often happened, Art got busted and disappeared off the scene. Being a junky, he was not the most reliable person in the world, but he loved playing so much that I can only remember him missing a couple of nights at the Tiffany club. When it came time to play, nothing else existed for him. He was one of my very best friends, easy to get along with, and marvelous to make music with.

In 1954 I spent six months with Stan Kenton, but truthfully I didn't like the band, although I adored the man. We were on different musical paths; that is not to say he was wrong, but his muse was not my muse. He actually hired me to write for him, and I was going to submit some of my originals like "Credo," "Pretty," "Speakeasy," and "Listen, Hear." I sketched them out on the long Kenton bus rides, but I changed my mind because the band was just too loud for my material. "Credo" was very ephemeral and delicate, but they would have destroyed it, totally losing the inner voices. "Listen, Hear" was a double fugue, and I couldn't imagine Stan playing it the way I wanted. Until you play in one, you have no idea how damned loud a big band can be, and Stan's could be pretty overwhelming.[9]

I rearranged all those numbers for my 1955 sextet album with Conte Candoli and Bob Gordon.[10] Paul Moer was the pianist, and Bob and I liked his playing so much that he did three albums with us. I have never found anyone else who could play those sextet charts as well as he could. He came from Florida, and I first met him at the Cottage Italia, where they used to have marvelous jam sessions. Shelly Manne was on the date, and he was a prince of drummers, but Bob Gordon didn't like his playing at all. Bob preferred the New York school, like Philly Joe Jones and Art Mardigan, because he was an aggressive player and he liked aggressive drummers. We had both played with Philly Joe when he had come out to the Coast, and Bob especially liked the way he used his hi-hat on two and four, something Shelly didn't always do, which occasionally led to arguments on record dates. It's strange how some people don't get along. Bob and Art Pepper didn't like each other, and as far as I know, they never worked together. As Herb Geller told you, Joe Maini and Art actually hated each other, and I was there the night they nearly came to blows.

A few weeks after we recorded the last titles for the sextet album, Bob was killed in a car accident. I met his parents at the funeral, which is when I discovered that his real name was Bob Resnick, and I don't know why he changed it. His wife, Sue, wanted some of us to play at the service, so Jack Sheldon, Bob Enevoldsen, Joe Maini, and I played my arrangement of

"Goodbye," which under the circumstances was very difficult to perform. If he hadn't died, things would have been a lot different in my life, because we were only just beginning. We had great plans for the future and would have certainly carried on playing together; I actually had another album already written for us. We were a partnership, and I have never missed anyone as much as I missed Bob Gordon.[11] Sue eventually went to live on Staten Island, and she died a few years ago.

In 1956 Art Pepper and I were supposed to make an L.P. called "Blues and Vanilla."[12] We rehearsed it, but I think he got busted again, so I called Joe Maini, and he was bebop incarnate, doing it so well and so naturally. I played a lot with Joe, and he was great fun and a wonderful player who didn't get recorded enough. We did studio sessions together when Marty Paich hired us for some Mel Tormé recordings, but Joe was on lead alto, so he didn't get any solos. Mel Tormé of course had the best phrasing, the best ears, and the best breath control; he was just superb, and I think Marty's writing for him and that little band was excellent. Marty had a way of understanding singers very well, and although it was not my kind of writing (I would have done it differently), those records still sound very good. I know that Corky Hale told you that Mel was hard to get along with, but I never saw it. I was on many dates with him and found him to be pleasant, and everything was as efficient and musical as could be.

All through the fifties I did a lot of writing for Dick Bock at Pacific Jazz, and he had a considerable input regarding players and repertoire, but he could not have been easier to get along with. He was a marvelous man in the right place at the right time to be part of the regeneration of jazz on the West Coast. However by 1960 something happened, because suddenly all the recording stopped and jazz seemed to be out of favor. I was still working in jazz clubs and strip joints where the girls were all jazz fans, so it was great practice. I also did some rock 'n' roll dates, but I don't want to talk about them at all—they were painful. That music started edging us out, although some of the jazz guys had a lot to do with turning off their audiences with their terrible arrogance. They started turning their backs on the customers, for instance, and I don't just mean Miles; a lot of lesser players were doing it. Also the *avant-garde* movement was too inaccessible and tough to take, and probably still is. Tastes were changing, but not being a social scientist, I could do nothing except suffer the results. I tried the Hollywood scene, but I couldn't make the deadlines; they just debilitated me. An agent would call and want three arrangements for the next day, and that isn't how I like to work. I'm not suited to turning out material without regard to its quality, so I was ready to quit by that time.

I decided to move to Las Vegas in 1971 because, if I had to do commercial work, Vegas provided a more relaxed atmosphere. I started playing in the shows, which were first class at the time, and acts like Sinatra, Steve and Eydie, Dean Martin, Sammy Davis, and Tony Bennett were certainly as good as the music could get in show business. I didn't rail against it, and I didn't mind going to work every night. This is when I met my wife, Zena, who was a violinist in house bands, and we still work together sometimes. Although I was embroiled in making a living in show business, I didn't stop playing jazz. The union had a rehearsal hall with a bar that stayed open all night, and after the second show, everyone would go down there to play. That carried on until about 1985, when we lost the musicians' building during a strike. There is not much work left in the casinos now, because most of the acts we used to accompany are no longer there.

Don Byas was the man who made me want to play the tenor, but Charlie Parker has to be my all-time favorite instrumentalist. He was absolute perfection as a creator, and any player who grew up during that time would have to admit there was no denying Bird. His solos were actually compositions on a level far advanced from anyone else, and some guys became so taken with him that they became cripples; they couldn't play anymore. They missed the message, which is to be yourself and not be a copy. Funnily enough, the first time I heard him, I wasn't really impressed with his sound, but I soon realized that his ideas required that particular sound. When I understood that, Bird became a fixture in my consciousness, as did John Coltrane later on. John had a sound without historical evolution—totally unique, and it went with what he played. The ideas couldn't have been produced with any other sound, which is true of every great player.

There are some marvelous writers in jazz, but nobody has influenced me as much as Duke Ellington and Billy Strayhorn. I would also have given anything to have played in Duke's band, and if it exists in another lifetime, I want to be in it!

NOTES

1. Russ Freeman died two years after this interview took place, on June 27, 2002.

2. Steve White's album on Nocturne OJCCD-1889-2, where he is accompanied by the incomparable Jimmy Rowles, confirms Jack's enthusiasm.

3. In 1945 Dave Madden recorded with Stan Kenton's band, where he sat next to the eighteen-year-old Stan Getz. He also worked with Tom Talbert, Woody Herman, Jerry Gray, Si Zentner, Dave Pell, Frank Capp, and Harry James. He and Gail Madden were what the gossip columnists refer to as an "item," although they never married. Gail later had a similar relationship with both Bob Graettinger and Gerry Mulligan.

4. *Chet Baker Ensemble*. Fresh Sound FSR CD 0175.

5. Bob Gordon, *Memorial*. Fresh Sound FSRCD180.

6. Leonard Feather and Ira Gitler, eds. *The Biographical Encyclopedia of Jazz* (Oxford University Press).

7. Clifford Brown, *Jazz Immortal*. Pacific Jazz CDP 7468502.

8. Art Pepper, *The Complete Discovery-Savoy Master Takes*. Definitive Records DRCD 11218.

9. Jack left the Kenton band in October 1954. He was replaced by the obscure Varty Haritounian, whose only commercial recording was with Serge Chaloff and Dick Twardzik in Boston a month previously, titled "The Fable of Mabel" (*The Complete Serge Chaloff Sessions.* Mosaic MD4-147).

10. Jack Montrose Sextet. Pacific Jazz 7243 4 93161 2 6.

11. In Gerard J. Hoogeveen's discography of the great Bob Gordon, Jack Montrose had this to say about his friend and colleague: "Bob Gordon was an inspiration to every jazz musician or aspirant who ever heard him play, or was perhaps fortunate enough to share the bandstand with him. Fortunate enough to partake of the fire that roared, the sparks that flew and the proclamations of the Gods that sounded, when he put his big horn to his lips and made the world abound with life, zest, and unbounded love. For the world was a better place to live in when he played and perhaps this singular ability to make it so, was in itself his greatest gift. . . . His feeling was contagious, his sound indomitable, his time impeccable, the beauty and logic of his thought inexplicable. I learned to write through playing and it was largely through Bob's influence that I learned how to play." Jack Montrose did not exaggerate, for Bob Gordon was, indeed, *a giant*.

12. Jack Montrose, *Blues and Vanilla*. Fresh Sound NL45844.

Chapter Nineteen

Gerry Mulligan

Gerry Mulligan was born on April 6, 1927, in Queens, New York City. By the time he was seventeen, he was contributing arrangements to Johnny Warrington's band for their broadcasts on WCAU, a local radio station in Philadelphia. Over the next few years his writing for Elliot Lawrence, Gene Krupa, Claude Thornhill, Miles Davis, and Stan Kenton showed him to be one of the best of the young postwar generation of arrangers. Although he played in all those bands except for Kenton's, he was far better known as a writer than as an instrumentalist. It was not until his move to California in 1952 and the formation of his first quartet that he really started to develop as a baritone soloist. We met on two occasions at his suite in London's Ritz Hotel in May 1994, and we concentrated on his career until the demise of the Concert Jazz Band in 1964. I hoped to continue our discussion at a later date, but Gerry died on January 20, 1996.

In the late forties I played in a group with Kai Winding, Brew Moore, and George Wallington, in clubs like Bop City in New York. We also recorded quite a lot, and we visited Kansas City in 1947, which is where I first met Bob Brookmeyer, when he sat in on valve trombone. At the same time I was playing and writing for Elliot Lawrence, and I was featured in a quintet from within the band, with Phil Urso on tenor. When I wrote "Elevation" for Elliot, he claimed a joint-composer credit, which was the convention with bandleaders in those days, but it was my tune. A little later that band became very good when he had Charlie Walp on lead trumpet with Ollie Wilson and the Swope brothers on trombone. Those guys were known as the "Washington brass section," and Herbie Steward was there, too, on lead alto. I remember walking into a rehearsal when they were playing one of my charts, with Tiny Kahn on drums, and it was the first time I heard a big band make my things

143

sound really great. The first time that happened with a small group was Georgie Auld's little band, with Serge Chaloff and Red Rodney.

For the Miles Davis nonet I actually arranged seven of the twelve numbers that were recorded, although I have seen most of them credited to somebody else over the years. There were two other titles not included on the *Birth of the Cool* album, "S'il Vous Plait" and "Why Do I Love You?" which were John Lewis arrangements. You may have heard that Miles wanted another trumpet to play lead so that he could concentrate on soloing, but that is quite untrue. He didn't want to know about another trumpeter, and remember, if we had someone else on lead, they would have phrased the band into another area. Miles wanted to do it his way, and I wanted him to do it his way. If you were writing for him in that band, you knew exactly where you were, and I only wish I had written more for it.[1]

A lot of these things seem easy in retrospect, because in 1992 we went on the road with the "Rebirth of the Cool" band and worked with those charts. That's really why I did it, because I finally wanted an insight into those pieces, to see where we might have taken them. Before the tour I thought a lot about the instrumentation, because I didn't see any reason to be nailed to Miles's nine-piece. The tentet arrangements I had from California, for instance, had two trumpets and two baritones, and I liked the idea of two baritones. You can have them playing unison in the ensemble, and it's like a cello section, which is fun. I really wanted a baritone doubling clarinet, but finding somebody to do both became a problem. Ken Peplowski was supposed to be with us, and he was a nice guy and a beautiful player, but I didn't want to push him into switching from tenor to baritone. Unfortunately on the day of rehearsal, he telephoned to say that he'd been running for a plane at a small airport somewhere when he slipped on the wet tarmac and broke his ankle. That's when I got Mark Lopeman, who is a fine musician, and he had done a lot of the transcribing for me.

Getting back to Miles's band, we originally wanted to have Danny Polo on clarinet, but he was on the road with Claude Thornhill all the time. During most of the years of Thornhill's success, he had two clarinets, Irving Fazola and Danny Polo, and they both had this great wood sound because they played "Albert" system. This was not "Benny Goodman" clarinet you know; we're talking about something much darker and richer, which were the timbres we were looking for. Anyway, Gil Evans and I decided not to mess around with the clarinet if we couldn't have Danny. Miles liked the idea of having a singer, so he had his friend Kenny Hagood sing a couple of numbers, one of which, "Darn That Dream," was recorded. For the 1992 "Rebirth" tour, I rewrote that arrangement, although what I actually did was to finish it, because I wrote it in too much of a hurry for Miles. The other ballad we featured on the tour was "Good-bye John," which I dedicated to Johnny Mercer.

Before I left the East Coast for California in 1951, I had already started experimenting with a pianoless rhythm section, using trumpeters like Don Joseph, Jerry Lloyd, or Don Ferrara, with Peter Ind on bass and Al Levitt on drums. It was actually Gail Madden who suggested the idea. She played piano and percussion, and as a matter of fact I've recently been trying to find out what happened to her. It was her experiments that helped me when I got to L.A., since I already had an idea of what would and wouldn't work. The last record date I did before leaving New York was in September for Prestige, playing my compositions with Allen Eager and George Wallington, among others. Gail played maracas on some titles, but the atmosphere was spoilt by Jerry Lloyd, who couldn't pass up the opportunity of making jokes about her boobs bouncing up and down when she played. Jerry was an old-guard male chauvinist and couldn't help it, but after a while, I sent the band home except for the saxes. I didn't want to do that thing with just Allen and me, but I had to complete the album.[2]

I decided to leave New York because the drug scene was a little out of control and the work was rapidly drying up, so I sold my horns and Gail and I hitchhiked to California. I did a little work along the way, using borrowed horns, mostly tenors, and I remember playing in a cowboy band outside Albuquerque for a while. I was lucky, because I knew a guy who was teaching at the university there, and he helped us keep body and soul together. When we reached L.A., I sold some arrangements to Stan Kenton, thanks to Gail, who arranged the introduction through her friendship with Bob Graettinger. She was really responsible for Gracttinger's survival up to that point, because he was nearly "done for" with alcohol, but when I met him, he was absolutely straight. I liked him a lot, and he was in the thick of a reworked "City of Glass," and he was also writing a cello and a horn concerto. As a matter of fact, I had heard the original "City of Glass" when they were rehearsing at the Paramount Theater in New York a couple of years before.

When I first got to L.A., I did some playing with Shorty Rogers at Balboa with Art Pepper, Wardell Gray, Coop, and June Christy. Shorty was very good and always used me whenever he could, and I remember Bob Gordon was around at that time, and I liked him a lot. I soon met Dick Bock, who was in charge of publicity at the Haig, and I started working there with Paul Smith, who was the leader on the off-nights, when the main attraction had a night off. We worked opposite Erroll Garner's trio, and when he left, they brought in Red Norvo with Tal Farlow and Charles Mingus. That's when I took over as leader on the off-nights, using Jimmy Rowles until I got the quartet together with Chet Baker, Bob Whitlock, and Chico Hamilton. I had encountered Chet at jam sessions in the San Fernando Valley, so when it came time to put the group together, I wanted to see how he would work out. Gail had already told me about Chico, who was just finishing a gig with Charlie Barnet's seven- or eight-piece band at the Streets of Paris down on Hollywood Boulevard. Carson Smith took over from Bob later, and being an arranger, a lot of the good ideas in the early quartet were his. For instance the way we did "Funny Valentine," with that moving bass line which really makes the arrangement, was Carson's idea. Chico thought of doing some *a cappella* singing behind Chet on a couple of numbers, but Chet never sang solo with the quartet. We played opposite Red Norvo for a while, then went up to the Blackhawk in San Francisco for a few weeks before returning to the Haig, this time as the main attraction.

Bernie Miller wrote "Bernie's Tune," but I never knew him. As far as I know, he was a piano player from Washington, D.C., and I think he had died by the time I encountered any of his tunes. He had a melodic touch, and he wrote a couple of other pieces that musicians liked to play. The recording company wanted to put "Bernie's Tune" in my name but I refused, because I always objected to bandleaders putting their names to something that wasn't theirs, so I wasn't going to do it to Bernie Miller whether I knew him or not. I told them to find out if he had a family so that the money could go to his heirs. If he didn't have one, I would have claimed it to stop it going into the public domain. A few years later Lieber and Stoller wrote a lyric for it, which I thought was a little presumptuous; I hated the damn thing. They were nice enough fellows, but I really resented them doing that.

Chico liked using brushes, because he was an admirer of the great brush-artists like Jo Jones, who was incredible—also Gus Johnson and Shadow Wilson. It would be a mistake, though, to think that the records are a total indication of what the group sounded like, because the drummer didn't always use brushes, even though a lot of the pieces were recorded that way. You know, when you examine the recordings of the twenties, you find that Bessie Smith never used a drummer at all, but nobody ever comments on that. Until it was possible to isolate instruments through multitracking, a set of drums was hard to balance with the rest of the band. This was especially so with the cymbals. A lot of recordings, even in the forties, had cymbals that tended to drown the main attraction, hence the beauty of brushes in recording. I remember when we first started rehearsing in Chet's house down in Watts or somewhere in southeast L.A., Chico would just use a snare, standing tom-tom, stand cymbal, and a hi-hat, and that's all, but when I looked in his trunk as he packed to go to the Haig for our first date, he had a whole set of drums. I said, "Where are you going with those?" and he said, "We're going to work." "Oh, no you're not," I said. "This is not what you rehearsed with. I don't want to get to the club and find a surprise waiting for me." So he came to work with the very minimum kit; then, as time went on, he figured out how he could add to the set without changing the sound. It was always a kit geared to what we had rehearsed with and not a whole big band set of drums.

Very little of what we played was written, although my originals sometimes were. Chet and I often put the arrangements together driving to the Haig, which is how we did "Carioca," for instance. He used to like singing the parts as we drove from his house, and we worked out that arrangement by singing it. A lot of movie people used to come and see us at the Haig, and one of the most regular was Jim Backus (Mr. Magoo), who often brought his buddy David Wayne. Mel Ferrer and Anne Baxter also used to come, and in fact, Anne had the quartet over to play at her birthday party.

Some months after our first records were released, Stan Getz showed up, playing at the Tiffany club with Bob Brookmeyer and John Williams, who was a good piano player. Stan used to sit in with us at the Haig, and I remember a jam session at somebody's house, probably Chet's, where Stan, Bob, Chet, and I were the front line, and we worked really well, improvising on ensemble things that were great. Stan decided that we should all go out together as a group, only he wanted it to be *his* group. Musically it was too bad that we couldn't do it, but personality-wise, I don't think it would have worked. Stan was peculiar; if things were going along smoothly, he had to do something to louse them up, usually at someone else's expense.

Early in 1953 we did the tentet album, and because I didn't think Chet wanted to play lead, I brought in Pete Candoli so that he didn't have that responsibility. In the event, Chet wound up playing most of the lead parts anyway, so I had Pete, who was a high-note man, on second trumpet! Somehow this myth has grown that Chet couldn't read music, but people love myths. It's more fun that way. There are lots of myths about Chet and the gothic, romantic life he lived and died; it's grist for that whole "Dark Prince" mode.

Both Dave Brubeck and Paul Desmond had recommended Dick Collins as a good replacement for Chet when I was reforming the quartet at the end of 1953, but he wasn't available. By this time I had become angry with L.A. anyway, so I telephoned Bob Brookmeyer in New York and asked him to come out to California for rehearsals, and bring some New York musicians with him. Bringing guys from the East was obviously expensive, but after rehearsals, we only had a couple of dates booked before going back to the East Coast to work. He arrived with Bill Anthony and Frank Isola, who had both been with Stan Getz. Before leaving town, we did our one and only engagement with the tentet at the Embassy Theater in downtown L.A., and that was quite an experience. When I looked through the curtains at 8 o'clock, it seemed as though we had bombed out, because there was hardly anyone in the house. We decided to get the show underway when someone came backstage very excitedly telling us to wait, because people were lined up around the block. Apparently, the newspaper advertisement for the concert quoted the wrong time. We wound up with a full house, and it really was quite an evening. It was so exciting that some fans stole a couple of the books, including mine, and it was at that point that we started to be more careful with the music.[3]

I had a second baritone as well as the tuba in the tentet, because they do different things, although the baritone is used in today's big band setup as if it were a tuba, but it's not at all. However, I've finally realized that I don't need a tuba, because laying in all those bottom notes gets in the bass player's way. Later on, when I was organizing the Concert Jazz Band, I had intended to include a tuba, but at that point, there was nobody I could count on who could cut the book to go on the road with us. The third trombone was supposed to be a tuba, so Alan Raph came in on bass trombone. What I really wanted was Bob Brookmeyer, bass trombone, and tuba, which would have given me a complete scale and palette, starting at the bottom and going chromatically to the clarinet on top. I could have used flutes, but they depended on amplification to be heard in that kind of band, and I didn't want to mess with that. I would have liked to have a couple of clarinets or possibly a soprano sax and maybe even C trumpets to sustain higher tones.

When the quartet reached New York early in 1954, I replaced Bill Anthony with Red Mitchell, who was one of the best bass players I've had. Frank Isola was with me for most of that year, and his thing really was to play time and keep out of the way, which worked out alright. Most of the drummers approached the quartet like that, which I accept. I hired guys because I liked the way they played, and Frank's approach established a precedent for the band, whether I wanted it or not. It's not quite what I wanted, because I would rather have had a little more activity or aggression in the rhythm section.

I had become used to playing with drummers like Max Roach, and when we were in Kai Winding's group, he was wonderfully considerate, thinking like an arranger by injecting melodic interest into what was going on. Very few drummers could do that. Most of them were aggressive but didn't add musical things that a writer would appreciate, and as a soloist, I didn't appreciate it either. Everyone should be working together, and if anything, the soloist should dictate where the solo goes. If you were playing with Buddy Rich or Art Blakey, for instance, and they felt it was time for the soloist to be pushing and getting into something climatic, *they'd* start pushing, whether you were ready or not. Max didn't do that because he listened to the soloist, and that is the kind of player I would have really welcomed.

That was one of the reasons why I always had problems with drummers. I needed somebody who was walking a thin line between playing the non-aggressive smooth thing that, say, Lennie Tristano wanted, where the drummer just kept time without any comments, but on the other hand, not dropping bombs all over the place. Even Chico used to do that, which is one of the reasons I took his bass drum away from him. He did it in Charlie Barnet's band and I said, "I'll kill him if he does that to me!" You have to remember that we were a totally acoustic group, and getting a balance to include the bass in the overall sound meant coming pretty far down in volume. I always needed a drummer who thought in terms of the ensemble sound, which is why Dave Bailey and Gus Johnson played the way they did with the quartet. Now if a drummer has a way of doing that and being busy, like Mel Lewis, for instance, that's fine. Mel never actually played with the quartet, which is a pity, because he carried on that chattering conversation underneath your playing which I always liked. There would be punctuations, and it would relate in a way that meant something in the construction. Gus Johnson's feel with the group was a lot different, but I had remembered how polished he was from seeing him with Count Basie. He was fun, and he loved playing brushes. As time went on, I was after drummers to play louder and use more sticks, but I never really pressed the point.

Later on in 1954 I was between trumpets and trombones, since I needed a replacement for Bob Brookmeyer, and being in the East, I decided to try Tony Fruscella. Now Tony had that fuzzy, introverted tone that Chet had, although Chet's was more outgoing while Tony's was very inwardly directed. It sounded nice, but one concert at the Newport Jazz Festival was enough for me to realize that having Tony travelling with me and being onstage together night after night would have driven me crazy. He lived in a world of his own, and when someone is a real introvert, it can take all your strength just to survive. They seem to have a magnet sucking in your energy but nothing comes out, which is what shyness does to people. For the professional life of concerts in a band that works and travels, your energy has to be *up* for it, and you can't live in a world of your own because you have to deal with the *real* world. Having a guy like Tony meant I had to deal for myself and him too. It was too bad it didn't work out, because he was such a lovely player, but he just did that one concert with me.

It's funny because Stan Kenton was the M.C. at Newport that year, and he always had the amazing ability of giving a speech that sounded so serious. You would be listening attentively, until you suddenly realized that he's not saying anything! I don't know how he did it, but it was all delivered with such oratorical sincerity that you felt it was your fault for missing the point. Towards the end of that year, I recorded some titles with John Graas and Don Fagerquist in California. I loved the way Don played, and he would have been an ideal trumpeter for the quartet, but he wasn't available when I needed him. At the end of 1954 I disbanded the quartet to go home to New York and write some new music.

In 1955 I sometimes played as a guest in Chet Baker's group, and I seem to remember a date in Detroit with him and Mose Allison. I also worked at Basin Street for a few weeks with Al Cohn, Gil Evans, George Duvivier, and Herb Wasserman. Now Stan Getz was around the corner at Birdland, and he drove Al crazy. Every time he was free and we were playing, he would come and watch Al from the Peanut Gallery, staring up at him and making him feel uncomfortable.[4] What he really wanted was to take Al's mouthpiece and have it copied over at Otto Link's. Al kept refusing, but Stan pestered him for about ten nights until he finally gave in. They met during the day, and Stan had it copied so that he could get a sound like Al's.

Later on that year I formed the sextet, and initially Idrees Sulieman was on trumpet, but he just did a couple of dates with us because we had a hard time getting together on a style for the ensemble. I think he was an interesting choice, and the group would have sounded a lot different, but we weren't comfortable with each other, because our stylistic approach wasn't compatible. I have often wondered what the sextet would have sounded like if we had aimed it in that direction. We ran the group for quite a while, although I don't remember all the reasons for not continuing with it. Zoot Sims may have wanted to leave, because a soloist like that would have found it to be a straitjacket after a while, and I certainly didn't try to replace him; Zoot was Zoot.

After the sextet I was "between groups," and "between everything" at that point. I was really at a low ebb, having had enough of being a bandleader for a while, because being the leader can be a pain in the neck. You have to lay out the focus of the thing, decide what to play, and arrange the transportation and hotels as well. There have been periods when I have been fed up and looked for somebody else's band to play with, which happened much later when I worked with Dave Brubeck. I was just going to be a soloist on one date; then we played in Mexico. One thing led to another, and I became the saxophone player who came to dinner and didn't leave for about seven years! In 1956 I did a little campaigning for Adlai Stevenson, who was the Democratic nominee for the presidency, when he ran unsuccessfully against Ike. The following year, I worked a little with Mose Allison, and I think that Chet and I took a group out together, although it was primarily his group. We also recorded a couple of albums, but there was never any talk of us getting back together permanently.[5]

Over the next couple of years I did a lot of recording. I remember a studio session with Manny Albam, which was a nice L.P. with a good group of musicians, and it was fun playing in the ensembles.[6] I did a date with Stan Getz, which Norman Granz wanted us to do. He was recording Stan, but you can tell from the material that we really didn't have anything prepared. The jam session idea is alright, but it has never been my bag, and it wasn't my idea to switch horns on some numbers; Stan or Norman suggested it. I liked Zoot's and Brew Moore's mouthpieces, but I never liked Stan's, and I didn't like the sound I got on it.[7] I did an album with Monk, and having Thelonious as an accompanist was a challenge.[8] We only played together a couple of times, but I remember a jam session I finally dragged him to, where we played "Tea for Two" and one other tune all night. He was trying to get us to play "Tea for Two" the way Tatum played it, where the progression goes up and then down in semi-tones, and we had to try and follow him. In the mid fifties we lived near each other in New York, hence my original "Good Neighbor Thelonious," because he lived on 63rd and I was on 68th Street near Columbus.

I also recorded with Paul Desmond, who always wanted to do the piano-less quartet thing, with the alto playing lead instead of trumpet.[9] Dick Bock produced an album with me, Lee Konitz, Al, Zoot, and Allen Eager, which he called *The Mulligan Songbook, Volume 1*, although I told him that title was a little optimistic. I used Freddie Green on guitar, because I was always messing around with the rhythm section, trying to find out what to do with it, and I loved the idea of playing with Freddie. The Annie Ross date was Dick's idea, and although we hadn't worked together before, I liked her and the album came out well. My favorite record from the "Mulligan Meets . . . " series was the one with Ben Webster, Jimmy Rowles, Leroy Vinnegar, and Mel Lewis. We played quite a lot with that group, including a feature on the Dinah Shore T.V. show, and everybody could be called a co-arranger because they all made a contribution. Jimmy Rowles was wonderful, and what he does is so deceptively simple, fitting things in so that they become part of the whole. Unfortunately he is now very ill with emphysema.[10]

In 1957 I did a big band album which I didn't complete, and consequently it wasn't released until about twenty years later.[11] I wasn't pleased with the way things were going, because on the fast numbers I couldn't get my rhythm section together. I had Dave Bailey on one set of dates and Gus Johnson on the other, and I realized that I had to write more for them, because there wasn't time for them to get to know the pieces like they would in a small band. It created a problem which I couldn't overcome, and George Avakian, who was the A and R man for CBS, said to postpone everything until later. He then left CBS, and it wouldn't have come out at all if it hadn't been for Henri Renaud. I remember Don Joseph played beautifully on "All the Things You Are."

When I formed the Concert Jazz Band in 1960, Norman Granz's financial input was pretty extensive. He paid for a tour in the States to prepare us for a European trip, but I paid for everything else, which is how I always ill-spent any profit I was able to make; I've always been a sucker that way! Judy Holliday did an album with us, although she never sang live with the band.[12] She should have done, because she would have been more comfortable when we got into the studio. Judy always joked, but it was only half-a-joke, that her way of going to work was to go to the theater, heave, and then start to get dressed. Recording for her was worse, but as she got to know the material, her sound would evolve, so it would have been good if she could have sung with the band at some point. Phil Woods didn't record with us, but he was a regular in the band whenever we could get him. He was always pretty busy, but he played quite a lot with us at Birdland. Later on, in the seventies, I formed another big band, and although I never really dropped the name, the Concert Jazz Band was a particular band and instrumentation in my mind.

After the CJB I went back to the pianoless quartet with Bob Brookmeyer, until we finally disbanded the group in 1965. Later that year I played with Roy Eldridge and Earl Hines in Europe. I would have loved to play more with Roy, but they booked the tour in such a ridiculous way, I wound up getting flu or something and I gave the whole thing up. The sixties were turbulent years.

I have always played a Conn baritone, but in the early sixties I used a Selmer for about a year. Jerome Richardson was funny, because when I started playing the Selmer, he said, "You sound peculiar. Why don't you get your Conn back and sound like you're supposed to. That sounds awful!" Eventually the Selmer got damaged, so I went back to the Conn, and Jerome came into the Vanguard one night and said, "Finally you've got your Conn, and everything's back to normal." I never did like the Selmer anyway, because of the way it was balanced, with the short neck on it.

Coming right up to date, in January 1994 I was elected to the *Down Beat* "Hall of Fame." Somebody said, "What took so long?" and it's true, things do seem to happen slowly for me, but I guess I'm not considered to be a fashionable elder. Popularity polls can be strange, because I started out as an arranger and always think of myself as one, but I don't show up in that category at all, which used to bug me. Have you noticed in the *Down Beat* polls that nobody ever votes for my present quartet? If I don't have a pianoless quartet, it's as though I don't have a quartet at all. You know, these things are fun to talk about, but I'll have to stop, or we'll be here all night.

NOTES

1. Johnny Carisi, who contributed "Israel" to the project, once said, "Gerry wrote more than anybody." For the record, he arranged the following: "Deception," "Rocker," "Godchild," "Venus de Milo," "Budo," "Darn That Dream," and "Jeru." Cap DT 1974.

2. One complete side of the original L.P. was devoted to an improvised blues called "Mulligan's Too." It lasts for eighteen minutes, and Gerry's thirty-five choruses represent his longest solo on record. *Mulligan Plays Mulligan*. Prestige OJCCD-003-2.

3. During a long and leisurely lunch with Arlyne Mulligan in a little town called Celebration, Florida, in September 2001, she told me that she and Gerry had asked Mel Tormé to sing with the tentet at the Embassy Theater. He didn't appear because he apparently wanted too much money, but he did attend the concert as a member of the audience. She also said that the tentet was her favorite of all Mulligan's groups and bands. Later in 1953 she and Gerry married, and she became his personal manager for most of the fifties. Incidentally, Celebration is a uniquely picturesque Disney town which was created in 1994. It looks as though it could easily have been part of the set for two Doris Day fifties films set in 1917, *On Moonlight Bay* and *By the Light of the Silvery Moon*.

4. Clubs often had chairs on the side where customers could sit and nurse a beer all night. It was less expensive there and was known as the Peanut Gallery.

5. Others have seen the situation differently. See Dave Bailey's interview in this book.

6. *Manny Albam and the Jazz Greats of Our Time*, vol. 1. Coral CRL 57173.

7. *Stan Getz Meets Gerry Mulligan in Hi-Fi*. Verve 849 392 2. Stan Getz chose the rhythm section for this session. He also seems to have had a major influence on the material recorded, because numbers like "This Can't Be Love," "Too Close for Comfort," and "I Didn't Know What Time It Was" were all part of his repertoire at the time.

8. *Gerry Mulligan Meets Thelonious Monk*. OJC20 310-2.

9. *Gerry Mulligan–Paul Desmond Quartet*. Verve 519 850-2.

10. *The Complete Gerry Mulligan Meets Ben Webster Sessions*. Verve 539 055-2. (Jimmy Rowles died two years after this interview with Mulligan, on May 28, 1996.)

11. Gerry Mulligan, *Mullenium*. Columbia CK 65678.

12. *Judy Holliday with Gerry Mulligan*. DRG Records SL 5191.

Chapter Twenty

Gerry Mulligan Quartet, 1952–1953

Early in 1952, after spending several months hitch-hiking from New York to Los Angeles with Gail Madden, Gerry Mulligan obtained a regular Monday night booking at the Haig, a small club opposite the famous Ambassador Hotel on Wilshire Boulevard.[1] Erroll Garner was the featured attraction during the week, and Mulligan played there with pianists like Jimmy Rowles, Paul Smith, Donn Trenner, and Fred Otis when Garner had the night off. After Erroll's engagement, owner John Bennett moved the concert grand piano from the Haig's cramped stage into storage, to accommodate Red Norvo's vibes when Red's trio took over the residency. Mulligan was now faced with a problem on Monday nights, since he didn't want to use a guitar or the small studio upright that Bennett offered to hire for him. His solution of a pianoless quartet featuring Chet Baker's trumpet, with his own baritone sax not only as a solo vehicle but also as an accompanying voice, created one of the most arresting and distinctive sounds in small group jazz.

Just prior to the fiftieth anniversary of the formation of that group, I interviewed the surviving members—drummers Larry Bunker and Chico Hamilton and bass players Carson Smith and Bob Whitlock—for their impressions of working in such an unusual ensemble. I met Chico Hamilton when he was playing in London's Jazz Café with his group Euphoria, but the others replied to my questions on cassette tape.

BOB WHITLOCK

The original bass player with the quartet was Bob Whitlock, who was born in Roosevelt, Utah, on January 21, 1931. In the early fifties, he knew Mulligan only by reputation as an arranger with the Miles Davis nonet, but he and Chet Baker had been friends since 1948.

When Gerry and Gail first arrived in L.A., they were both enthusiastically reading *The Fountainhead* by Ayn Rand, which tells the story of an idealistic architect clashing with big business. It had been released as a film with Gary Cooper and Patricia Neal, and they really saw themselves in those roles! Anyway, it was around January or February 1952 that Gail telephoned, asking if I would be interested in coming to an audition with Gerry Mulligan. The audition was successful and I was offered the job playing Monday nights with him at the Haig, opposite Erroll Garner. A little later, when we were rehearsing at the Cottage Italia in North Hollywood, it became obvious that the trumpeter Gerry was using, whose name I have now forgotten, wasn't working out.

I should explain that the Cottage Italia was an ordinary Italian restaurant which happened to have a bandstand, and it became a jazz "gladiator" school, where musicians jammed regularly to keep in shape between gigs. It was packed every night, and as far as I know, no one was ever paid a dime. The public was allowed in, but for the most part, musicians and "wannabes" far outnumbered non-musicians. In order to get a feel for the place, it is necessary to understand that nobody organized sets or determined who would play with whom. It was all done very much like choosing sides to play ball in the street, a real grassroots approach resulting in a strange mixture of democracy, anarchy, and survival of the fittest. It was also a surefire way to determine status in the hierarchy of Los Angeles jazz musicians. I once had the dubious distinction of being caught by surprise with a Sunday punch from an angry bass player while combing my hair in the lavatory. He felt slighted about being passed over, and we fought from the lavatory through the bar and restaurant, out onto the street, in front of one of the most attentive crowds I ever performed for. I remember this very well because of a record date the following evening with Gerry for Gene Norman's label at a little second-floor studio on Vine Street. By then my muscles were so stiff and sore, I could barely make it up the stairs with my bass, and the recording session turned out to be a catastrophe. I don't think we ended up with one good take, and as far as I know, nothing we did that night has ever been released.

Gerry needed a new trumpeter, and I persuaded him to consider Chet, assuring him that he would be perfect for the group, as he was one of the best trumpet players on the West Coast. Gerry agreed to an audition and asked me to arrange it as soon as possible. I was excited and I knew Chet would be, as we were both in awe of Gerry's work. Imagine my horror at what happened the following day. Chet had a dreadful habit of warming up at extreme decibel levels. It was irritating, but those who knew him were used to it. After a few earsplitting blasts, Gerry simply went berserk, and there is no other way to describe it. He turned on Chet, screaming, "Don't ever do that around me again!" Chet angrily put his horn away and told Gerry in no uncertain terms where to go and what to do when he got there. They were still raging at each other as Chet stormed out of the audition; it really was quite unbelievable.[2] The drummer at the session might have been Lloyd Morales or Alvin Stoller, and I think Gil Barrios was on piano. Gerry still hadn't decided what to do with the piano, as there was a large grand onstage at the Haig for Erroll Garner, and anyway, I always felt that the pianoless concept wasn't planned: it evolved.

On his Monday night gigs at the Haig, Mulligan used a number of musicians, like Sonny Criss, Ernie Royal, Dave Pell, Howard Roberts, and Art Pepper. Pepper sat in on half a dozen occasions, but Whitlock did not recall anything beyond a working relationship between Pepper and Mulligan.

I seriously doubt if they had any social contact to speak of. My guess is that they probably had some musical respect for one another, but knowing both of them, I suspect there would have been a good chance of clashing egos. The one thing they had in common was a great admiration for Zoot's playing. I recall Gerry playing tenor and clarinet at some of our early rehearsals, and although he didn't use the tenor much, I was thoroughly enchanted by the sound he got on his old metal clarinet. I have often wondered why he didn't have a tryst with the bass clarinet, and one can only imagine what he might have done with it.

He occasionally played piano at the Haig and at some of our rehearsals—and as you might expect, his approach was totally individual and distinctive. It was fascinating listening to his highly personal rhythms and harmonies, the best of which were the result of strong, independent voice leading, with a predilection for contrary motion, often producing wonderfully dissonant and strikingly original results. To my ears, he sounded like a superlative arranger attempting to realize some of the richness of his ideas at the keyboard, although I must confess to a preference for leaner textures. Surprisingly, it was when jamming that the complexity and density of Gerry's piano work tended to conspire against swinging, despite the axiom that complex ideas often require complex means. At his best, when he was comfortable with the tempo, he sounded extraordinarily inventive and interesting. At his worst, one had the impression that he was in over his head, especially if the tempo overtaxed his technical facility. I often found in his piano playing a sense of humor similar to Erik Satie, especially when he was parodying older styles. At rehearsals he used the piano as a tool to explore, evoke, or convey a certain mood or feeling.

When we were rehearsing, Gail had a tendency to try to dominate initially, which took some getting used to. Gerry often had his hands full, but many of her observations were very astute, and she made some valuable contributions, in my opinion. How could a bass player fail to appreciate her obsession with transparency, buoyancy, precision, and balance within the group? That was her major concern and the focus of a good deal of her criticism. Gail was nothing if not flamboyant, and she was most certainly in the vanguard. I also found her to be intelligent, resourceful, rebellious, bold, opinionated, and altogether fascinating. She could also be a major pain in the ass sometimes, but at the end of the day, I thought she was great and I give her five stars! I might add that I secretly admired Gerry for his anti-chauvinistic manner of relating to her. Despite some moments that had to be uncomfortable and deeply embarrassing for him, I think he held her in high regard and valued her in many important ways. It wasn't long, though, before she just vanished from the scene, and I never quite understood what went awry. After she was gone, I missed her, because she always managed to generate an aura of excitement that I found very much to my liking.

We sometimes rehearsed at the Haig, but more often we played at Charlene's parents' home, which was in Lynwood, in the southern part of L.A. Aside from the twenty-mile commute, we enjoyed these workouts. Charlene was Chet's wife at the time, and if weather permitted, and it usually did, we played outside on the rear patio. Gerry wrote practically all the originals, but on standards, show tunes, and ballads he not only encouraged but *expected* everyone to improvise, or improve-ize if you will, and that was the beauty of it. The charts weren't static — just no anarchy, please! When everyone was on the same wave, listening and responding with acumen, it could be very exciting. Having said that, it was Gerry's inimitable presence that drove and defined the character and flavor of the group, and I loved working with it. I couldn't wait to get to work each night, because it was great being out there, totally exposed to the challenge of inventing melodically interesting bass lines, strong enough to eliminate harmonic ambiguity and simple enough to swing. I thrived on that challenge!

Of course Gerry's abilities as an accompanist were phenomenal, and he had that vast pool of ideas to draw upon, from all those years as an arranger. His forte was building spontaneous arrangements, because he was something of an architect. It was really exciting to walk a bass line and discover him moving along a tenth above, totally enhancing the whole effect. He always had his ears open and expected the same from his cohorts. With all due respect to the other guys, without Gerry's accompaniment, there is no Gerry Mulligan Quartet.

CHICO HAMILTON

Just as Gail Madden had recruited Bob Whitlock, she was also responsible for introducing Foreststorn Chico Hamilton to Mulligan. Hamilton, born in Los

Angeles on September 21, 1921, had been working for Lena Horne since 1947. He was taking a sabbatical from the singer, and Gail heard him at the Streets of Paris, where he was playing with Charlie Barnet.

Gerry wasn't in too great a shape at the time, and he used to hang out at the Streets of Paris nearly every night. We befriended each other, and I often invited him home for dinner with my family. One night he said to me, "Foreststorn, if you play for me the way you play for Charlie Barnet, I'll fire your ass!" I was doing a lot of things with Barnet, like dropping bombs, but he let me do them because Charlie was cool.

Gerry's group with Chet and Bob got together, and we started rehearsing over at my house. The historians can say what they like, and they usually do, but we just happened to be four guys in the right place at the right time. It was destiny, and those recordings still sound fresh today because we were all listening to each other. Suddenly the Haig was the hottest joint in town, with wall-to-wall people every night.

Two months after Mulligan and Chet Baker's first acrimonious meeting, and as a result of what Bob Whitlock has described as some serious apologizing, the Gerry Mulligan Quartet recorded their first titles at Phil Turetsky's bungalow in Laurel Canyon. Phil was an amateur recording engineer, and he produced those initial sides, "Bernie's Tune" and "Lullaby of the Leaves," with just two microphones. The quartet was still doing the off-nights at the Haig when they were booked to play for a week in September at the Blackhawk in San Francisco, opposite Dave Brubeck's Quartet.[3] Just prior to this engagement, Whitlock decided to leave the group because, he says, "I was broke and needed income, so I left town with Vido Musso's band." The new bass player was Carson Smith.

CARSON SMITH

Carson Smith was born in San Francisco on January 9, 1931. Just three months before he died in 1997, he talked about his time with Mulligan.

I had been following Gerry's career for several years before I joined the quartet, because he was one of my heroes. His arrangements on those Miles Davis recordings were among my favorites, and I played them until I wore them out. In early 1952 I was living in Long Island, New York, and spending all my time looking for him in jam sessions, until I discovered that he had already taken off for the Coast. I was feeling homesick for California, so a friend and I drove my 1936 Ford across country. When we reached L.A., I found that Harry Babasin was having a little session down in Inglewood and Chet Baker was there. This was the first time I played with him, and we had a ball. During the break we went outside to smoke a little grass, and he asked if I would like to team up with a guy called Gerry Mulligan who had a quartet without a piano. I said, "You have to be kidding. I have been looking for him for the past year." Gerry had a rehearsal a couple of days later, and I sure liked what I heard. I did my best with what little musical experience I had, although I knew a lot of tunes, which impressed Gerry. That meant that he didn't have to teach me a lot, and he seemed to take a little bit of a liking to me. Except for some originals, very little of his stuff was laid out on paper.

I never met Gail Madden, as she and Gerry had split up before I joined the group, but I knew she was a little strange from the stories I heard from everyone who knew her.[4] She was what you might call a hippy, before the hippies came in. She apparently pushed Gerry pretty well, like most of his female associates, who were all strong women.

It was while the group played in San Francisco that they recorded part of an album for Fantasy Records, which included their celebrated version of "My Funny Valentine." Mulligan has said that this is the only album he didn't receive royalties from, and it is arguably one of the best he made with Chet Baker. Smith told me about the recording session.

Those sides were recorded by having us stand around a single 440 mike, which looked like a small football placed about nine inches above the floor. We had actually run out of things to play, and Gerry asked if anyone could think of something. I suggested "Funny Valentine," which nobody knew, so I quickly sketched out a lead line, and it almost became Chet's theme song for the rest of his life.[5]

I used a rented bass whenever we recorded, because my instrument at the time was literally falling apart, so I had to get a new one. When the quartet got back to L.A., I bought an old French bass from Joe Mondragon for $300, which doesn't sound much now, but you couldn't touch that bass for $8,000 today. Thanks to Ralph Peña, who was leaving Billy May, I had the chance to go on the road with the band for a three-month tour. I arranged to send Joe $50 a week from my paycheck until I paid him off, and of course I told Gerry why I was leaving the group.

BOB WHITLOCK

In October 1952 the quartet returned to the studios to complete their first album for Pacific Jazz, with Bob Whitlock again on bass. He was in town after working with Vido Musso, whose big hit at the time was "Come Back to Sorrento."

Gerry asked if I wanted to return, and I accepted. After a few weeks of "Sorrento," I was ready to go back as his gardener if necessary. We were mostly working at the Haig, except for two engagements at the Blackhawk and some Sunday afternoon sessions in Hollywood at the Tailspin on Cahuenga Boulevard. We eventually lost the job at the Tailspin when Steve White showed up one afternoon in rare form. He was a brilliant tenor player and a legend in his own time, and I think Gerry wanted to shoot him on the spot, because the group was just beginning to really make it. There may have been a few other minor casual dates that I don't recall.

The quartet had become very popular and the reason was "Show-Biz," plain and simple. Gerry knew the importance of variety in material and treatment, and he had an uncanny sense of pacing. We not only played standards and originals but also everything from Latin sambas to tunes from Disney movies. There was something for everyone, and the caliber of musicianship was always convincing. Also, it would be naïve to ignore some of the more obvious gimmicks that Gerry used. For instance, the slightest disturbance in the audience was his cue to stop the band in its tracks and make an example of the poor perpetrator, and how the rest of the crowd ate it up! It reminds me of when Miles used to turn his back on the audience, play a few bars, and then walk off stage. Audiences, especially "hip" jazz audiences in the fifties, loved the melodrama, even when it involved being insulted, or maybe because of it. It's no wonder that we were often referred to as "the Chamber Music Society of Lower Wilshire Boulevard"! Of course, there's no denying that just the idea of a pianoless group got Gerry plenty of attention, as well as a lot of free publicity, and you can rest assured that he was not oblivious to the fruits of controversy. I also sensed that audiences were able to feel the excitement of our newfound independence and felt a certain connection with us, which they weren't used to, and they liked it. Then, when the group really started to catch on, it was a *fait accompli, oui*?

Ironically, what makes performing without a piano so exciting is the very thing that can bring you to the abyss, because you are always exposed. If the creative juices aren't flowing or you are otherwise compromised, it can be devastating, and even a minor fault in intonation can make you want to run and hide. There is also some limitation in material, because certain pieces almost demand a chordal approach to be effective and can be tough to handle. Others lend themselves to a more linear treatment and do just fine with a couple of moving lines—a *basso ostinato*—or some other unifying device, to define and clarify. Obviously it is from this type that you draw most of your material, because no one likes swimming upstream for too long. One of the worst problems for me involved tuning, especially at the outset of the evening, when changes in temperature and humidity were wreaking havoc on the instruments. Since the horns' pitch was dominant, it was on me to adjust, and it isn't easy playing while reaching for the tuning pegs!

I remember William Holden and Deborah Kerr used to visit the Haig, and what a class act they were. Their behavior was impeccable, and they really seemed to enjoy being there. After paying so many times to see them on the screen, I couldn't believe they were actually paying to see us. One of the most important visitors I can recall, although not a star *per se*, was Leonard Rosenman, the film composer, who later wrote those haunting Berg-like passages in the opening of Kazan's *East of Eden*. I reckoned if people like Rosenman were interested in us, we must be doing something right.

It is a well-known cliché that England and America are two countries separated by a common language. I wanted to ask Bob if he had ever sent in a dep while he was with the group. Not sure if the abbreviation would be totally understood, I used the word "deputy" instead.

Deputy. I love that word. Californians hear it and ditch their pill bottles! The only dep I sent in was Red Mitchell, who was a class act and an absolutely incredible soloist. He sat in with the group a few times and was perfectly at ease.

As far as personal relationships within the group were concerned, I got along great with Gerry at first. He was friendly and charming and I was very much in awe of him; after all, he was the chief arranger on one of the most historically significant jazz recordings in history. Unfortunately, our relationship eventually took a downward turn, and it just went from bad to worse. As far as he and Chet were concerned, Gerry liked to create the impression that Chet was his discovery and protégé and fancied himself as some kind of mentor, which didn't sit well with Chet at all. He was having none of it and didn't resist an opportunity to repudiate any such suggestion, often in open revolt against Gerry.

Chet was one of those rare birds who learned to read music but never had any real training in harmony. Most of us play by ear, assisted by some knowledge of harmony and counterpoint, but since he didn't have the benefit of those tools, he was forced to do it *all* by ear, and therein lies his genius. Naturally, there is a price to pay with this approach. It requires the bravado to run through minefields and the courage of Hannibal, because the perils are endless. The reward comes in the form of refreshing vitality, breathtaking melodic invention, freedom from exasperating clichés, extraordinary sensitivity to shading and color, and a lyricism second to none. Not a bad trade-off if you are willing to take the risks, and Chet greeted the challenge like a gladiator. Of course, Gerry's trade winds blew from the opposite direction. He had all the tools at his disposal, and he made impressive use of them, especially in the area of accompaniment, where he was probably without peer. In Chet's case, he was my closest friend. We would spend whole days together, and we always knew we could count on each other. As for Chico, he thought he was my big brother. Every so often after work, he would take me to one of those after-hours speakeasies on the south side, where everyone knew him. I guess you could say we were socializing, but whatever we were doing, I enjoyed it. I liked Chico and was always happy to see him coming down the pike.

I stayed with Gerry until the night before Christmas Eve 1952. We had just returned from the group's second stint at the Blackhawk, and I remember going out to Chet's car during intermission at the Haig. A police cruiser came by our parked car in time to see sparks flying from a furtively lit joint tossed out of the window. One of the officers turned out to be from Chet's home state of Oklahoma, and he told him that if there was no more weed in the car, he would release us with a warning. Chalk that up for male bonding, I thought, but when they searched the car, they found two full lids in the door panel. We were summarily arrested and spent the Yuletide in jail, during which Chet took all the weight and had me cut loose. This incident led to a bitter confrontation with Gerry in the dressing room at the Haig, where he decreed that Chet and I were bad news for each other. By this time our personal relationship had deteriorated beyond redemption, but up to this point we had never threatened each other physically. I guess we were bluffing, because it all ended with a childish exchange of "You're fired!" and "I quit!" What can I say? Boys will be boys! My heroin habit was way out of control by this time, and some concerned relatives intervened. Three of my closest cousins were visiting for the holidays and came to the Haig to surprise me, but they were horrified at my condition and nearly kidnapped me. A few days later I was on my way back with them to my birthplace in Utah, and although it was cold turkey and tough for a while, I stayed there for nearly a year and got my health back.

CHICO HAMILTON

Chico Hamilton was still with the quartet at this time, and towards the end of January 1953 he and Larry Bunker shared the drum duties on Mulligan's ten-tet album. His personal circumstances, though, were quite different from his colleagues'. At thirty-one, he was by far the oldest, and he was the only one to have a wife and family. The job at the Haig paid union scale, but he could clearly earn far more with Lena Horne.

I was under contract to Lena, and when she was ready to go back to work, I had to leave the group. I have often wondered what would have happened if I had stayed, because they were good times and Gerry and Chet became virtual superstars. Most people don't realize that Chet was a phenomenon, and he was not just an imitation Miles Davis; he was a hell of a player. He could play like any trumpeter you can name, but he had his own thing going. And Gerry, after Harry Carney, reinvented the baritone. He had a flowing, swinging style, and you could say he applied Lester Young's approach to the instrument. He was one of the most melodic baritone players ever, and with his soft, well-rounded, smooth sound he could almost sound like Johnny Hodges on that thing! I have a tremendous respect for Gerry and his abilities as a musician.

Eventually, there was friction between Gerry and Chet, and I would sometimes stay in the middle of them to keep them apart. Some nights we would come off the stand, and Chet would stand one way at the bar and Gerry another, so that they were back to back.

LARRY BUNKER

Larry Bunker was born in Long Beach, California, on November 4th, 1928, and joined the group after Chico Hamilton left to resume working with Lena Horne. Chico described Larry's playing to me this way: "He is a good player. On some of those records, I can't always tell if it's him or me playing."

I had already met Gerry before I joined the group and played with him at a few sessions. I had also worked with Chet at a club in Inglewood where Harry Babasin ran things. Of course I knew Chico casually and had seen him play around town, but we were not particular friends, because we traveled in different circles. I had already seen the quartet a few times when Gerry asked me to replace Chico, and I thought it was an interesting concept. I was bowled over by Chet particularly, and if truth be told, I was a bigger fan of Chet than I was of Gerry. I don't know why the group was so popular with the public, but it seemed to be the right thing at the right time. There was an enormous influx of musicians who had recently left the Kenton and Herman bands, and suddenly the whole "West Coast Jazz" thing seemed to start. Gerry, with his sensibility and musicality, showed up right in the midst of that, and soon there were lines around the block at the Haig to hear the quartet.

I don't remember rehearsing with them before joining; I just started immediately at the club. I could learn the material from the records, but there wasn't that much to learn really, because nearly everything, even Gerry's originals, was in a song format—AABA. They had their repertoire down, and it was up to me to jump in and chug along, but it was difficult at first. I was so oriented to what a rhythm section with a piano should sound like that it took some getting used to, but the transparency became very appealing and I liked it. Gerry, Chet, and Carson, who was a good bass player, had some kind of magic chemistry in delineating the harmonic structure with just three voices, so that after a while I didn't miss the piano.[6] Of course Gerry's abilities as an accompanist were very important, because he and the bass outlined the harmonic structure while Chet was playing. Gerry would indicate the notes of the chord, but Chet's approach while playing backgrounds to Gerry was very different: much more linear and across the changes.

There wasn't very much sitting in, but I remember when Stan Getz and Bob Brookmeyer were playing at the Tiffany, Gerry went over to visit Stan and came back raving—*raving*—about Bob. Those guys would take it in turns sitting in with us, and Gerry would go over there to play with them on intermissions. Lee Konitz of course played with us, and I seem to remember Oscar Pettiford sitting in on cello.[7]

I was with Gerry from January to June 1953, and that was my only job: six nights a week with Mondays off. I never sent in a dep, even though I was starting to get into the freelance field of recording in films and early T.V. That was daytime stuff, so I didn't have to take any nights off. I got along with him O.K., although we never talked about art, literature, politics, or the issues of the day. He was very bright and he was aware that he was very bright and he could use that to knock you off balance, which made him a bit intimidating. Although we didn't hang out together, he was nice enough to me—friendly, though not overly so. I showed up and played, did what I was told, and took the money—but I had a good time. He and Chet were both a little bit into the drug thing, which didn't seem to impair their ability to perform. I have never done drugs. I had my own little bout with the bottle, but not drugs. If you are not a "druggie" and you are hanging out with people who are, they can manifest an "outsider" thing to you, no matter how nicely it's done. Even then, and I was only twenty-five years old, I had known too many people who were dear to me found face down in the gutter, dead from an O.D., so I was petrified of any of that.

As for Chet, he was a brilliantly talented juvenile delinquent and not someone I could get next to, because I couldn't abide his attitudes. He was married to a lovely lady named Charlene at the time, and he was just a chauvinistic pig to her. At intermissions, she would be waiting at the bar for him while he was in the back seat of someone's car with a groupie, and if she dared to ask where he had been, he would kick her ass. That didn't appeal to me, and whatever else he was interested in also didn't appeal to me. Sometimes he would come into work with his mouth all cut from having been in a fistfight during the day, but that was Chet. The paradox was that he could be incredibly sensitive in his playing. He was a more linear player than Gerry, probably because of his lack of technical knowledge about what he was doing; so much of it was a magical, intuitive thing. Even without piano harmony to guide him, he could sail across the changes when they were merely implied. Some people thought he couldn't read music, but he certainly could, though not very proficiently. He had been in an army band, so he would have had to read marches, and in the few situations I was with him when he had to read, he did O.K. He couldn't read chord changes, though, and he didn't know what they were, except for that amazing ability he had that enabled him to hear where they went. Gerry was right on the money when he said, "Chet knew everything about chords; he just didn't know their names."

When other musicians realized that he didn't have any theoretical knowledge, they would sometimes try to get him at jam sessions by calling tunes in ridiculous keys that nobody was familiar with, hoping to trap him. They would try "Body and Soul" in G-flat, for instance, but it didn't matter at all, because they could have said Q-flat and Chet would still have been able to play it. After a while that all stopped, because the guys couldn't transpose that fast from their accustomed keys, so they were trapping themselves, but not Chet. They backed themselves into corners that they couldn't get out of, but he would just sail through all of it because he didn't have those kinds of constraints. His mental apparatus worked in a different way, and that was what was so amazing about him, the fact that he could do what he did with such limited theoretical knowledge.

Gerry, on the other hand, was enormously knowledgeable and skilled in harmonic structure and chord changes—all of that. He could solo in a very linear fashion as well, but he may have wanted to play in a more vertical way because we didn't have a piano. He played the piano sometimes himself, and although he wasn't a great pianist, he knew what he wanted to do on the instrument. On baritone he was amazing, but sometimes it was a little hard to play with him, especially on a double-time thing where he would blow so many notes that he would get behind the time. I would be scuffling along, trying to drag him with me, but that was because of that big, awkward horn he was playing. Unlike an alto or tenor, it takes a long time for the air to get through. I have great respect for him both as a writer and a player.

I remember he did something really wild when we recorded those tentet things. We rehearsed one of the pieces, and after we made a take on it, we listened to the playback. Gerry flopped down on the floor in the middle of the studio, concentrating in a really dramatic, Christ-like pose, with his arms outstretched and his eyes closed. When the recording was finished, he got up off the floor and said, "O.K., guys—pencils." He then proceeded to dictate a new road map for the chart, which completely rearranged it, and when he counted us in, it was like a brand new piece of music. His writing had a magical quality, and he probably influenced both Bill Holman and Bob Brookmeyer, because he was a fantastic arranger. He acquired a lot of his knowledge when he was very young, certainly before he was twenty, and if you examine his earlier music side by side with a Gil Evans chart, you can see they probably influenced one another. There are definite similarities in their chord voicings and ways of voice leading.

One of Gerry's originals on that tentet album was called "A Ballad," which I wanted to learn. After the album was released, I kept listening to it, and I asked him to play it for me on the piano. When I went behind him to see the voicings, he stopped playing immediately. "Oh no you don't," he said. "You have to learn it by hearing it." He knew I had good ears, so he wasn't going to *show* me the voicings; I had to learn them by hearing them. I was able to learn an enormous amount about harmonic structure from him, but I had to do it the hard way. The experience of working with Gerry Mulligan was very valuable in my own musical development.

CARSON SMITH

The final piece in the jigsaw concerns Carson Smith again, who rejoined the quartet when Bob Whitlock left to go back home to Utah.

It was Christmas 1952 when I got back from the ninety-day tour with Billy May. I went straight to the Haig and saw Chet and Bob during their break. We went outside to smoke a little grass in Chet's car just as the cops drove by. That was Chet's first ever bust, and he took the fall because it was his car. A couple of days later, Gerry called and asked me to return to the group because Bob was leaving, and I stayed for the duration of the quartet with Chet. Mulligan of course was known as the driving force behind Miles's "Birth of the Cool" project. He was a very popular *Wunderkind*, and those first singles with Bob Whitlock were saturating the airwaves. Chet was initially unknown, but he was becoming a legend because he played so beautifully.

Weekends at the Haig, we had a line of about three hundred people waiting to get in, and all the jazz musicians in Hollywood came to hear us. I tend to play with my head down and eyes closed, and one night when I looked up, Miles Davis and Charles Mingus were standing next to me. I couldn't believe it! They had flown in from Manhattan just to hear the group. Oscar Pettiford sat in several times with us on cello, and he even had me sit down and play the instrument while he played bass, which was a laugh and a half, but it was fun. One of our regular customers every night after the second show at the Ambassador was Freddy Martin, who just loved us. I understand that he used to be a pretty good jazz tenor player. I saw everyone at the Haig at one time or another.

By the time I rejoined Gerry, we didn't rehearse much. I think in the six months I was with him, we might have had about four rehearsals for new material. He often introduced something new by just turning round on the stand and asking me if I knew it. One night he really stumped me, because he wanted to play "Polka Dots and Moonbeams," which I didn't know. He got madder than hell and, on the next break, he took me outside and told me that as a bass player I was supposed to know the repertoire. He finished up by saying that the next time he asked me if I knew a tune, I better know that tune! The following day I bought the sheet music—and learned it so well that I have been playing it as a solo ever since.

"Carson City Stage" was the only original I wrote for the group, and it was my biggest hit! Funnily enough, Gerry didn't like the tune but he loved the introduction, so the intro became the tune, which is all you hear. He decided on the title because he was good with words. I also wrote most of "Freeway," which is actually credited to Chet and not me, but you can't take credit for everything, can you? I used to stay at his house, partying all night, and then crash out on the sofa—"With a Chesterfield," as they say. One day Chet sang some little riffs which I played on his old beat-up piano. I wrote them on paper, adding a bridge which I was going to use for something else, and Gerry recorded "Freeway" while I was away with Billy May. Mostly, though, everything was Gerry's; we just followed him. He conceived the idea of the group and the arrangements, and although we had every opportunity, nobody contributed more than just serious playing. I wish I had known how to write in those days, but I didn't.

Gerry's abilities as an accompanist on the baritone was the most important factor as far as the group's success was concerned. I didn't miss the piano at all, because he had such an arranger's mind, he could always pick the best notes to back a soloist. The bass plays the bottom of the chord, and the most important harmonic note above is the seventh leading to the third, and Gerry was always right-on; I have never heard anyone play that way, and certainly nobody could have done it as well as Gerry.

While I was with him, I never sent in a dep. If I had, the only one he would have let me get away with was Joe Mondragon—but that is a whole different story, which I will get to later. Some of my favorite records had Lee Konitz with us, and his version of "Lover Man" is one of the best Konitz solos I ever heard. I'm still a big fan of Lee's. When Chico left to return to Lena because he couldn't turn down the money, some of the best drummers in town tried out, including, as I recall, Chuck Flores. Gerry just didn't seem to find anyone he liked until he heard Larry Bunker, and we all agreed that Larry had the best sound for the quartet. He was a marvelous player, especially on brushes, which that group needed. I had worked with him on Billy May's band when he took Alvin Stoller's place, and at first we didn't get along, but quite soon I realized what a great musician Larry was. He was a master percussionist and a very crisp drummer, whereas Chico was more of a showman, although I loved his "Jo Jones" style with the hi-hat.

Gerry was a bit of an oddball in those days because he was young, very tall, and probably didn't weigh more than ninety-five pounds! He was an imposing sight on the stand, with his huge baritone sax, which he loved to swing up and down while he played, if you remember, just like a bent straw. People were in awe of him, and when they sat down, they really paid attention to the music. Occasionally, though, we would get a table where customers were talking. He would stop everything and lecture the audience: "If you don't like what you came to hear, we would like you to leave right now." And the crowd would applaud him for it. We'd pick up without losing a beat and play the rest of the tune out. He didn't socialize much and I rarely saw him off the job, but Chet and I were the best of friends.

Chet was very sports-minded and, as everybody knows, he loved to race cars, not on the track but on the highway, and he scared the hell out of me many times. Once in San Francisco around 2 a.m. he showed me Lombard Street, which is a hill famous for the numbers of Z bends it has. We drove down there in what seemed like half a second flat, and it was so much fun, we did it two or three more times, until all the lights started going on around the neighborhood. We often went skinny-dipping after work, and I remember once, when we were leaving the Haig, he decided we should go skiing on Bear Mountain. We rented some skis, and although he had never skied in his life, he took off down the hill as though he had been born on them. Chet seemed to be good at everything, and the girls went crazy over him. He really knew how to have fun, and he lived life to its fullest, never wanting to miss out on anything. I know Chico has said that there were personal problems between him and Gerry, but I didn't witness any difficulties at all. Towards the end, just before Gerry got busted, they were living together, and I know Gerry loved Chet, and Chet felt that Gerry was one of the greatest musicians he had ever met.

In January 1953 Gerry recorded his tentet album with Joe Mondragon on bass instead of me. I knew that he loved Joe, as everybody did in the music business. Joe was a perfectionist who played beautifully, and I will never forget him, because he was always wonderful to me. I learnt a lot from him, and even though I was a complete unknown at the time, he used to send me as a sub if he couldn't make a record date. Anyway, one night at the club, Gerry seemed a little hostile to me and I asked him what the problem was. He said, "I've been really listening to you the last few nights, and I'm not getting the feeling I want. There is something wrong with this rhythm section because you and Larry aren't playing well together. I'm not happy and I'll be looking for a new bass player in the next few days, Carson; that's where it is right now." I told him that I thought we'd been playing better and better each night, but if there was something he wanted me to change, I would change it. He wouldn't listen, and I was heartbroken. Then it turned out that he had this tentet date and he started rehearsing with Joe Mondragon. I was there for each of the three nights they recorded at Capitol Studios, and it was magnificent. When I came to work after the last night, Gerry said, "Carson, you've been playing considerably better lately. I don't know what changed your attitude, but I like what you're doing, and I wish you'd stay with the group." That was the end of that! I've often thought about it, and I think that Gerry was unable to say to me, "You've been my bass player for a long time, but I want to use Joe Mondragon on a record date." He found it easier to fire me for three nights and then rehire me, and to this day I still laugh about it because we never had any problems.

Anne Baxter, who was an adorable person, often came to hear us, and one night her agent asked if we would play at her birthday party. At the end of the night, at 2 a.m., we set off for her house in the Hollywood Hills, where we played for about an hour. She wined and dined us and couldn't do enough for us, because she loved the music. Later, I sat down at the piano and started fooling around with her score of Ravel's *Mother Goose Suite*. She asked if I liked the piece, and when I told her it was one of my favorites, she insisted that I take the music home.

I remember arriving at the Haig one night to find that Gerry had eloped to Palm Springs with one of the waitresses, called Jeffie Lee Boyd. She was a friend of Dick Bock's, and I had tried to date her a few times, but I guess I wasn't her style. The marriage lasted for about a month before they had an annulment, and I could never figure it out, although I've heard several stories. We didn't know that Gerry was messing around with drugs, and one rumor was that he had gone down to Palm Springs to dry out and Jeffie was there to help. I don't know if I believe that or not, but it could be true, because it sure was a strange marriage! She was still working at the Haig when Gerry got busted, and shortly afterwards Arlyne Brown arrived on the scene from New York. She was the daughter of the great Lew Brown of the DeSylva, Brown, and Henderson songwriting team, and she and Gerry had known each other for years. It seemed that within a matter of days Arlyne had taken over and become Gerry's manager, with the intention of showing him the way to a new life. She was a real New Yorker and, man, was she strong that woman!

One night, two plainclothes detectives named Hill and O'Grady came into the Haig and sat down right in front of the bandstand for two whole sets. Chet pulled me aside and told me they were cops and Hollywood was their beat. Their great fame came from going around busting celebrities like Robert Mitchum and Lenny Bruce and, let me add, they were a couple of assholes.

If the club hadn't been full, they would have arrested us there and then, but they waited until a quarter to two, when it was time to close the joint up. They herded us into the office and looked up our sleeves, checking for needle marks. I was bewildered, because I didn't know what they were talking about, but after checking Chet, Larry, and me, Gerry just broke down, saying, "I've been screwing around with drugs again," just like that. He didn't have to say a word, but he was like a beaten man. He took the cops to the house that he and Chet were renting in East Hollywood near Sunset Boulevard and Western, showed them his paraphernalia, and went off to jail in handcuffs. I know now that he was desperate to get away from the drug scene and that was the only way he knew how to do it.[8]

Gerry's lawyer kept the case bouncing around from court to court for a couple of months while we carried on playing at the Haig. By this time he and Arlyne were renting a tiny house in the Hollywood Hills. The night before his final court appearance, when he fully expected to get the case kicked out for good, we all went up to Gerry's place for a little party to cheer him on. The next day the judge gave him six months at the Sheriff's Honour Farm, and that was the end of the first Gerry Mulligan Quartet.[9]

The Honour Farm was in Saugus, which is about thirty miles out of L.A. on the road to San Francisco, and I was Arlyne's ride when she visited Gerry. He would arrange for me to see one of the other prisoners, usually a musician, while he and Arlyne spent their hour together.[10] We all expected Gerry to reform the quartet when he was released, and in the meantime, Chet and I got to play with Charlie Parker for a while. We also did some things on our own with Russ Freeman and Bob Neel, because Dick Bock was preparing Chet to become a bandleader, although Chet didn't want to be a leader. We were keeping fairly busy, not busy-busy, but hanging in there and paying the rent. We were both astonished to find that, on the day Gerry was released, Arlyne picked him up and took him right to the airport. Somebody said his final remark was, "Good-bye, Los Angeles, you will never see me again.[11]

It has been said that Gerry and Chet didn't get back together again because Chet wanted more money, but I was his closest friend and I never heard him talk about money. As long as he could have a little bit of weed every day, he was happy; money was the last thing he thought about. I will never figure out why they didn't get back together.

I did play with the group once more a few years later, in 1964, when Gerry organized a reunion at the Hollywood Bowl with Chet and Chico. At the last moment, Art Farmer took Chet's place, and when Gerry made the announcement, a lot of the audience assumed Chet was getting stoned somewhere, because by that time, he had a bad reputation as a junkie.

I think that Gerry, along with Duke, Gil Evans, and Bill Holman, was one of the best arranger/composers in jazz, and nobody will ever replace him. When it comes to people in that position, you can name them on the fingers of one hand. He did so much in music, and he will always stand out as the greatest musician I have met in my entire life, bar none. He was the very best on baritone, although I may be a little prejudiced, but he just got better and better. In recent years when he wasn't writing so much and concentrating on playing, he was the strongest and the best. As for Chet, I can't say enough about him. He was the most musical and melodic trumpeter I've ever played with. He and Gerry were magnificent together because they had "The Magic."

On a discographic note, all the Pacific Jazz recordings by Mulligan's quartet and tentet are available on Mosaic MD3–102. The quartet's San Francisco date, which included "My Funny Valentine," can be heard on Fantasy - OJCCD-711-2, and their final studio session, which was produced by Gene Norman, has been reissued on Jazz Society (F) 670511CD.

NOTES

1. Some bizarre and also some historically important events occurred at the Ambassador Hotel over the years. Albert Einstein once rang reception to complain about room service, and on another occasion Scott and Zelda Fitzgerald set fire to their room, creeping out in the confusion to avoid paying the bill! In 1952, while Gerry Mulligan was still appearing at the Haig, Richard Nixon composed his famous "Checkers" speech at the Ambassador, which saved his position on the Republican ticket as Dwight D. Eisenhower's running mate. Sadly, the hotel achieved a different notoriety when Bobby Kennedy was assassinated there after having just accepted victory in the California primary during his campaign for the presidency in 1968.

2. This incident occurred early in May 1952, just before Chet Baker joined Charlie Parker for a two-week engagement at the Tiffany club.

3. In an enthusiastic *Down Beat* review titled "Mr. Mulligan Has a Real Crazy Gerry-Built Crew," Ralph Gleason said, "the group turned San Francisco into the modern music center of the country . . . they are a musical sensation."

4. According to Carol Easton in her book *Straight Ahead: The Story of Stan Kenton* (Da Capo), Carson's description of Gail Madden being "a little strange" may be an understatement. Easton says, "From 1947 to 1949 Gail was living with Bob Graettinger. She was a frustrated pianist who saw herself as the woman behind the genius (whomever he might be at the moment). She looked even freakier than Graettinger, in mismatched shoes, men's clothes, whatever took her fancy. She shared Graettinger's oblique perspective on life and was one of the few people who could make him laugh, but she was volatile and erratic if not downright psychotic. Graettinger came home one day to find everything dyed pink—bedspread, towels, curtains, clothes, shoes, everything."

5. It shouldn't come as a surprise that both Mulligan and Baker were unfamiliar with "My Funny Valentine." Rodgers and Hart had written it for a 1937 show called *Babes in Arms*, and despite earlier recordings by people like Cab Calloway, Mel Tormé, and Eddie Condon, it remained in obscurity until revived by the Mulligan quartet in 1952. The following year, Frank Sinatra sang it on his very first L.P., *Songs for Young Lovers*—and the rest, as they say, is history.

6. Towards the end of the fifties, when Art Farmer joined the group, his initial reaction to working without a piano was: "It's like walking down the street with no clothes on!"

7. In his excellent book *Bird's Diary: The Life of Charlie Parker 1945–1955* (Castle Communications), Ken Vail mentions Joe Maini sitting in with the quartet. He quotes the following letter to Parker from Maini, who was visiting Los Angeles with Jimmy Knepper: "Jerry [*sic*] Mulligan is making a lot of money out here. He's got a small group with no piano. I played with him the other night on his gig and it was a lot of fun." The letter is dated January 23, 1953.

8. In a long 1959 Mulligan profile by Nat Hentoff in the *New Yorker*, he confirmed that Gerry expected to be sent to the Federal Hospital in Lexington, Kentucky, where he hoped to be cured. That is why he so readily gave himself up, and in a more tolerant society, that is where he would have been sent, rather than to jail.

9. James Gavin, in his book *Deep in a Dream: The Long Night of Chet Baker* (Chatto and Windus), points out that the judge who sentenced Mulligan also sent Barbara Graham to the gas chamber for murder in 1955. Susan Hayward took the role of Graham in the 1958 film *I Want to Live*, which featured Mulligan on the soundtrack as well as in some early nightclub scenes.

10. Mulligan has described his incarceration as "sheer torture," but Robert Mitchum on his release from an Honour Farm in 1949 said, probably tongue in cheek, "It was like Palm Springs without the riff-raff!"

11. It was a long time ago, and understandably Carson's memory is a little at fault here. Mulligan remained working in California for a while after his release, before returning to the East Coast with Bob Brookmeyer.

Chapter Twenty-One

Lennie Niehaus

In 1955, Lennie Niehaus won the Down Beat *magazine award as the "New Star" on alto, and during the rest of that decade, he made a series of fine albums for the Contemporary label. He was also the principal arranger and lead alto for Stan Kenton. In 1963 Niehaus stopped playing entirely, preferring to concentrate on writing for film and television, but he has now started to perform again, when his writing commitments allow. This interview took place in December 1997, when he replied on cassette tape to my list of questions.*

I was born on June 1, 1929, in St. Louis, Missouri, and my family, which was a musical one, moved to Los Angeles when I was about seven years old. My sister Agnes became a concert pianist, although she hasn't played for many years, and my father had been a professional violinist in symphony orchestras. He encouraged me to take up the violin when I was eight, and a couple of years later, I switched to the oboe before trying the alto. I did things a little backwards because it was after taking up the alto that I learnt the clarinet. I also became interested in the bassoon, which I played in high school and college, and I was still playing it when I was in the Army.

In 1945, while I was still in high school, I worked in a bebop band, playing mostly stocks, and I was also doing a lot of writing for the band. Later on we switched to a Latin American style because we couldn't play bebop at dances. There was a riff called a *Montuno*, which was a two-bar repeated pattern that could go on indefinitely, allowing the jazz players to get up and blow over a Latin beat, and that was kind of fun. Some of the musicians who came through that band included Teddy Edwards, Warne Marsh, Herbie Steward, Herb Geller (who was playing tenor), Jimmy Knepper, and Billy Byers. Even in those days, Warne Marsh was hearing different things to the bop that was happening. He was already playing a little like he did when he was with

Lennie Tristano, and of course, when you listen to their music now, it doesn't sound so far out as it did at the time.

In 1946 I went to L.A. City College for two years, with Jack Sheldon and Jack Montrose as fellow students, and we played at a lot of clubs around town with Russ Freeman. We were gradually learning the new bop tunes, and Russ was a big help because he knew a lot of that music. The college had one of the few jazz programs in the country, and we had a jazz group with some of the part-time students like Dodo Marmarosa, Tony Rizzi, and a drummer called Jackie Mills. I then studied at Cal State for three years, where I graduated *cum laude* in composition, and while I was there I auditioned for Jerry Wald, which would have been in 1951. The book, which was mostly written by Al Cohn, was fun to play, and Jerry was using a *Four Brothers* sound with a tenor lead, even though he had a conventional five-man sax line-up. We played for dancing at a club called the Moulin Rouge, and although I wasn't with the band very long, I managed to write three charts for the girl singer, whose name escapes me now.

I auditioned for Stan Kenton one morning early in 1952 when he was putting a new band together. Many of the players who had been with him a long time had left and he was looking for a jazz alto to replace Art Pepper. Although he had used woodwinds in the Innovations Orchestra, it was just an alto chair with no doubles, because Stan didn't like the clarinet. He also didn't like trumpets in cup mutes.[1] The first arrangement we tried was Gerry Mulligan's "Limelight," which I sight-read and also played a solo, and then Stan did something unusual. Dick Meldonian was the lead player and, as I said, I was auditioning for the second alto, the jazz chair. In those days the two parts were quite separate, but Stan wanted me to play lead on "Deep Purple." To my knowledge, that was the first time he did that, and later on when Charlie Mariano was in the band with me, we both played some lead and some jazz.

Mulligan had written some really great charts for Stan, like "Limelight," "Walkin' Shoes," "Young Blood," and "Swinghouse," which were a lot of fun to play, and they represented quite a change for Stan. He wasn't used to the swinging type of arrangements that Mulligan was writing, but he really liked them and he often featured them. Gerry rehearsed the band, and despite what you may have heard, I didn't witness any personality problems between them.

After three months with Kenton I was drafted into the Army in April 1952, serving two years at Fort Ord in Monterey. Hamp Hawes and Ed Thigpen were there for a while, but they didn't stay long. I played oboe in the concert band, and being influenced by Mulligan, I had a pianoless quartet with a tenor player. I also wrote some octet arrangements, which we used to play at the officer's club, where Clint Eastwood tended bar. We had met at basic training, where he was a swimming instructor, and had become friends because we had a lot in common, having been to J.A.T.P. concerts, listening to people like Bird, Prez, Illinois Jacquet, and Flip Phillips. Along with Oscar Peterson, they are still some of his favorite jazz musicians. During my time in the Army I would sit in at the Haig or the Lighthouse whenever I got back to town. I played with Shorty Rogers, Jimmy Giuffre, and Shelly Manne, and it was Shelly who convinced me to sign for Les Koenig of Contemporary Records when I left the service in 1954. Shelly told me that Les would give me complete artistic freedom, and it turned out to be a great move, because he was wonderful to work for. He let me record anything I wanted, with any size and type of group, and altogether I did five albums for him.

I had been playing a lot with Jack Montrose and Bob Gordon, so I used them on my first album in a pianoless group with Shelly Manne and Monty Budwig.[2] I liked the pianoless concept because it gave the improviser freedom to play different chords over chords, almost polytonality. Bob of course was a wonderful baritone player and a lot of fun to play with and to be around. He also had a great sense of humor, which was reflected in his playing. Jack Montrose still plays his tenor and lives in Las Vegas, where everyone used to be busy working in hotels six nights a week. That's all changed now because a lot of shows are prerecorded so the bands aren't needed, or the stars come in with their own self-contained groups. Years ago, guys like Jack and Billy Root moved to Vegas and had some good years, but they mostly do casual work now.

In 1954 I also played with Chico O'Farrill's Latin band, which I enjoyed, and that was the year I rejoined Stan Kenton. For the next few years, I was very busy, working with the band and writing for my own recordings, which included two octet dates and a string album.[3] Whenever Kenton took a break, I usually worked in a quintet with Bill Perkins around town. I remember being thrilled one night when I heard a tenor player warming up in the kitchen at Jazz City, where we were appearing opposite Miles Davis. I said to Perk, "Listen to that guy play," and he said, "Yeah, it sounds really interesting." It turned out to be John Coltrane. I also played with Chet Baker at jam sessions, who was a great player with an unbelievable ear. You could call any tune and he would be able to play it, although I never asked him what chord he was playing, because he didn't think chordally, but he played beautifully.

When I first started playing with Kenton again, jazz clubs were beginning to die out, so we played a lot of dances. Unfortunately he didn't have enough dance charts, so he had to play his concert material, leaving the audience who came to dance standing around in front of the bandstand. That's when I started writing dance arrangements for the band, because I thought it would be a great idea to play charts that people could dance to, while still sounding like Kenton. Funnily enough, it took him a little while to realize I was back in the band and Lee Konitz was no longer there. I remember in 1954, when I had just taken over from Lee, we did a tour called "A Festival of Modern American Music," with Shorty Rogers, Art Tatum, Charlie Ventura, and Mary Ann McCall. We appeared at the Chicago Opera House, and because it was such a formal occasion, we wore our alternative band uniforms of dark blue suits. I had solo spots on "Lover Man," "Cherokee," "Stella by Starlight," and "The End of a Love Affair," and I would just turn to the band and tell them what I wanted to play after Stan announced me. As I was about to play, he came over to the band and said, "Lee's music," forgetting that Lee had left. Bob Fitzpatrick, our first trombonist, said, "Stan, it's Lennie, not Lee," but Stan couldn't hear him. He said to the audience, "We would like to feature one of the greatest alto players around today, please welcome—Lee Konitz." As usual, Stan was looking particularly striking, but when he saw me walking to the mike and realized his mistake, he didn't say a word but just crawled off the stage on all fours!

Boots Mussulli was on baritone with the band, and I loved him because he was such a great guy. I wasn't one of the poker-playing bunch, but I could usually hear some of the guys in the back of the bus getting pretty angry with him, because he always seemed to win.

It was around 1957 that Stan had the idea of changing the sax section to one alto, two tenors, and two baritones. This meant that all their music had to be rewritten, because it wasn't as simple as getting one of the baritones to play the second alto part. I did a lot of the rewriting, and I was on lead, with the first tenor playing the original second alto part. The second tenor had the original first tenor part, and one of the baritones played the original second tenor, while the other baritone had the conventional baritone line. He liked extreme highs and extreme lows, which is the only way I can explain it. The trumpets were always "way up there" with high-note specialists like Maynard Ferguson, Ernie Royal, and Bud Brisbois, and he had five trombones instead of the usual four, even though Ellington had used three for years. Later on he went to two bass trombones, with one doubling tuba, and he did the same to the saxes when we had two baritones—one doubled bass sax. It was what Stan wanted, but I still prefer the conventional saxophone line-up, and although we couldn't play as loud as ten brass, we held our own because we were a pretty loud section.

As far as Kenton's other arrangers are concerned, Bill Russo experimented with the different sounds that can be achieved from a jazz band without woodwinds, by using various combinations of instruments. For instance, he had something he called the "Gazelle" sound, which featured the lead alto with a trombone and two tenors creating a very graceful voicing, just like a gazelle. I always liked his arrangement of "Fascinating Rhythm" as well as some of the more serious things he for wrote Stan. Gerry Mulligan showed both Bill Holman and me that there could be a different approach to writing for the band by thinning it out and making it swing a little more. We didn't *have* to write fully voiced chords. We could give the soloists a chance to be heard with nice linear lines in the background, and three-part chords instead of loud five-part punctuations. Mulligan's writing for the "Birth of the Cool" sessions and for Stan was a big influence on me. Bill Holman, too, wrote some marvelous things that still sound as good today as they did back then. Gene Roland was a very talented and imaginative arranger who was always trying to get a hit for Stan. He wanted to be the "hit-maker." He wrote "Opus in Chartreuse" as well as a whole series of "Opus" titles in every color you can imagine.

I played in a lot of Stan's bands that I liked, but my favorite was the 1953 edition with Lee Konitz, Zoot Sims, Richie Kamuca, Frank Rosolino, Conte Candoli, and Stan Levey. They recorded my first arrangement of "Pennies from Heaven," which I had written before leaving the band to go in the Army.[4] Other soloists in later bands that I liked were Bill Perkins, Carl Fontana, Sam Noto, and Rolf Ericson.

I must tell you a favorite story about the Dizzy Gillespie Big Band coming to L.A. around 1955. His jazz alto player got sick, so I was recommended because I could sight-read. Dizzy called "Groovin' High" and whispered to me, "Hey, stand up." I wondered what was going on—just me, stand up? I didn't know the arrangement, but I stood up after the introduction, and it suddenly struck me that I was playing "Groovin' High" with Dizzy, a number I had first heard him play in the forties with Bird, and it was probably one of the biggest thrills of my life. I can't remember now who else was in the band, but Charlie Persip was on drums, and the baritone was Billy Root.

As I mentioned earlier, I took Art Pepper's place when I first joined Stan Kenton. Art was very influenced by Lester Young, and in the early days I liked his playing a lot. He had a lovely sound. But many years later when I went to hear him, I was a little disappointed. I don't think that everyone has to play the same as they did when they were twenty-one, but it sounded as though he was trying to play in a style that wasn't him—just playing a lot of notes that weren't in the chord, running up and down the horn and squeaking out a high note once in a while. When I listen, I try to find the best in musicians, and I don't expect them to play the way I think they should, so maybe he was just experimenting.

My biggest influences on alto were Lee Konitz and Charlie Parker, and Parker of course was the foundation for all alto players, because we all play Bird, even to this day. It's like building a house. We add a wing, which makes it a little more ourselves, but he is still the foundation, and everybody I hear still plays *Bird.* There are some exceptions, like Paul Desmond, who I enjoyed when he was with Brubeck, and I also liked some of the recordings he made with Jim Hall. The more I listen to Paul, the more I can appreciate what he played back then, because he played beautifully, although usually on the same emotional and dynamic level, without ever getting louder; rather like a conversation when nobody gets angry. You know, everybody is into playing high notes now, but Paul did it really musically back in the fifties, but today, I hear a lot of sax players going for a high note for effect's sake.[5]

I also have a great deal of respect for Benny Carter as a player and arranger, but that school was never an influence on my playing, although I hear a little of Benny in some of the bebop alto players. During the fifties I knew Joe Maini, who later played lead with Terry Gibbs's "Dream Band," and he played very good bebop, as did Sonny Criss.

After I left Stan in 1959, I continued playing the saxophone until 1963, which is when I put it aside to concentrate on writing, although I did miss it. I also started teaching, and students were coming to me, wanting to know how to play jazz, because at that time there was nothing published. I started to write different exercises and *études,* and pretty soon I had enough material to have a series of books published called *Jazz Conception for Saxophone.*[6] One of my students was a very talented young man called Quinn Davis, who later played with Kenton.

I was getting into studio writing, and in 1967 I did a T.V. series with Mel Tormé, who was great to work with. He had a good concept of chords and could make suggestions about moving from one chord to another, and I remember he could even sing some of my octet arrangements from my recordings. He was a very talented, well-rounded musician and one of the last of the really great scat singers, like Ella and maybe a few others. I started playing the alto again because of the movie *Bird,* when I had to teach the actors how to pretend to play. During preproduction I had a little sax class in Clint Eastwood's office on Saturday mornings, with Forest Whitaker and his brother, who played "young" Bird, along with some other alto players I was teaching.

As far as favorite instrumentalists are concerned, it is very hard to think of all of them, but on trumpet you would have to include Dizzy Gillespie, Miles Davis, and Clifford Brown. Trombone would be Frank Rosolino, Carl Fontana, Bill Watrous, and J. J. Johnson. My favorite alto is still Charlie Parker, although Phil Woods is a fine player, as was Cannonball Adderley. On tenor it's John Coltrane, and Stan Getz with Gerry Mulligan, and Pepper Adams on baritone. Clarinet is Eddie Daniels and Ken Peplowski. Milt Jackson and Lionel Hampton always come to mind on vibes, although I'm not really too keen on the instrument. Piano would be Oscar Peterson, Bill Evans, and Kenny Barron, who is doing some fine things. Guitar is Jim Hall and Joe

Pass, and on bass it starts with Ray Brown and you can take it from there. On drums, again, there are so many, but you would have to mention Shelly Manne and Max Roach. Favorite singers are Frank Sinatra, Mel Tormé, Carmen McRae, Sarah Vaughan, and Irene Kral. As far as big bands are concerned, in L.A. we have two of the finest around, led by Bill Holman and Bob Florence, who both write great arrangements in different styles. When I was in New York in 1996, I was greatly impressed by the Carnegie Hall Jazz Band, whose musical director is Jon Faddis. They played at a concert called "Eastwood after Hours," which featured a suite I wrote about the music he listened to as a teenager, and his use of jazz in his movies.

I'm playing more regularly now, and for the past year I've been working on material for a new CD with Bill Perkins, which also includes Jack Nimitz on some tracks. Altogether, we put in about fourteen years with the Kenton band in the fifties, and I've arranged one of my favorite tunes, "It Seems Like Old Times," which will be the title of the album, celebrating the three of us together again after all these years.[7]

NOTES

1. There was something else that Kenton didn't like. Gerry Mulligan has said that when he was writing for the band, Stan complained when one of Mulligan's scores called for Shelly Manne to play brushes on cymbals. After listening patiently for a while at the rehearsal, Kenton shouted out, "No! No! No! We don't use brushes on cymbals in this band; that's faggot music!"

2. Lennie Niehaus, *The Quintets*. Contemporary C3518.

3. Lennie Niehaus, *The Octets*. Contemporary C3540 and C3503. *The Quintet and Strings*. Contemporary C3510.

4. Apparently the first time Lennie heard the recording was when he was in the Army and "Pennies from Heaven" was played on the jukebox one night. Not surprisingly, he played it over and over for the rest of the evening.

5. The saxophone has a normal range of two and a half octaves. Desmond could play an octave above this, until a fan asked him to demonstrate the fingering required. When he tried to show him, Paul apparently lost the octave forever. This may be apocryphal, but true or not, it's typical of the self-deprecating humor of the witty Mr. Desmond, who once said that he really wanted to be a writer rather than a musician. He had to stop, he explained, because he could only write on the beach and kept getting sand in his typewriter.

6. Try Publishing Company, Los Angeles.

7. Lennie Niehaus Quintet. Fresh Sound FSR 5016CD.

Chapter Twenty-Two

Jack Nimitz

Jack Nimitz is a name that will be thoroughly familiar to most jazz record col-
lectors. His fine baritone sound has been heard on countless recordings, un-
derpinning the bands of Woody Herman, Stan Kenton, Gerald Wilson, Terry
Gibbs, and Oliver Nelson. He is a founding member of Supersax, and he has
recorded with Frank Sinatra, Peggy Lee, Ella Fitzgerald, and Sarah Vaughan.
Nimitz was born in Washington, D.C., on November 1, 1930. This interview
took place just prior to an engagement at London's Pizza Express, where he
was appearing with Buddy Childers in April 1997.

I started my professional career down South, with territory bands like
Bob Astor and Johnny Bothwell, before coming back home to Washington
to join the Willis Conover Orchestra in 1952. Charlie Walp, Marky Markowitz,
and the Swope Brothers were there, and although drummer Joe Timer was
really the leader, Willis used to introduce the band, because he was well known
from his "Voice of America" broadcasts and his name carried more clout. We
played on Sunday afternoons at the Club Kavakos, and people from New
York — like Al Cohn, Stan Getz, and Bird — would often guest with us. There
is a recording of Parker playing with the band in February 1953.[1]

I stayed with Willis until late 1953, which is when I took Sam Staff's place
with Woody Herman. Woody had heard me at an after-hours club in D.C. in
a quintet with one of his former bass players, Mert Oliver, and when Sam became ill, he called and asked if I would join the band for a couple of weeks
until he got better. Sadly he never did, and although he was only in his twenties, Sam died from cancer. Woody was getting the Third Herd together, so
there was a big turnover of musicians coming and going, which can be pretty
terrible until it shapes up. The Conover/Timer band, on the other hand, was a
good, hot, happening band, with fine charts and guys who had been with El-

liot Lawrence, Buddy Rich, and Woody. I wasn't sure whether to stay with Herman, but in the end, I made the right decision and remained.

It was while I was with the band that Nat Pierce tagged me with the nickname "The Admiral," after Chester W. Nimitz from World War II. Dick Hafer was on lead, because we used three tenors and a baritone, which was Woody's "thing," and although there is more color and versatility with the conventional five saxes, Woody's sax section was nice to play in. Of course we did "Four Brothers" every night down in front of the band, and it took me months to memorize it, because there are a lot of repeated notes for the baritone, which makes it difficult. I was featured on Ralph Burns's "Cool Cat on a Hot Tin Roof"[2] and Bill Holman's "Mulligan Tawny,"[3] which had Dick Collins on trumpet and was rearranged by Woody to give it that Gerry Mulligan/Chet Baker feel at the beginning. I was also on "Mambo the Most,"[4] but I don't have any of my records—because once you hear how terrible you sound, it's onward, and who wants to listen anyway! Red Kelly was the bass player, and he still plays in a club and restaurant he owns in Tacoma, Washington.

During my time with the band I was involved in two car accidents. The first when Cy Touff was driving was not particularly serious, but the second, when we were on our way to Chicago with Dick Collins at the wheel, was pretty bad. A tire blew and I was thrown clear, but the car rolled over and landed on my back, which resulted in me being hospitalized. Dick was a good trumpeter, who still plays casuals, but he had a degree in library science so dropped out of full-time music to work at the main library in LA. Incidentally, I was quite unaware of the financial problems caused by Woody's manager, Abe Turchen, when I was with the band, and I think that Woody was unaware of them too.

Woody broke the band up towards the end of 1955, when he took a small group into Vegas for a while. That's when I went to New York to join Stan Kenton, and playing in that band was completely different, as the brass and drums were so loud. The baritone usually sat under the drums, which were on a raised platform, and you had to put cotton wool in your ears, because when that theme started, with all the cymbals rolling—!!

With Herman, it was like a whole bunch of guys hanging out together, but Stan's band had cliques and factions. He paid more, though, and he was also a very nice man and sincere in what he was doing. He was very tall and charismatic, and when he stood in front of the band, he was really impressive. Dave Schildkraut, who was a quiet, introverted guy, was the lead alto for a while, and he was a great sax player but a rotten poker player. He used to lose all his money in games on the bus, unlike Charlie Mariano, who was very good at cards, really slick. I only met Bob Graettinger once while I was with the band, and that was at Zardi's, when he came over and introduced himself.

We never played his "City of Glass," which became something of a joke, because if we were at a club and unsure what to do next, someone would always say, "Right, 'City of Glass' in B-flat!"

Early in 1956 the band came over to Europe, so I suppose I'd better tell you the story of how Spencer Sinatra and I came to be sent home by Stan. It was all because Spencer had become very friendly with Ronnie Scott's girlfriend, Joan, which quite naturally upset Ronnie. There was talk of other things going on, so Ronnie complained to Stan. You have to remember that we were the first American band to visit England in a long time, and Stan was scared to death about any adverse publicity, so he panicked. He called a meeting, and even though everyone spoke up for us, he said Spencer and I would have to go back to the States.[5] I was involved because Spencer and I were roommates and I had been hanging out with them. I'd got Spencer on the band in the first place, because we were friends since growing up together in D.C., and his father used to give me lessons. Spencer was a good musician, and he played the flute in the National Symphony, until he got sick of that and asked me to get him into Woody's band. He and Joan got married, and he carried on playing in pit jobs on Broadway, but he had a lot of problems. He eventually committed suicide by jumping off a building in New York.

When I returned to the States, I worked in a quintet that played for dancing at the Savoy Ballroom in New York, opposite Cootie Williams, which was a great gig. I also played on Quincy Jones's first record date, and sitting with all those giants like Zoot, Lucky Thompson, Hank Jones, and Charlie Persip was a little intimidating, because I was pretty young and in awe of those guys.[6] Towards the end of the fifties, I went home to D.C., which is when I got a call from Gerry Mulligan, who was organizing the Concert Jazz Band. I had known Gerry since 1949, when he was living in Washington with a friend of mine. He wanted me to come up to New York for rehearsals, but I was really broke at the time, and he didn't say anything about sending me some money to get there. A drummer friend agreed to drive me, but the next morning, when I waited at a street corner for him, he didn't show. I phoned Gerry and told him I wouldn't be able to make it, and that's when he called Gene Allen, who was a good player. I'm really sorry that I missed playing with the CJB.

Guys like Red Mitchell were coming through D.C. and saying that I should go out to L.A., as there was plenty of work there. Around that time, Stan Kenton called and said all was forgiven, and would I like to come back on the band? It seemed like a great way to get to California, so I took Don Davidson's place, and after I settled in L.A., I gave my notice. I think that Don might have returned.

I played a lot of solos with the band when we were on the road, but they weren't written into the charts. Stan would just point to me. Consequently, whenever I play at these Kenton reunions, I don't get to solo on some of the things I played on. It was while I was with Stan the second time that he changed the sax section to an alto, two tenors, and two baritones, which I hated. He was always changing things. I much preferred the band with a conventional sax line-up, but he got into that two-baritone thing, then the mellophonium thing. He didn't want a swing band; he wanted an *orchestra*. Lennie Niehaus was the lead alto, and he wrote most of the dance charts, because we played a lot of dances. When he left, Charlie Mariano took over on lead, and Charlie is a great player.

Just before I rejoined Kenton, I had run into Mel Lewis, who was with Mulligan. He told me that if I ever came out to L.A., he would get me into Terry Gibbs's band, and in 1961 I got to play with Terry alongside guys like Richie Kamuca, Charlie Kennedy, and Joe Maini. Joe of course was a great soloist and lead player, and a real free spirit. Later on in the sixties I co-led a quintet with Bill Hood, who was another talented guy—fine baritone player, composer, arranger, copyist, and he could sing as well. He did some studio playing, but he was his own worst enemy because he didn't always know when to be quiet, so he tended to put his foot in it sometimes. Bobby West was the bass player, Jackie Wilson was on piano, and Nick Ceroli was the drummer, although Frank Capp took his place later on. We kept the group together for a couple of years, and we worked Shelly's Manne-Hole every night for months, but unfortunately we never recorded.

I must tell you about one of the greatest musical experiences of my life, which occurred towards the end of the sixties, when I was doing the Della Reese show. Harry Edison was also on the show, and he asked if I wanted to play with the Count Basie band, who were in L.A. at the Whiskey-A-Go-Go on Sunset Strip. It was just one night, because Charlie Fowlkes had an illness in the family and had to go back East. Marshall Royal and Eddie "Lockjaw" Davis were in the section, and it was like being swept up in a tornado. Of course that's never happened to me, and I hope it never does, but you get the picture!

I joined Supersax pretty much from the beginning in 1972, and it just started as a fun thing, where we got together to play the charts. We didn't expect to work or record with the group, and to start with, we didn't even have a rhythm section apart from Buddy Clark on bass. As you know, most of the time the baritone doubles the lead, although there are some arrangements where it's five-way, but mostly it's double lead, so I'm always saving Med's ass. Only joking, Med![7] We aren't working now as much as we used to, because I don't think that Med is really looking for it, and you have to play those charts regularly to make them sound right. You just can't sit down, pull the library out, and play, because it doesn't work that way. When we used to tour,

Conte Candoli, Frank Rosolino, or Carl Fontana went out with us, and they usually got to solo, which gave the saxes a rest. After playing about three pages of one of Bird's lines, we needed a rest, believe me, and anyway who wants to listen to us after Bird's choruses?

I'm playing more jazz now, and I recently went to Vienna with Gerald Wilson's orchestra, and he definitely has his own thing going. I've worked with him off and on since the early sixties, and I've been on a lot of his albums. I got to solo with the band while we were in Europe, because he features the baritone, which is nice. In 1996 we went back to Washington, D.C., with his band, because Gerald was being honored in having his music housed in the Library of Congress, and I got to see my family. He writes and teaches a jazz history course at UCLA, but he doesn't play at all now.

There is still a lot of studio work in L.A., but I'm not interested in doing it anymore if it isn't fun. I would rather play jazz. In 1993 I recorded with Bud Shank, Conte Candoli, and Bill Perkins,[8] and I have also made a couple of CDs with Frank Strazzeri's group, Woodwinds West. The first had Bob Cooper, and after he passed away, Pete Christlieb took his place on the second recording, which is very good.[9] I sub with Juggernaut and Bob Florence, but not regularly, because I hate just sitting there, playing parts all night. I've really got sick of it. I've worked with just about all the main singers, like Ella, Peggy Lee, Sarah Vaughan, and Frank Sinatra—and Frank of course could be different at different times. He was always very professional, though, just a couple of takes and that would be it. He wouldn't put up with any incompetence, because he knew his stuff and you had to know yours. Sometimes he would take a band out for a couple of weeks, and I did that a few times. It was always first-class travel and hotels, with good money, and the charts were great, too, by people like Billy May, Nelson Riddle, and Don Costa.

My favorite arrangers include Al Cohn, Johnny Mandel, Bill Holman, Gerry Mulligan, Bob Brookmeyer, and Manny Albam. As far as the baritone is concerned, you can't say that any one guy is better than another, as they all have something to say, which has added to the lore. Harry Carney of course was a monster, and Serge Chaloff was very impressive. Cecil Payne was underrated, but after a few notes you knew it was him, because he had a great time-feel. When Gerry Mulligan came along, he was very innovative, too, influencing Lars Gullin for instance, another fine player. Incidentally, Gary Smulyan told me recently that he was doing a tribute to Gerry with Nick Brignola and Ronnie Cuber, just three baritones and rhythm, and the intention is to play some festivals together.

I play a Buffet saxophone with the low A, which you must have for commercial work, which means that I have completely switched from Selmer; I got tired lifting my leg over the bell to get that A! Buffet actually sent four altos, four tenors, and a baritone over to Supersax, but I was the only one of the group who kept the Buffet. I don't care for the keyboard, because it is very stretched, but the horn has a real big bore and I like the sound I get. I also like the way it tunes so well, because when a Selmer or Conn get cold, you have to push the mouthpiece on a lot to make a difference, but with the Buffet, a small move is enough to change the pitch. The baritone weighs about 15 pounds, so I don't put the sling around my neck anymore, because I have a compressed vertebrae from years of doing that. I have a shoulder sling, which works a lot better, and a lot of guys use them now.[10] Some baritone players use a stand, but I don't care for them because it doesn't feel as though you're playing, since you have no contact with the instrument.

Finally, I must tell you that in 1995 I made my first recording as a leader, with Lou Levy, Dave Carpenter, and Joe LaBarbera, and I'm very pleased with it.[11] Teddy Edwards once told me that you can make hundreds of records, but it doesn't mean a thing unless you have one out there yourself, and he's quite right.

On the sleevenote, Bill Perkins says the big question is, "Why did so many years have to pass, for Jack to make his debut as a leader?" Hopefully this CD will let the record-buying public in on the secret shared by his playing colleagues for years, that Jack Nimitz is not only a wonderful section man but also a superb baritone soloist.

NOTES

1. *Charlie Parker with the Orchestra*. Electra K 52359.
2. Woody Herman. Capitol EAP3-658.
3. Woody Herman. Columbia CL 952.
4. Woody Herman. Verve MGV 8216.
5. Two local musicians were drafted in as replacements. Harry Klein played baritone, and Tommy Whittle initially took Sinatra's place. When Whittle had to leave because of a prior engagement, Don Rendell completed the tour.
6. Quincy Jones, *This Is How I Feel about Jazz*. ABC Paramount ABC 149.
7. Med Flory plays lead alto with Supersax.
8. Bud Shank Sextet, *New Gold*. Candid CCD 79707.
9. Frank Strazzeri, *Somebody Loves Me*. Fresh Sound FSR 5003 CD.
10. Bill Perkins even used a shoulder sling for his alto.
11. Jack Nimitz, *Confirmation*. Fresh Sound FSR 5006 CD.

Chapter Twenty-Three

Hod O'Brien

Hod O'Brien's musical C.V. is an eclectic mix of the old and the new. He has played with Russell Procope, Sonny Greer, and Aaron Bell as well as Warne Marsh, Roswell Rudd, and Archie Shepp, but despite making his debut on the New York jazz scene in the late fifties with Oscar Pettiford at the Five Spot, this talented pianist has maintained a low profile with the record-buying public. His latest release on Fresh Sound Records should help correct this. He was interviewed in June 2000, when he replied on cassette tape to my questions.

My full name is Walter Howard O'Brien, and I was born in Chicago on January 19, 1936, and adopted six weeks later. My biological family on my mother's side was musical, and by the time I was ten years old, I was listening to records my stepparents had by people like Meade Lux Lewis, Albert Ammons, and Pete Johnson. I just flipped over boogie-woogie and learned to play it by ear. I also liked Fats Waller and Teddy Wilson. Later, Nat Cole got me going in another direction, but by the time I was fourteen, I was hooked on bebop through listening to "Jazz at the Philharmonic" records. By then, Billy Taylor and Hank Jones were influences, but Bud Powell was a little harder for me to fathom at first, because the music was so fast, with discordant harmonies that I didn't pick up on right away. It was powerful music, and more complicated than Nat Cole for instance, but Bud was the source for all the pianists who subsequently became my influences—like Tommy Flanagan, Barry Harris, and Claude Williamson. It was Claude who really got me into the "Bud" mode, because he was the distillation of that style, and I could understand Bud better by listening to Claude's early records.

I was seventeen when I attended Hotchkiss School in Lakeville and met Roswell Rudd for the first time. In those early years he was playing Dixieland trombone, and we used to jam with his father, who was a good drummer, and Jim Atlas, who later played bass with the Jimmy Giuffre Three. Roswell and I parted company in the late fifties and didn't meet again until the mid sixties in New York, by which time he was playing totally out, with people like John Tchicai and Archie Shepp. In 1954 I spent a semester at Oberlin College, but I was very neglectful and didn't finish my studies by a long shot. Dave Brubeck had recorded there the year before, and I used to listen to that album because I liked Brubeck's quartet. Some of us would go into town and listen to Max Roach with Clifford Brown, Coleman Hawkins, Billy Taylor, etc. Oh boy, the old days were great!

In the summer of 1955 I did my first professional gig, subbing for Randy Weston, with Willie Jones on drums. Willie invited me to New York, where he was playing with Charles Mingus, and I once went over to Mingus's house to listen while J. R. Monterose and Jackie McLean rehearsed the "Pithecan-thropus Erectus" album. It was Willie who introduced me to the New York loft scene, where everything was happening, and that's when I first met all the Detroit guys like Tommy Flanagan, Kenny Burrell, and Pepper Adams. I also remember listening to Freddie Redd, who just knocked me out. I stood by the piano, watching him with his head thrown back, a cigarette dangling from his mouth, playing all that rich, beautiful bebop.

In the fall of 1956 I started studying at the Manhattan School of Music. I met Donald Byrd there, but the only time we played together was on a recording for Teddy Charles at Prestige the following year, and it was really thanks to Hal Stein that I was called for the date. He was playing alto with Teddy at the Pad in Greenwich Village, and he knew me from a loft session, so when I visited the club, I was invited to sit in. Teddy liked my playing and said he could use me on an album he was producing for Prestige called "Three Trumpets," with Donald, Art Farmer, and Idrees Sulieman. It was my first record date, and I was a little nervous. I remember playing a big fat B-minor 7th on the first chord of the bridge on "Cherokee," and Idrees cocked his head and smiled when we listened to the playback. I loved Idrees, man, although Art's playing was beautiful, especially from that period, when he was with Gigi Gryce. But Idrees stands out as being the most interesting in terms of ideas, sound, and energy.[1]

Later on in 1957, at the recommendation of Red Rodney, I had the dubious distinction of replacing Bill Evans with Oscar Pettiford because Oscar didn't like Bill's playing. Bill had a new and unusual approach to time and harmony, and Oscar was apparently getting very put out with him. One night he got so mad that Red had to calm him down, which is when I was hired, because I played straight-ahead bebop, which Red and Oscar liked. I worked for about eight months with Oscar, and although he could get pretty rumbustious and difficult, he never got out of hand while I was with him. Eventually, Red's drug habits caused Oscar to change trumpeters, and Johnny Coles came in, sounding great. Sahib Shihab was in the group on alto and baritone, with Earl "Buster" Smith on drums, and sometimes Oscar added Betty Glamman on harp. She was known as "Betty Glamour" because she looked good onstage, which Oscar liked, and anyway, he thought the harp made us look distinguished!

We worked mostly at the Five Spot and Smalls, and when Oscar left for Europe in the summer of 1958, I started playing with J. R. Monterose. At first we used Al Levitt and Buell Neidlinger, but later on, Elvin Jones and Wilbur Ware were with us for several months. I'll tell you a funny story about Wilbur, who was a wonderful bass player. We were at a concert in some town where J.R.'s in-laws lived, and he naturally wanted to impress them, but Wilbur was in his famous drugged and drunk state, and I wasn't much better. I was trying to play, but he kept falling over his bass, finally ending up slumped on top of me. The two of us were sprawled on the piano, and Elvin and J.R. finished playing by themselves. Elvin got mad, and J.R. wasn't too happy, but we all loved Wilbur—he was "Mr. Time." That group also played on weekends at a rather infamous club in the red-light district of Albany, called the Gaiety.[2]

In 1960 I did an album for Decca with Gene Quill, Teddy Kotick, and Nick Stabulas, which unfortunately was never released. I had come into contact with Gene because "Phil and Quill" were happening at the time, and I remember learning "Things We Did Last Summer" the night before the recording. It's a great tune, and Gene played a nice version of it. Just prior to the album, I'd worked with Phil Woods at the Cork 'n' Bib, which is where I first met Chet Baker. Everybody came out to see Chet, and I had never seen the club so full. For the next three years until 1963, Don Friedman and I were the resident pianists at a club on Staten Island called the Totten Villa. We usually had Vinnie Ruggiero, who was a great drummer and probably the white man's answer to Philly Joe Jones, and when he couldn't make it, Art Taylor would take his place. It was Teddy Kotick's gig, and he booked people like Phil, Freddie Hubbard, Charlie Rouse, Lee Konitz, Al Cohn, Stan Getz, and Bob Brookmeyer. We played "common denominator standards," in other words just calling tunes and blowing, with no arrangements and nothing written down, which is just as well, as I'm not a sight-reader. I liked Brookmeyer a lot, especially from those days, and I loved the "Interpretations" album he did with Getz, partly because of Johnny Williams, who was the pianist on the date. He was one of my favorites at the time because he had a rhythmic approach in his solos and his comping that was really impressive.

I started studying with Hall Overton, who was an authority on Thelonious Monk. He was also a nodal point between modern classical and the jazz world, and that is when I became interested in *avant-garde* electronic music, which I studied with Charles Wuorinen and Milton Babbitt. I dabbled in free jazz for a while, which can be great when it's coherent, but with a lot of players, it's just plain gibberish. Roswell Rudd, though, is an exception, because he plans structured sections which can be played freely, making his music successful. By the middle of the sixties I found interest in jazz falling away, partly due to the *avant-garde* and partly because of the popularity of groups like the Beatles, and this is when I dropped out of the music scene for a while.

I enrolled at Columbia University and eventually graduated with a degree in psychology, but I was still playing occasionally with Nobby Totah, who was a good friend. He used to invite me down to El Morocco to sit in with Chuck Wayne, and then around 1973 I rekindled my relationship with Roswell. He was teaching at a college in upstate New York with my ex-wife, and we decided to open our own club in Greenwich Village. We called it the St. James Infirmary, and it became quite a saga. His wife, Mosselle, knew all kinds of people in the Village, and as she had a gift for public relations, she became the manager. Unfortunately she was not very organized, so we ended our partnership after three months. Mosselle was very persuasive, though, and convinced the club's rhythm section, Beaver Harris and Cameron Brown, to go on strike along with Roswell! I was left without a band, so I called Richard Youngstein, the bass player, who brought in Jimmy Madison on drums, along with altoist Bob Mover, and we had a great time.

Bob was also playing with Chet at Stryker's Pub, so for a while Chet came into the St. James and did two nights a week with us. Sometimes we had Archie Shepp on weekends, and the only time the club went into the black was when Chet and Archie played together. We would actually be about $300 or so above the overhead for the week, whereas most of the time we lost money. Archie didn't play much free stuff at that time, because he had been through all that in the sixties, and he sounded great when he played straight-ahead music. Pepper Adams also played the club, and he was a big influence on me. His melodic lines were so impressive that I tried to incorporate them into my own blowing licks, so to speak.

Getting back to Chet, I think playing at my club had a lot to do with him getting back on his feet after that terrible beating and all the problems he had with his embouchure. Every night he seemed to get better and stronger, and that was when the real depth of his music started for me. He was fairly easy to work for, and we often played together when he came to New York, but for some reason, he didn't always like the way I comped. It was difficult to satisfy him sometimes, which made me resentful, because I think my comping is pretty damn good, as most people do. The only other person who doesn't is Frank Morgan, and there may be something in the fact that they both had similar ways of life. Working with Chet, though, was a privilege and honor, because he is a very important part of our jazz family and one of the great poet laureate musicians of all time. By the summer of 1975 Chet, Archie Shepp, and a lot of other guys we were featuring went over to Europe to play the festivals. That was when I decided to close the St. James, and that was the end of my career as a club owner. I started playing with Marshall Brown, who had a great book, and we had a long-lasting relationship until he died in 1983.

In 1977 I did three months at Gregory's with Russell Procope and Sonny Greer. I took the place of Brooks Kerr, who was hospitalized, and although it was just a trio job, Aaron Bell used to sit in on bass sometimes. Brooks was almost raised with the Ellington Orchestra, because his mother could afford to have them play at her apartment when he was young. When he was older, he used to go on gigs with the band, and if Duke forgot something, he would have Brooks play it for him, because he knew everything that Duke had written. Brooks often had Ellington sidemen play with him, but the mainstays were Russell and Sonny. Russell made no bones about not liking bebop or Charlie Parker, but I managed to turn him on to "A Night in Tunisia," which he eventually liked a lot.

When they left, I stayed on with Joe Puma and Frank Luther. The job lasted until 1982, but Joe let Frank go after a couple of years because Frank's playing was getting too outlandish. Joe said, "I'm trying to play Dixieland and he's playing Stravinsky!" Although when Frank buckles down and plays time, he's one of the best there is. A lot of fine guitarists like Jim Hall, Jimmy Raney, Attila Zoller, and Chuck Wayne used to sit in, and whenever Joe Pass was there, he and Puma would really go at it. We had some great times, especially when "Papa" Jo Jones came by and played brushes on a newspaper, which was a real trip. Stan Getz sat in one cold January night when the club was nearly empty, and a guy came in looking for girls. When he saw there weren't any, he stood listening for a while and, walking to the door, said to the owner, "Well, he ain't no Stan Getz!"

In 1982 I recorded with Allen Eager on his first record date in about twenty-five years.[3] He had been involved in racing cars and hanging around with society people, and when he started playing in the studio, it was as though he had never blown a sax before. I was pretty shocked, but he kept at it, and slowly but surely, the lines got longer and clearer. It was as though he learned to play again in the space of half an hour. He didn't sound anything like I remembered from the forties or fifties, when he was with Fats Navarro or Tadd Dameron, but as he loosened up, he became more coherent from tune to tune. In fact at the end of three hours, when we did "Just You, Just Me," which was our last title, he played something that was worthy of Lester Young. It was a gem, just a perfect solo. He was a temperamental guy, though.

Phil Schaap brought him to the West End in Manhattan around that time, and Phil booked a straight-ahead rhythm section for him. Halfway through the first night, Allen decided that he didn't want to play that way, so he fired the band because he wanted to play completely free. He hired a new group of free players for the next night and continued the gig in that bag. I don't know what he's doing now, but I think he's living and playing down in Florida.[4]

In 1984 I recorded with Warne Marsh and Chet Baker in Holland.[5] Warne was a very important saxophone player who used the upper partials, which are the tones above the sevenths, and his ability to handle that part of the harmonic spectrum was remarkable. On the record date Chet really didn't know what to do, so Warne took charge and ran the whole show. He picked the tunes, blew on the changes without stating the melodies, then retitled everything so he could get the royalties. It was around this time that I began collaborating with Fran Landesman by putting music to some of her poems,[6] and my wife, Stephanie Nakasian, recorded one of our tunes, "Mystery Man," on her 1988 CD with Phil Woods.[7] Fran and I made a demo of eight songs, which we sent to Bette Midler because they would have been perfect for her, but I don't think they ever got past her henchmen.

I have already mentioned some of my early influences, but there are many other pianists who are important to me, like Red Garland, Wynton Kelly, George Wallington, Duke Jordan, and especially Al Haig, who almost defined the sound of bebop piano. I love Jimmy Rowles, who was a sort of white version of Thelonious Monk. He had an offbeat way of coloring and harmonizing that was uniquely his. Dave McKenna, too, is incredible. I love the way he gets that walking bass line going with the right hand comping and blowing a melodic line, while making it all sound smooth and fluid. It's amazing that anyone besides Art Tatum can play that much solo piano; he's a one-man orchestra. Dave is just as good in an ensemble setting, and he makes his cohorts feel needed, unlike Art, who I'm told used to make them feel superfluous.

At the end of 1999 I recorded a trio album for Fresh Sound that is my best yet.[8] It has Tom Warrington on bass and Paul Kreibich on drums and should help publicize the West Coast tour that Stephanie and I are undertaking later this summer. She and I work a lot together and will continue to do so.

NOTES

1. *Trumpets All Out* (originally issued as *Three Trumpets*). Prestige OJCCD-1801.

2. Nick Brignola dedicated his original "Green Street" to the club on Reservoir RSR CD 159.

3. Allen Eager, *Renaissance*. Uptown 27.09.

4. Since this interview, Allen Eager passed away, on April 13, 2003.

5. Chet Baker/Warne Marsh, *Blues for a Reason*. Criss Cross 1010.

6. Fran Landesman of course has written many fine lyrics, and none better than "Spring Can Really Hang You Up the Most," with music composed by Tommy Wolf. It was originally featured in a 1959 Broadway musical titled *The Nervous Set*, a satire on the Beat Generation, with Larry Hagman as Jack Kerouac and Del Close as Allen Ginsberg. The score also included "The Ballad of the Sad Young Men."

7. Stephanie Nakasian, *Comin' Alive*. V.S.O.P. 73.

8. Hod O'Brien, *Have Piano . . . Will Swing!* Fresh Sound FSR 5030 CD.

Chapter Twenty-Four

Bill Perkins

This interview with Bill Perkins took place at the 1999 "Stan Kenton Rendezvous" in Egham, England. He reminisced about Kenton and Woody Herman as well as colleagues like Dave Madden and Steve White, who are almost forgotten today. He was also quite happy to discuss the dramatic stylistic change that occurred in his playing during the early eighties.

I was born on July 22, 1924, in San Francisco, and my first big-time job was around 1951, when I worked with Desi Arnaz and Lucille Ball. He was a fiery Latin type who would punch first and ask questions later, so it was quite an experience, because I was pretty green. Lucille, of course, was a great comedienne, but Desi had a lot more to do with their success than he has been credited with. He was a brilliant man and the brains behind *I Love Lucy*. Later that year, thanks to Shorty Rogers, I joined Woody Herman. Shorty was often my benefactor, because he also recommended me to Stan Kenton, although I didn't know it at the time—I had to find out from someone else.

I took Phil Urso's place with Woody and showed up at the L.A. Palladium still wet behind the ears and scared to death. He put up with me for a long time, so he must have figured I would amount to something, and God bless him for that. Jack Dulong, who has since passed away, was the lead tenor, and he was a lovely player, although he didn't get much solo space with the band. He also played baritone and later on became a copyist in the studios for many years. Don Fagerquist, Doug Mettome, and Dick Collins were in the trumpet section, and they were just remarkable. Don was also an outstanding lead player, and Carl Saunders, who plays with me in Bill Holman's band, idolizes him.

Woody disbanded around Christmas 1953 and Dave Madden, for whom I had a great regard and respect, eventually took my place. He and his partner, Gail, were a couple at the time, and they were really *avant-garde* in every way. Dave and I had been to the Westlake School of Music together with Bob

Graettinger, and I was very impressed with the sound he got from his old Conn. I recommended him to Woody, which turned out to be a mistake, because he'd changed his approach and become pretty far out. Today his playing would be fascinating, but everyone was in that "Stan Getz" groove at the time, and I don't think Woody was too pleased with him.[1]

I was very lucky to be part of the Stan Kenton band, which I joined after I left Herman. Dave Schildkraut, who was a personal favorite, was on alto along with Charlie Mariano. One of our concert tours featured both Charlie Parker and Lee Konitz as guests, which was a great experience for me, still a pretty dumb kid. Anyway the player Bird liked the best was Davey, who was a complete original, and he played tenor well, too, although in a totally different way. We got along beautifully, but he was a worrier, always bugged with himself. I felt privileged to be playing Bob Graettinger's music with Stan, and I try to dispel the myth created by those who only know "City of Glass." He was not like a monkey with a brush tied to its tail, producing something that is subsequently sold as modern art. I really appreciate that piece now, although at the time I didn't know what to make of it. When we were at Westlake, he wrote every type of music and wrote it well, and whether you like "City of Glass" or not, he knew exactly what he was doing. I like it because I enjoy twentieth-century composers, and boy, was he a twentieth-century composer!

While I was with Kenton, Mel Lewis was my roommate, and he was one of my dearest friends. Times have changed, but he was one of the great big band drummers, and everyone got a little from Mel, just as he did from people like Tiny Kahn. He was the most unselfish drummer I've ever heard, though his personality was about as abrasive as sixty-grit sandpaper. He didn't bother me because I used to pull the pillow over my head and just go to sleep! Inside, though, he was very kindhearted and he played for *you*. He worked out much better in New York than in the L.A. studios, where you have to keep your mouth shut and do what you're told; individualists don't really make it in L.A. I wish I could have played in the band he had with Thad Jones, because the writing gave it a small band feel, which I like.

Towards the end of the fifties, Kenton decided to drop one of the altos and add a tuba and two French horns. Being the first tenor with a four-man sax section, I became in essence the second alto. That was great for my chops, especially with Charlie Mariano on lead, because he plays like there is no tomorrow, but it was tough competing with all that brass. The conventional sax section has been around for a long time with good reason, but Stan wanted a different sound. Not wanting to stand still, he was always looking for a new approach, but it made things very difficult for us. We kept telling him that we wanted another saxophone, so he got a *second* baritone, which we needed like a hole in the head, because it made the band even more bottom heavy. While I was with him I also worked in local L.A. clubs with Bob Gordon in George Redman's little group, and we also tried to get Bob on the Kenton band.[2] He was the "Zoot Sims" of the baritone but was tragically killed in a car crash in 1955. He was a marvelously ebullient player and a really neat guy to be around, but he could get pretty down on himself if he thought he wasn't playing well.

Another legendary guy from those days was Steve White, who played clarinet, all the saxes, and he sang as well. On tenor, which was his primary instrument, he sounded like Lester Young, and I mean the *real* Lester from the late thirties recordings, when Prez was awesome. That's the way Steve played, just a complete natural. He was a real character, and there have been a lot of stories about him, which are all true! I remember staying on Hymie Gunkler's powerboat after a New Year's Eve gig, when I had been working with Murray McEachern's band on Catalina Island. We were woken up around 3 a.m. by the sound of a baritone coming from Avalon Harbor, which turned out to be Steve playing alone on the pier. Unfortunately, he stumbled and the baritone went over the side into the ocean, but he managed to fish it out the next day. He lives in San Fernando Valley and still plays, as far as I know. Stu Williamson, who died in 1991, is someone else who is forgotten today, which is a tragedy because he was a remarkable soloist. He was a gentle man and a real sweetheart, as is his brother Claude, who I'm glad to say is playing again quite beautifully.

Al Cohn and Zoot Sims have always been heroes of mine, and along with Richie Kamuca, I recorded with Al in 1955.[3] I tended more towards Al, I suppose, because his mournful sound appealed to my personality, whereas Zoot was always so happy in his playing. Everybody knows Al had a great sense of humor, but Zoot could be pretty funny, too. Stan Getz once said to him, "Al prefers your playing to mine," and Zoot replied, "Don't *you*?"

I recorded with John Lewis in 1956, and that was a marvelous experience, because he had heard me play and knew exactly what my pluses and minuses were.[4] I have always been grateful to John for arranging that date with Dick Bock and for making it so easy for me, just like falling off a log. Afterwards, when I went out into the real world, I found that record dates were not usually like that; they don't set them up just for you. Later that same year, I did an album with Richie Kamuca and Art Pepper, and one of the titles was my arrangement of "All of Me."[5] I remember saying on the sleevenote that for all the effort I put into that chart, I could have had an original. Unfortunately you can't copyright an orchestration, which is something a lot of people regret, and that's why Bill Holman writes so many originals now. Jimmy Rowles played on that date, and he was another hero of mine, because he was a towering giant of individuality. A single bar on a record is enough for me to recognize him, which isn't easy on a piano. His daughter Stacy is a beautiful flugelhorn player, and I would love to do an album with her. She doesn't work much because she is dedicated to jazz music, and she is a girl on top of that, which is two strikes against her right there!

What a fine player Art Pepper was, and what a writer. People who remember his playing today have probably forgotten what beautiful lines he wrote. We were not close, so I didn't see him that often, but many years later we used to rehearse at my house, along with David Angel. That's when I really appreciated him, because when you are older, you stop focussing on yourself quite so much, and whatever chair Art played, alto or tenor, he always gave his part such life. Everybody around him responded to that, and Bob Cooper, whose tenor I have today, was the same sort of guy. Players like that can sit in the section and just lift you up. Towards the end of Art's life he could hear all the new stuff going on around him, and I think he felt left out. If he had lived, he would have assimilated the *avant-garde* things, and with his genius for playing, the results would have been priceless. I like guys that can add change to what they already have.

In the mid fifties I often worked with Lennie Niehaus at Jazz City and the Tiffany, and Hampton Hawes sometimes played with us. At the time I was usually bugged with myself too much and worried about my own playing, but in recent years I've begun to appreciate just how good some of these people were, which is the only advantage from growing old I suppose. Hampton was marvelous, and I only wish I could play with him now. He had his problems, like a lot of others, but he was a very nice and gentle man. It's funny, but when I listen to the album I made with him and Bud Shank in 1956, I wonder where I got all that energy.[6]

In the early sixties I played quite a lot with Marty Paich in his Dek-tette, and I really loved him. He did a lot for my career, and just like Bill Holman, he never wrote a note in haste or turned out a schlock bar. He was an old bebop piano player, but he was so dedicated and intense, he became a martinet on the podium. That could be misunderstood, but he thought it was the best way to get discipline. I was on a few albums with Marty and Mel Tormé, and almost until he died, Mel's singing was right on the money. He was one of the best in-tune singers ever, just a paragon of excellence, although he sometimes forgot lyrics towards the end, but then, I forget a lot of stuff too! He was also a good arranger and drummer, but for my personal taste I prefer baritone singers like Joe Williams, because I don't care for high-pitched voices so much. You can't take anything away from Mel, though, because he started it all, influencing groups like the Hi-Los with his own Mel-Tones. He was a very exacting guy, but you can accept a lot from someone who can sing like that, with his intonation.

While I was working with Marty Paich, I was also playing in Terry Gibbs's Dream Band with one of my all-time favorite musicians, Joe Maini, on lead alto. Sadly, through his own fault, very few people are aware of him today, but those who played with him will never forget him. Along with Lanny Morgan he was the greatest, most dynamic jazz-oriented lead alto I ever played with. He was also a wonderful soloist who didn't get much exposure, but every now and then some young player will say, "I heard a solo by this guy Joe Maini which was terrific." He was a larger than life character who would do anything without fear, living life on the edge, just a great person to be around and someone who could light the room up.

During the sixties I worked mostly in the studios, and I was on some Frank Sinatra singles like "Strangers in the Night," which is best forgotten. Chuck Berghofer was on that, and he also did Nancy's hit, "These Boots Are Made for Walking," and we are *never* going to let him forget that! Sinatra of course was a pro, none of this twenty-take business. By the time he had done three, that was it and you'd better be right, too. It was always an experience with him, because he would have a big entourage with lots of attractive girls in the studio. I remember once seeing a beautiful lady standing by herself, looking very quiet and lonely. She smiled at me, and it was Marilyn Monroe.

In the early days of Supersax, they rehearsed in my garage, and we were casting around, looking for a second tenor. Med Flory may deny this (and he's bigger than me!) but I recall him saying, "Warne Marsh is available but he doesn't play so good." Anyway, Warne joined the group, and one night Med turned him loose on "Cherokee" and the rest is history, because after about six choruses it was obvious just how good Warne really was. Supersax was hard to play with, and there wasn't much solo room for the saxes, but I had to leave anyway, because of my studio commitments. I don't do studio dates anymore, as I have retired, except for playing jazz.

In the early eighties I started changing my approach because I felt I had to do something else. I'm not ashamed of my previous style and sound, but I wanted to move on, even if it was sideways, and jazz is all about being able to adapt, otherwise you become stagnant. Of course you can't change overnight, and at first it was painful and I didn't play well. I remember in 1983 when Zoot Sims and I were touring Switzerland with Woody's band, I was already striking out in a new direction, and sometimes *really* striking out. Zoot, though, was very nice and supportive to me. Hopefully things have smoothed out a little, because you have to be true to yourself; you can't be another person. In recent years I have started to play the baritone, and I've been very influenced by Pepper Adams, although I don't have his technique, because he was a monster. He was a true original, and even when he was with Kenton, he was such a radical player that he really turned me around. He's still the daddy of guys like Gary Smulyan and Nick Brignola, who are wonderful players, incidentally. Pepper grew up in Detroit with Tommy Flanagan, and this may surprise you, but their playing is very similar. I know it's hard to equate the baritone and piano, but their lines are very close, and it was Frank Strazzeri who pointed it out to me.

I currently play with a marvelous young trumpeter, John Daversa, whose father, Jay, played with Stan Kenton. Everyone in the band is about half my age, and I keep handing in my resignation but he won't accept it. John's writing is fascinating because he uses a lot of mixed meters, which makes things interesting. I have to admit, though, that I'm tired of playing in big bands, although I make an exception for Bill Holman, who is an absolute genius. I play second alto with him and it is tough music, but he has given me a chance to learn the book and kindly given me solo space. Some of today's bands are so regimented, almost Kentonian, whereas I prefer bands that are loose, like Duke Ellington's was. Part of the problem is the college system, where Stan performed an invaluable service in his desire to educate, but there is now a tendency to discipline music too much. I'm tired of playing regimented music, and that was the only aspect of Stan's band that became burdensome. A lot of the stuff we did with him *sounded* better than it played, I'll tell you that. With Bill's band, not only do the charts sound great but they play great as well.

What must be respected, however, is that Stan Kenton always looked forward, often at great financial hazard to himself. They were totally different personalities, but Woody Herman was just the same, and that's what makes them heroes.

Four years after this interview took place, Bill Perkins died on August 9th, 2003. A memorial was held for him at the Local 47 Musicians' Union on Vine Street in Los Angeles, where a packed crowd heard, among other attractions, Bill Holman's big band.

NOTES

1. Dave Madden's career with Woody Herman seems to have lasted for about three months in 1954. He left after the band played the Hollywood Palladium in September and was replaced by Richie Kamuca. He went on to play with Jerry Gray, Si Zentner, and Harry James.

2. Bob Gordon did a studio recording with the Kenton band in 1954 but, unfortunately, did not solo.

3. Al Cohn, *The Brothers*. RCA Victor LPM 1162.

4. John Lewis, *Grand Encounter*. Pacific Jazz CDP 7 456 592.

5. Bill Perkins, *Just Friends*. LAE 12088 (subsequently issued in Japan on Toshiba TOCJ 5427).

6. Bud Shank/Bill Perkins. Pacific Jazz CDP 7243 4 93159 2 1.

Chapter Twenty-Five

Bud Shank

Clifford "Bud" Shank was born in Dayton, Ohio, on May 27, 1926, and his primary instrument is the alto saxophone, although for many years he doubled very successfully on the flute. During the fifties he made several fine recordings on the baritone, and none better than a 1954 Chet Baker L.P., where he fashioned a lyrical solo of quite exquisite beauty on "I'm Glad There Is You."[1] We met in July 1995, when he was appearing at London's Pizza Express, and I began by asking him why he no longer played the baritone.

That was such a short period in my life because it was never an instrument that fascinated me. I was always attracted to the alto saxophone, and any explorations on the tenor, baritone, or even the flute were just sidetracks. The alto was always my main thing. The reason why my recordings on the baritone came off so well was because I really didn't care; I just picked up the horn and played it without getting too involved. It was the same thing about ten years ago when I stopped playing the flute. I woke up one day and asked myself what I wanted, and I realized that all I ever wanted to be was an alto saxophone player, so I put the flute in the case and it hasn't been out since, which doesn't please Linda, my wife. All my flutes are in a safe deposit box, and I will probably start selling them soon. There's a lot of money invested in them, so why not? Bill Perkins has my Conn tenor and Conn baritone, which he borrowed for a recording date.

To start more or less at the beginning, I auditioned for Stan Kenton at the Capitol Records studio in L.A. in 1949, thanks to a recommendation from Buddy Childers. Stan had a whole sax section set up, with parts that included woodwinds, and it was actually my flute playing that got me the job. He had already hired Bob Cooper, Art Pepper, and Bob Gioga, so the only open spots were lead alto doubling flute and second tenor doubling bassoon. He kept alternating both chairs with several players until he settled on Bart Caldarell and myself, and that was the only time I auditioned for anything in my life. On the road, Art played all the alto solos because that was his job and mine was to lead the section. As you know, it was a very loud band, not just because of the ten brass but also because of the way it was written, and when I first joined during the "Innovations in Modern Music" period, there were two French horns and a tuba in addition to all that other lovely noise. It was thrilling, though, to hear that mass of sound behind you, although I don't know if anybody actually heard the saxes when the brass were playing. I was on the second recorded version of Bob Graettinger's "City of Glass," which I thought was marvelous, and still do—and even today, people don't realize how great that piece really was.[2]

Bob's girlfriend was Gail Madden, and she was also Gerry Mulligan's girlfriend too. There were some others that used to hang out with them, and they were all a bunch of free-thinkers, especially Graettinger, Gail, and Gerry. They didn't think or act like anybody else. But Gerry, being Gerry, was able to survive in the everyday world, whereas a lot of that group just kept right on going! Graettinger died in 1957, and those of us who knew him felt that it was from a broken heart, although he had physical problems as well. He never found anyone to really understand him, and although Gail used to minister to him, she was just as out of it as he was. They weren't married, but she took her name from a tenor player called Dave Madden, who was also pretty strange. She and Graettinger lived together, and Gerry and Dave were involved: just one, big, happy, funny family! I don't know all the inside details, and I probably wouldn't relate them if I did, because they must have been pretty odd. As far as Gerry was concerned, he cleaned up his act and very soon got a handle on reality, and even after all these years, he is still playing marvelously. Getting back to Kenton, I think the best album he ever did was *Contemporary Concepts*, with the Bill Holman and Gerry Mulligan arrangements. The peak was reached with that band and that writing.[3]

After I left Kenton in 1952, I worked in a group fronted by a drummer called George Redman. We played rhythm 'n' blues six nights a week for about a year around a circuit of L.A. clubs, and it was just me on alto and tenor with a rhythm section. Occasionally, Maynard Ferguson and Bob Gordon would play with us, and if I couldn't make it, Bill Perkins used to sub for me. Bob Gordon was my closest personal friend. He was a great person and a superb player, and it was a terrible loss to the music when he was killed in 1955.[4] I also used to dep for Herb Geller and Joe Maini at a burlesque club called Duffy's Gaiety, where Lenny Bruce was the M.C. I was a fan of Lenny's because he was hilarious, but I didn't hang out with him like Herb and Joe, who had a free seat every night.

While I was with George Redman, I also made some rhythm 'n' blues records with "Boots Brown" and his Buddies. Not everyone knows this but

"Boots Brown" was actually Shorty Rogers, who was recording that material for a laugh. It was just a put-on, and I'm probably letting some tales out of the closet here, but there were some very good players on those dates, like Zoot, Gerry, Marty Paich, Milt Bernhart, and Jimmy Giuffre—good musicians playing pretty raunchy music, but doing it well. It all started with a piece that Jimmy wrote for the Lighthouse All Stars called "Big Boy," which was a takeoff of the sort of thing the Lionel Hampton band used to do. Jack Lewis, the record producer, asked Shorty to write some more material in that style, and we got to make quite a few records with "Boots Brown."[5]

During 1953 when Gerry and Chet were at the Haig, I played there on Mondays, which were the off-nights, with Laurindo Almeida, Harry Babasin, and Roy Harte. The Haig was where that group with Laurindo was born, and it was Harry's idea for us to get together. We used to rehearse in Roy's drum shop, and after about six Monday nights, we made that first record for Pacific Jazz.[6] I also played on Mulligan's tentet album in '53, which is when I recorded my first alto solo, on "Flash."[7] Chet was on the date, and he could certainly read music, though not as fast as everyone else. During the fifties I worked a lot with Claude Williamson at the Lighthouse, and when I left there, Claude came with me. We toured Europe and South Africa and stayed together until about 1958. Later on in the sixties, he did a lot of television work as a rehearsal pianist on shows like *Sonny and Cher*. Both Claude and his brother Stu, who was a marvelous trumpeter, had personal problems, but Claude is beginning to resurface as a jazz player and is recording again. Unfortunately, Stu gave up playing, and before he died a few years ago, I believe he was driving a truck. I knew them both very well and was very close to them in the fifties.

In 1958, along with Art Farmer, Gerry Mulligan, Frank Rosolino, Pete Jolly, Red Mitchell, and Shelly Manne, I played on Johnny Mandel's first film score for the Susan Hayward movie *I Want to Live*.[8] I recently taped it off the T.V., but I couldn't watch it all because it's so depressing. The group played in some nightclub scenes, and our set was next to the gas chamber set where the Susan Hayward character was executed at the end of the film. It was right there while we were playing, just made out of plywood, but it looked awful! I also did the writing for a couple of films myself: *Slippery When Wet* in 1959, which was a surfing film, and Robert Redford's first movie, *War Hunt*, in 1961.

In the fifties there was a long stretch when I was very close to Frank Rosolino—and what a player he was, just fabulous. When he was doing all that fast playing, the slide didn't seem to be moving; somehow it was all done with his lip and tongue. I remember, at the Lighthouse, he always sang at least one number every night where he would be yodeling and doing all those crazy things, and the crowd loved it, as did the band, because he was a very funny guy. I didn't see him very much towards the end, before his suicide in 1978, because he never made it much as a studio player like the other jazz musicians. It's horrible, dumb music, and he would have found that kind of work very difficult, especially as you spend a lot of time just sitting there, doing nothing. None of that would have impressed Frank, who was so active and always bubbling around. He was probably not playing that much jazz in the seventies, which might have been part of the problem. He'd also been through a couple of wives, but shooting his kids and then killing himself was a dreadful shock. The whole thing was scary, because he was torn up inside, despite the front he presented of all humor and fun. He was a proverbial clown, like Pagliacci; a very sad clown, but nobody knew it. One of his children survived in a terrible state and is supported by an organization called "Musicians' Wives Inc.," which my former wife was instrumental in starting.

From about 1960 to 1963 I often played at the Drift Inn in Malibu, usually with Carmell Jones, Dennis Budimir, and Gary Peacock. Dennis and Gary were very adventurous, especially in their conception of time, and being the early sixties it was a little early for that, so I used to hire some very straight-ahead drummers to keep it all together. I didn't want to tell them to cool it, because I wanted them to have their freedom. So the drummers tended to vary, but more often than not, we had Frank Butler with us. Lee Marvin used to come to the club all the time, as did a lot of movie people, because many of them lived in Malibu. We recorded for Richard Bock in 1961, and although I only played alto with the group at the club, Dick wanted me to play baritone on a couple of numbers, because I had just come second in the baritone section of the *Playboy* Readers' Poll.[9] We used Mel Lewis on the album because, on the morning of the date, Dick Bock telephoned to say that our drummer had just been busted, so I said, "Get Mel, real quick!" That was the last jazz record I made for a long time, because right after that our music seemed to disappear; it was the end of that era.

In January 1966 Duke Ellington came out to Hollywood to record the music he'd written for a Sinatra film called *Assault on a Queen*. I was playing in L.A. with Stan Kenton's Neophonic Orchestra at the time, and we were doing monthly concerts of new material which actually featured me quite a lot. Duke came to one of the concerts and asked me to join his orchestra on lead alto. Of course I was very flattered, but I wasn't in a position to leave L.A. at the time, and with the difficulties jazz was having, it wasn't a good time to be on the road with any band, even Duke's. I also had some family problems that would have made it difficult for me to be away, and I was just getting established in the studios, doing the better work. For the film score he had a nucleus of his own sidemen, like Cat Anderson, Cootie Williams, Jimmy Hamilton, Johnny Hodges, Paul Gonsalves, and Harry Carney, supplemented by local studio players, Conte Candoli, Al Porcino, Milt Bernhart, Buddy Collette, and myself.[10]

During the sixties a lot of young people, who were the potential new audience for jazz, were attracted to groups like the Rolling Stones and the Beatles, and the older listeners had become put off by some of the experimentation that was going on then. Eventually John Coltrane reached a level that wasn't accessible to the public, or even to other musicians, because the world wasn't ready for it, which is why we haven't had a Messiah since. Everything now has gone backwards with all this "return to the fifties" stuff, because with Coltrane we had gone as far as we could. The jazz-buying public wanted to go back and pick up the pieces, so guys like myself have been given a second chance. Historically we had gone from Louis Armstrong to Lester Young and Charlie Parker to John Coltrane in fairly quick jumps, but we've been in this retrospective phase now for about thirty years, which has never happened before. In the mid seventies, when we put the L.A. Four together, it was like putting your toe in the water, since Shelly Manne, Ray Brown, and I hadn't worked as jazz players for about ten years. We were a chamber jazz group rather than a straight-ahead jazz group, but it turned out that there was still an audience out there. That was when I phased myself out of the studio scene, because the more I was out of town, the less the phone rang. Soon they didn't bother to call at all, which was fine with me, since I didn't want to do it anymore.

One of my CDs that has recently been released, although we recorded it back in 1993, is *New Gold*, and it has Conte Candoli, Bill Perkins, and Jack Nimitz in the front line, who are old friends.[11] We had a pianoless rhythm section, with John Clayton on bass and Sherman Ferguson on drums, and playing without the piano gives you a lot of freedom. It's easier to get into the altered notes of a chord, because you don't conflict with the pianist, but you must pay attention. Before we made the CD, we worked a few jobs at the Catalina Bar and Grill, and the guys were really concerned at not having a piano, but by the second night they all loved it. Bill's playing has changed over the years, and on this new recording, he's really out there, but a lot of his friends are forever giving him sermons about going back to playing the way he used to. Dick Bank in L.A. arranged for him to make a CD featuring some Lester Young transcriptions and doing them in a Prez style.[12] Dick called me recently and played some of it over the phone, and it's marvelous. Lester used to play a Conn, and Bill asked if he could borrow mine, but in the event he used one of his old Selmers. He sounds just gorgeous, because he can change mouthpieces and go right back to the old Perkins, and I love him—he's wild! He plays a lot of baritone these days, and he is also amazing on soprano, because he finds it easy to play anything, but the *real* Bill Perkins is a tenor player.

Somewhere along the way there's going to be something new in jazz, but it won't come from the *avant-garde* guys, who seem to be saying: "I'm *it*, man. I'm the new Messiah. Follow me!" They make a lot of noise and forget about playing their instruments, and that really bothers me, because these people are leading us into another blind alley. It's going to take someone who masters his horn, because ego alone isn't going to make it.

The three people right now who are doing the most important writing are Manny Albam, Bob Brookmeyer, and Bill Holman.[13] They've been around a long time, but there is more adventure and advanced thought with those three as writers than with any horn player I know, and maybe that's going to be the next phase—the writing only.

NOTES

1. Chet Baker Sextet. Fresh Sound FSRCD 175.
2. *Stan Kenton Plays Bob Graettinger: City of Glass*. Capitol CD 8 32084 2.
3. Stan Kenton, *Contemporary Concepts*. Capitol 5 42310 2.
4. In 1954, Bob Gordon made a fine album with George Redman and Herbie Harper that is well worth trying to track down: *The George Redman Group*. Skylark LP20.
5. Shorty Rogers and His Giants, *The Rarest*, vol. 2. RCA 70110. Jimmy Giuffre was the principal soloist on the "Boots Brown" titles, and he showed that he could have had a very successful career as a rock 'n' roll tenor-man, in the style of Rudy Pompilli or Sam Butera.
6. Laurindo Almeida/Bud Shank, *Brazilliance*, vol. 1. World Pacific CDP 796339.
7. Gerry Mulligan Tentet. Mosaic MR5-102.
8. Gerry Mulligan, *I Want to Live*. United Artists UAL 4006.
9. Bud Shank, *New Groove*. Mosaic MD5-180 CD.
10. Duke Ellington said at the time that "Bud Shank is too much. I told him I had his contract ready but I can't get him to leave California. He was the greatest part of Kenton's Neophonic concert the other night, and he was even greater with us the last two days. He even shook up Johnny Hodges. Bud Shank is something else!"
11. Bud Shank Sextet, *New Gold*. Candid CCD 79707.
12. Bill Perkins, *Perk Plays Prez*. Fresh Sound FSR 5010 CD.
13. Manny Albam died on October 3, 2001, six years after this interview with Bud Shank.

Chapter Twenty-Six

Phil Urso

Tenor-man Phil Urso spent thirty years, off and on, playing with Chet Baker. He is also well known for his fine work with Elliot Lawrence and Woody Herman, and in the early fifties he was a regular at Birdland with Miles Davis, Charlie Parker, and Oscar Pettiford, among others. Urso once fronted the Jimmy Dorsey Orchestra, and just like Herb Geller and Zoot Sims, he has worked the burlesque scene, not to mention playing Dixieland clarinet with actor George Segal on banjo. This interview took place at his home in Denver, Colorado, during the summer of 1999.

I was born in Jersey City on October 2, 1925, but by the time I was ten years old, my family had moved to Denver to open a restaurant. I started on clarinet when I was thirteen, but my teacher encouraged me to switch to the tenor. He said that if I ever played in a big band, I would get more solos. My parents bought me a Conn for $150, which was a lot of money in those days, and I found the saxophone much easier, because the clarinet will drive you crazy. I actually stayed with my Conn until about ten years ago, when I switched to a Selmer Mark 7.

During World War II, I served in the Navy on an aircraft carrier in the Pacific which was hit by a Japanese suicide plane. By the time I was discharged in 1945, my family had moved back East to Elizabeth, New Jersey, and I started playing at Don José's, with people like Gerry Mulligan, Zoot Sims, Al Cohn, Lester Young, and Jerry Lloyd.[1] I did a couple of weekends with Herbie Fields, and believe it or not, Bill Evans was the pianist. Bill and I had a quartet for a while, which played at weddings and small jazz clubs, and he taught me a lot about the keyboard.

In 1948, with the help of the G.I. Bill, I enrolled at the Hartnett Music School, and Tony Fruscella and Al Haig were fellow students. We didn't stay too long because the lessons were pretty basic, and very soon Al left to go with Stan Getz, Tony started working somewhere, and I auditioned for Elliot Lawrence. The audition was at the Pennsylvania Hotel, and I had to play a solo with the rhythm section and read a part with the saxes. Afterwards, he said the job paid $120 a week, and the only question he asked me was what size jacket would I need. I was with Elliot for the next two years, and about six months after I joined, Gerry Mulligan, who was out of work and needed the money, came on the band.

Gerry was playing baritone, clarinet, and straight alto, which was very unusual, and to this day, nobody knows where he found that straight alto. His clarinet wasn't up to much either; in fact, it wasn't worth a dime! I tried playing it, but it was almost impossible to blow, so as we sat next to each other on stage, I loaned him mine. He was an arranging genius, of course, and did a lot of great charts for the band, including my very first recorded solo on "Elevation" in 1949.[2] Elliot used to feature Mulligan and me with the rhythm section as a quintet from within the band, and there are tapes of the two of us at Bop City and the Meadowbrook Club playing "Jeru" and "Goldrush." Gerry had a room near 56th and Seventh Avenue with an in-tune piano, and when the band was in town, he often invited me over and taught me a lot about chord voicing. When we were on the road, we roomed together, because it was cheaper that way, and when he left, I shared with drummer Howie Mann, who became a lifelong friend.

Once, when we were backing Frank Sinatra at the Paramount, he bought the band a case of Scotch, which was nice of him, but he was lucky to get away from the theater with at least a few clothes on his back, because the bobby-soxers were determined to steal some mementos from him. It was while we were with Sinatra that I went over to Birdland, which was a few blocks away, and met Al Cohn, who asked me to take his place with Woody Herman. He wanted to stay in town and get off the road, and Woody's band was a young tenor's dream, so I showed up for an audition the next afternoon at the Capitol theater at 3 p.m. Woody said, "How well do you read?" and I remember saying, "Just enough so it doesn't mess up my jazz!" Al was out front, rehearsing the band, so I took his place with the other saxes, who were Buddy Wise, Bob Graf, and Marty Flax on baritone. There were three sheets of music spread out on the stands, and Al counted us into "Music to Dance To." The tempo was really fast, with a lot of sixteenth notes that I let fly by, and the only one of us who read the part properly was Buddy Wise on lead tenor. I passed the audition, and Woody asked how much I was making with Elliot Lawrence. Then he offered me $175 a week to go on the road with him. I gave Elliot two weeks notice and met Woody's band bus at the Forest Hotel for our first engagement at an amusement park in upstate New York, and this would have been in 1950.

Conte Candoli and Don Fagerquist used to play split lead with the band, because it was too much of a strain for one guy to handle. Don of course is not so well known now, but he was a great improviser and everyone liked him. I was with Woody for about sixteen months, and Bill Harris with his great big sound used to sit right behind me. When he left, Woody gave me all his solos, and Bill had a lot of solos. Woody was a wonderful person, and if he thought you could play, he would feature you a lot, but the grind of one-nighters can really get to you, because there's no rest. After the gig you stop at a greasy-spoon, go to the bathroom, then jump back on the bus and drive another four hundred miles. Sometimes we took a shower with our shirts on when there was no laundry. I remember once, when we had done about seventy one-nighters in a row, Woody was out front, singing something like "Somebody Loves Me." I started quietly mimicking him and joking behind his back, just for something different to do, and it broke the crowd up, but he turned round and caught me. At the end of the set he called me over and said, "The audience loved it. From now on, when I sing that song, you go into the same act every night until I tell you to stop."

Jack Dulong was a very good lead tenor during most of my time with the band, but Woody wanted me to play lead on "Early Autumn," although we usually disagreed about the correct tempo. He liked it very slow, but as it was my solo, I wanted it a little brighter, and one night at the L.A. Palladium we had an argument over it. That's when I left, more or less by mutual consent, and the next day he and Abe Turchen drove me to the airport. Woody paid my fare back to New York, and my replacement was Bill Perkins, who was recommended by Shorty Rogers.

I started playing the Monday night jam sessions at Birdland in the summer of 1951. It only paid $17, but I didn't care, because it gave me the chance to play with people like Fats Navarro, Horace Silver, Kenny Clarke, and Charles Mingus. You never knew who would show up until you were at the club, and one night I sat in with Charlie Parker when Erroll Garner and George Shearing were in the audience, and that was an experience. Bird's ears were so much quicker than mine, although he came down to my level most of the time, but occasionally he went off where I couldn't follow. Like everyone else, I used to lend him money, and once when he had a job on 54th Street, he hired me with Jackie McLean, Duke Jordan, Oscar Pettiford, and Kenny Clarke because he owed us all, and the only way he could pay us back was to give us a gig. Of course a few days later he would see you somewhere and ask to borrow $20! The early fifties was difficult for everyone because we were all scuffling, and I remember Mulligan even had a necktie for a belt. Some of the guys, like Gerry, Red Mitchell, Billy Root, and Red Rodney, used to eat at our place in New Jersey, because my mother was doing their laundry.[3]

In 1952 I did two weeks at the Blue Note in Philadelphia with J. J. Johnson, Milt Jackson, Percy Heath, and Kenny Clarke, opposite Harry Belafonte.

J.J. was one of the all-time greats and a beautiful person who would really take time with you if you were learning something new. It was around this time that I did a six-month stint with Miles Davis, which started when Symphony Sid called to say that Miles needed a tenor player for a job at the Hi-Hat in Boston. For some reason Miles wanted me to room with him, and I remember once sitting by the window, reading a paper. He came out of the shower, drying himself, saying, "Say, Phil, what do you think about me being black?" It was obviously a test, but I told him that I couldn't care less; all I knew was that he was the greatest trumpeter I had ever heard. I don't know if he believed me, because nothing else was said, but one guy he couldn't get along with was Symphony Sid. He was the M.C. on the job, which was supposed to pay $1,500, but after the first week Miles only got $1,300 from Sid, who claimed that was all the club owner gave him for the group. The next week, even though Sid had some of his Mob friends to protect him from Miles, they both went in to get the money, and this time it was the right amount. Miles always said that Symphony Sid was one "M-F" he didn't like.

I spent nearly a year with Jimmy Dorsey in 1953, along with guys like Bill Anthony and Al Porcino. Jimmy was a nice guy, but he liked a drink, and one night when we were doing a coast-to-coast broadcast from the Colonial Hotel in Memphis, he was too drunk to do the show. He needed someone to take his place while he went upstairs to sleep it off. Even though I had never done it before, he called me over and said, "You front the band, and after you count off the tune, sit down and play the chart. When you get up, cut the band off and call the girl out for 'Green Eyes.' There's nothing to it." After the broadcast I went to see him in his room, and he said, "You did fine, Phil, pour yourself a drink!"

In 1954 I did a recording with Bob Brookmeyer, who was in town with Mulligan.[4] We had got to know each other well at Charlie's Tavern, which was a musicians' bar where you could have a beer and hang around with the rest of the guys. I needed a rhythm section, so I went to Birdland to ask Miles if I could use Horace Silver, Percy Heath, and Kenny Clarke. Now very few white people could just go up to him and ask a favor like that; you'd be asking for a kick in the ass. But Miles and I were tight and everything was fine. I wrote all the charts, but I didn't title them—Ozzie Cadena did that—and there were no rehearsals. Bob sight-read everything, and it was a great date, which got a five-star rating in *Down Beat*. Horace Silver and I had roomed together on Oscar Pettiford's band, and we used to flip a coin to see who had the bed and who slept on the floor. He showed me chords on gigs, and I would often stand behind him and catch different things he was doing, because you can learn a lot from pianists that way. His timing was impeccable, and he wrote great songs that were not easy, and yet they appealed to the public—at least the musically hip part of the public.

During those early days in New York I studied with Lennie Tristano for a while at his place on Long Island. He charged $10 an hour, and he would play behind me on numbers like "Out of Nowhere" and "Have You Met Miss Jones?" If he heard something he didn't like, we would stop while he played an alternative chord change. Lennie was a gentleman, but Mulligan's approach to writing and playing was more to my taste. Tristano liked you to go outside the chords every once in a while, atonal stuff, whereas I came from the same school as Gerry, Al, and Zoot, who stayed inside the changes.

I first met Chet Baker at Birdland in December 1954. His quartet was playing opposite Miles, and Gerry Mulligan introduced us while Chet was on a break. I used to keep my tenor in a booth at the club, so Chet asked me to sit in for a set with Russ Freeman, Carson Smith, and Bob Neel. When we finished, he invited me over to his room at the Bryant Hotel to meet his French girlfriend, and he put on Ravel's *Daphnis and Chloe* while we talked. Later in the lobby, on our return to the club, he and Russ Freeman had a nasty disagreement. Russ didn't like Chet's old lady, and Chet didn't like Russ's old lady, so Chet fired him there and then. The four of us finished the booking as a pianoless group, which was fun and challenging. The next day Russ came to Chet's room and started collecting his music, which was very depressing but nothing to do with me. Chet could have had any sax player in the world, but he offered me $175 a week to go on the road with him, and he said the Joe Glazer agency would keep us working for years.

Just before we left New York, we played on the *Tonight Show*. Then Chet drove us to our first gig at Baker's Keyboard Lounge in Detroit. We stayed at the Wolverine Hotel, and as Al Haig was in town, I started phoning around, trying to track him down. We were very close, and eventually Art Mardigan found him for me at his girlfriend's house. I told him we had a lot of steady work lined up and we needed someone that night, so he came over to the hotel. I had to loan him a tie with a clean white shirt, and he stayed with us for about six months. Carson Smith was a great bass player who did a lot of writing for us, and Bob Neel, who had been with Les Brown, was a good timekeeper.

Later, Joe Glazer booked us into Toronto, but he wanted Gerry Mulligan with us, because he was more of a leader-type than Chet.[5] Chet was very loose and relaxed on the stand and didn't mind Gerry taking charge; he actually liked it, because it meant he had nothing to worry about except his own playing. We were billed as the "Chet Baker/Gerry Mulligan Sextet," and although I wasn't included in the title, I was very happy to be in the band. The audiences liked us so much, they even applauded in tempo. By now, Jimmy Bond and Peter Littman had taken over from Carson and Bob, but Al Haig was still there, and he was phenomenal. Towards the end of 1955, Gerry sat in with us at Carnegie Hall when we played opposite Dave Brubeck and Carmen McRae. It was always fun playing with him, because he was a natural sparkplug.

Chet was a very good-looking guy, and the women used to go crazy over him. We got along fine because he was very friendly, and of course he had been raised by a nice family. While I was with him, I was the musical director, handling recording dates and rehearsals, and I wrote some of the charts. With his melody and my harmony, we made some good music. I usually hired the musicians, but I didn't handle the money; each guy discussed his own price with Chet. After Al Haig left, I hired Bobby Timmons when he sat in with us at the Showboat in Philadelphia, but he and Peter Littman didn't get along, so when we were in L.A., I got Lawrence Marable on drums and, man, what a difference he made! By now we had Scott LaFaro on bass, who was wonderful, but he used to drive me mad, because he liked to practice every morning about nine o'clock when I wanted to sleep. We recorded about five albums in L.A., including one with Art Pepper, as well as appearing on the Bobby Troup T.V. show.

We worked our way back across the country playing college dates, clubs, and festivals, and with Chet's reputation as an addict, he would sometimes have trouble from the local police. They would visit whichever club we were in and ask him to step outside for a "chat." One night at the Cadillac Lounge in Philadelphia, two guys in plain clothes called him down from the stand and took him out back to check for fresh needle marks on his arms with a flashlight. They didn't find any, but it was harassment pure and simple. We had a lot of fun, though, and I remember one incident, driving down in Texas, when the police stopped us on our way to play at San Diego State College. Chet and I were travelling in his brand-new Jaguar, and the rest of the group followed a long way behind in a 1954 Mercury, with a trailer carrying the bass and drums. Chet's car was like a jet on wheels, and driving along Route 66 he was doing about 140 miles an hour—and although he was a good driver, I'm lucky to be alive. A police car gave up chasing us but radioed ahead for a roadblock to be set up. We were pulled over and taken back to a little town where they got the judge out of bed. Still in his nightclothes, he looked down at Chet and said, "Fast little mother, aren't you. That'll be $50 or two nights in jail." Chet reached in his pocket, pulled out a roll of $100 bills thick enough to choke a horse, and said, "Got any change, judge?"

Another happy memory from those days was the Birdland All-Stars package in 1957, which toured sixteen cities before climaxing at Carnegie Hall. Zoot Sims, Bob Brookmeyer, Lester Young, Seldon Powell, Sarah Vaughan, Billy Eckstine, Bud Powell, Basie's band, and Chet's group were all on the bill, and Lester and I used to sit in the back of the bus, drinking gin, while we drove through the night. Soon after that tour finished, I went back to freelance in Denver, and I think that Chet went to Europe. Towards the end of the fifties I worked with Claude Thornhill, who was leading a sextet at the time, but he augmented to a big band for college dates, which is when we played those lovely Gil Evans and Gerry Mulligan charts. I used to drive with him to the jobs, and we became very close, especially as we had both been in the Navy during the war. Claude was a very nice guy and really smart.

In the early sixties I played at the Sands in Las Vegas with an act that did Al Jolson and Judy Garland impersonations, and I also jammed at after-hours sessions with Red Norvo. When things got a little slow, Charlie Mariano and I used to help out at the gaming tables as croupiers. Herb Geller was there with Louie Bellson, and we played tennis together in the mornings before it got too hot. The "Rat Pack" was in town filming *Ocean's Eleven*, and I'm on the soundtrack playing clarinet, but I never did get paid. I got to know Sammy Davis and Dean Martin, who were both really nice, but Peter Lawford never talked to you; he was a stuck-up son of a gun. Frank Sinatra offered me a job playing tenor with Nelson Riddle, which I decided not to take, because I would have had to move to L.A.

When Chet returned from Europe in 1964, he was living with his manager, Richard Carpenter, who at one time had managed Bird, Sonny Stitt, and Sonny Rollins.[6] I telephoned Chet at Carpenter's house, and he asked me to join him on a recording with Hal Galper, and it was one of the best dates I have ever played on.[7] Tadd Dameron had written some of the material, and we rehearsed at his house so that we almost had it memorized. Tadd and Chet had been in Lexington, Kentucky, together, where Tadd had a band with a lot of guys whose names we won't mention. Lexington was rather like a hospital where addicts were treated like sick people; they could swim and play basketball because everything was very loose. The next date Chet and I did, called "Baby Breeze," was in 1965, and Frank Strozier played alto with us.[8] "Baby Breeze" was an original of mine which I sold to Carpenter, and that's why it's credited to him on the CD. In between the two recordings, I was Chet's best man when he and Carol married in Reno, Nevada. Sometimes in the sixties I used to work at a burlesque club in Denver for a stripper who always asked for me when she came to town. Her name was Tempest Storm, and she was married to the singer Herb Jeffries. She liked me to back her on tenor while she took her clothes off little by little, and she made good money, something like $800 a week.

In 1973 Chet was on his way from California to New York, and he stayed with my wife and me in Denver for a while. We went to hear Dizzy Gillespie, who was in town, and he recognized us from the stage, giving us a very nice introduction to the audience. After the job, he invited us to his room at the Ramada Inn, and he sent Mickey Roker out for $25 worth of quarters, so we

could play poker. Chet told him that we were going to New York cold, looking for work, and he immediately picked up the telephone and called Rose-
mary Canterino at the Half Note. She always did have a thing for Chet, although she hadn't seen him since he had been beaten up and didn't know
what he looked like, which was about ninety.[9] Thanks to Dizzy, she offered
us three weeks at the club. Chet drove all the way to New York, but I took a
747 because, as I said before, he was too fast a driver; it was safer in a plane.
We played opposite Jackie Cain and Roy Kral, with the house rhythm section
of Harold Danko, Michael Fleming, and the great Mel Lewis, and I remember Gil Evans and Antonio Carlos Jobim came to hear us.

In 1976 I played clarinet in the film *The Duchess and Dirtwater Fox*, star-
ring George Segal and Goldie Hawn. Goldie was sweet and nice, and during
one of the breaks, I was playing "Sunny Side of the Street" when George
heard me and invited me to a private party he was having for the cast at the
L.A. Hilton. We had a quartet and he paid us $400 out of his own pocket and
sat in on banjo. He was an excellent player and knew all the Dixieland tunes
with the right changes.

The last time I played with Chet was at the Oxford Hotel in Denver in
March 1985, and there is a tape of some of the sessions. We were due to play
together at the North Sea Jazz Festival in 1988, in what was to be called "A
Set with Chet," but in May of that year he was killed when he fell from his
bedroom on the third floor at the Hotel Prins Hendrik in Amsterdam.

As far as my playing influences are concerned, Lester Young was obviously a major one, but by the early sixties I was listening to Sonny Rollins a
lot. I loved his approach and timing, but I could never duplicate his sound.
His ideas always make sense, and he can really control a rhythm section because he is so forceful and strong. Of course I like Stan, Al, and Zoot, and
also Joe Henderson, but Rollins is my top tenor. I'm no slouch, you know. I
have a great résumé, and I've worked with a whole bunch of wonderful people. I'm proud of what I did and I want to go on playing.

*Something else that Phil is rightly proud of is a letter Chet Baker sent him
from Paris in 1979. The last sentence reads: "Whenever anyone asks me who
my favorite tenor player is, the answer is always the same—Phil Urso."*

NOTES

1. Don José's was a studio on West 49th Street, between Broadway and Eighth Avenue. Musicians hired it for sessions, and its bright red door inspired Zoot Sims's
original of the same name. Years later, Dave Frishberg added an excellent lyric called
"Zoot Walks In."

2. Gerry Mulligan, *Mullenium*. Columbia/Legacy CK 65678.

3. In 1951 Gerry Mulligan had to rehearse a band that included Brew Moore and Allen Eager in Central Park because nobody could afford to hire a studio.

4. Phil Urso/Bob Brookmeyer Quintet. Savoy MG12056.

5. In the early part of 1955 Mulligan was between groups, having just disbanded his quartet with Jon Eardley, and he often worked with Baker at this time.

6. According to James Gavin in his book *Deep in a Dream: The Long Night of Chet Baker* (Chatto and Windus), Carpenter's specialty was "taking on strung-out black musicians and getting them to surrender their record royalties, and the rights to their compositions." One good example of this is Miles Davis's "Walkin'," which is still credited to Carpenter. Pianist Hal Galper is quoted as saying that Carpenter "had the air of a gangster, like he'd kill you in a second." Apart from the musicians mentioned by Phil Urso, Carpenter had also handled Lester Young, Gene Ammons, Howard McGhee, Elmo Hope, and Tadd Dameron. Although he preferred representing black players, he made an exception for Chet Baker, who readily signed over his future royalties. Gavin quotes Sonny Stitt telling Urso, "Richard Carpenter's a motherfucker—don't go near that guy, he'll burn you."

7. Chet Baker Quintet. Colpix CP 476.

8. Chet Baker, *Baby Breeze*. Verve 538 328-2.

9. Baker had been badly beaten in San Francisco in 1966 and needed extensive dental treatment to help him play again. The Half Note gig was his first booking in New York for eight years.

Chapter Twenty-Seven

Phil Woods

Herb Geller once told me, "People play the way they are," and anyone meeting Phil Woods for the first time will quickly realize that his personality is indeed reflected in his playing, which is characterized by its passion, humor, and warmth. Woods was born in Springfield, Massachusetts, on November 2, 1931, and we met on May 6, 1996, the day after he and Gordon Beck had recorded a duo set at London's Wigmore Hall.[1] He has a fund of stories and anecdotes, and he was more than happy to take a stroll down Memory Lane with me.

I love Memory Lane because I can give some of the guys their due, although Bill Crow is really our Boswell. I had a great teacher back in Springfield who used to give me transcribed Benny Carter solos to play, and the first well-known alto player I saw was Johnny Hodges. Duke's band came through town, and Hodges stepped out of the section to play "Mood to Be Wooed," which my teacher had just given me for a lesson. Later on when I was about fifteen, I had private lessons with Lennie Tristano. His lessons were essentially about improvisation, and they mainly consisted of scale exercises and piano harmony, and I found that I had a lot to learn. The journey to Lennie's place on Long Island was about 180 miles, and I used to travel there with a pianist named Hal Serra, who also studied with Lennie and later became Julie London's musical director. We had quite a clique of young musicians in Springfield, and I played in a little bebop group with Sal Salvador, Joe Morello, and Chuck Andrus, who later played bass with Woody Herman. I still see Joe, and we are talking about making a record together.

In 1948 I passed the clarinet entrance exam to Julliard, where the fees were about $500 a term, but with my parents' help and a lot of Italian wedding gigs, I got by. I also used to play at jam sessions in Teddy Charles's loft, which was on the corner of 55th Street and Broadway, and Tony Fruscella, Don Joseph,

Brew Moore, Jimmy Raney, and Frank Isola were all regulars there. I already knew Teddy because he was from Springfield, too, where he was known as Teddy Cohen. He played drums there, and we used to say even his watch couldn't keep time. Then when I got to New York, I heard him playing wonderful bebop vibes with Chubby Jackson's band.

I first met Gene Quill at Teddy's loft when I sat in for a super-fast "Donna Lee." Gene kicked if off, and when we hit the head, it sounded like a unison. Afterwards, we went to the bar to hang out, and Gene could *really* hang out! He became one of the very best lead alto and clarinet players, but unfortunately he self-destructed because he couldn't stand success, and I never forgave him for that. He was an ex–Golden Gloves boxer, and being a tough little Irishman, he got into a lot of fights, but he was mugged one night when he was drunk and that finished him. He went back home to Atlantic City, and years later there was a benefit for him. He was paralyzed down the right-hand side and didn't have a horn, so I bought him a new alto. He played his favorite ballad, "It Might as Well Be Spring," with me on piano—and there wasn't a dry eye in the house, I'll tell you that, because the sound and fire was still there.

Gene had a wonderful sense of humor, and even when he was at death's door, he was still a riot. Bill Potts and I used to visit him in the hospital, where he was lying in a semi-comatose state in an oxygen tent, with tubes connected to every orifice. I once leaned over his bed and said, "Is there anything I can do?" and he whispered, "Yeah, take my place!" Another time when he was coming off the stand with Gerry Mulligan's CJB at Birdland, some idiot said, "Gene Quill, all you're doing is imitating Charlie Parker." Gene offered him his alto and said, "Here, *you* imitate Charlie Parker!"

In my last year at Julliard I played with Charlie Barnet. Dick Sherman, who was a wonderful trumpeter, was in the band, along with Harold Granowski on drums. Charlie's family had shares in New York Central Railroad, among other stocks, and he was a rich man, but music came first with him. He was a great leader, and he was fine to the musicians as long as you took care of business. There is a famous story of Charlie telling a fixer to organize a band for a tour. When the fixer phoned back, he said, "I've got a good bunch of guys for you, Charlie," and Charlie said, "Fuck that shit. Get me some pricks that can play!" It was about this time that I became friendly with John Williams when Chuck Andrus introduced us, as they had both been in the Army together. John had that lovely bebop drive with a sort of Horace Silver punch, and he was the hot new piano player in town. We did a couple of records together[2] and have remained good friends ever since, and I see him whenever I'm in Florida. He is one of the nicest people you could meet.

I'll tell you my only Charlie Parker story. In 1954 he was booked at a club which is still there, called Arthur's Tavern on Grove Street in Greenwich Village, and I was playing just across the street at a strip joint called the Nut Club, with Jon Eardley, Nick Stabulas, Teddy Kotick, and either George Syran or Gil Evans. When somebody said that Bird was at Arthur's, I ran over to see him, and he was playing Larry Rivers's baritone because he didn't have a horn at the time. Larry of course has since become one of America's most famous artists, and his paintings sell for thousands of dollars. Anyway, it was just a little band, drums and piano, and Bird was obviously having a tough time on the baritone. I asked him if he would like to play my alto, and he said, "Yeah, that'd be great," so I rushed back to get it for him. Now you have to understand that like a lot of young sax players, I wasn't sure about my mouthpiece or the reed, and probably the alto wasn't right—in fact, the equipment was all wrong. Bird played "Long Ago (and Far Away)" and it occurred to me that there was nothing wrong with my saxophone—it seemed to be working just fine! When he told me to play, I did my feeble imitation of the Maestro, and I will never forget him saying, "It sounds real good, son." Man I levitated across Seventh Avenue to the strip club and played the hell out of "Harlem Nocturne"!

Incidentally, I must correct something that has become part of jazz folklore concerning my owning Parker's alto. When I was married to Chan, there was a time when we didn't have enough food to eat, and as I wasn't working, I hocked my horn to get some money to feed the kids. One day I had a call because somebody had cancelled at the Five Spot, so Chan loaned me Bird's silver King, with the engraved "Charlie Parker" on the bell. It wasn't in good shape, but I needed to make a buck now that I had responsibilities. Anyway, I'm up there playing and who walked in but Mingus. He recognized the horn, walked right up to the bandstand, and looked at me. He looked at the bell of the horn, then looked back at me and just walked away. I thought, "You S.O.B. I'm trying to feed Bird's kids, so what are you busting my nuts for?" It was Bird's plastic alto that was sold at Christies. The silver King remains in the family, so I do not have Charlie Parker's alto.

Getting back to the Nut Club, Nick Stabulas was the leader, and it was thanks to him that I first met Jon Eardley, so when I got a record date, it seemed logical to use the guys I had been playing with, like George Syran, Teddy Kotick, Nick, and Jon.[3] Jon was a wonderful player, but the rumor was that he eventually had to leave America, because the Mafia had a hit on him after he had apparently named some names in a drug bust. He did very well in Europe, playing with the Cologne Radio Band for years, and whenever I did workshops there, we would always arrange to meet. Another fine trumpeter from those days, in fact one of the best, was Tony Fruscella. I played with him and Don Joseph at the Open Door, and they both used to come and sit in at the Nut Club. Don was a lovely player, too, and he was very close to Gerry Mulligan. He was a brilliant man, very articulate, and very well read, into Hemingway, Faulkner, and Thomas Wolfe. He was quite an imbiber, though, and mad as a hatter, and until he died in 1994, he was teaching school on Staten Island.

Early in 1956 I took Jackie McLean's place in George Wallington's great little group, thanks to a recommendation from Donald Byrd. I remember that we rented a carriage and stayed up all night waiting for first light, so the photographer could get his picture for the album cover, *Jazz for the Carriage Trade*.[4] George's family was in air conditioning, which was quite new then, and business was booming. He took over when his father had to step down, which was a great loss to jazz. He had a percussive left hand with very strong accents, and luckily he did come back to playing before he died.

Later that year I made my first big-name tour with a group called "The East Coast, West Coast All Stars," featuring Al Cohn, Conte Candoli, Kenny Dorham, and Sarah Vaughan's rhythm section. We were hired as the opening act for the Birdland All-Stars. I remember showing up for the bus at 10 a.m. in front of Charlie's Tavern, and there was Count Basie's band, Lester Young, Bud Powell and his trio, Al Hibbler, and Sarah Vaughan, plus all the aforementioned. So where do you sit? I mean, some of the Basie guys had been sitting in the same seats for years and you had better not sit there! I was young and green, but I heard a friendly voice shout, "Back here Phil," and it was lovely Al Cohn, who had a seat at the back of the bus where the action was, right behind Lester Young and Bud Powell. Prez would sit there and roll joints. Bud just looked out of the window, and they never spoke on the whole tour!

Quincy Jones heard me on that tour, which is how I came to be picked for Dizzy Gillespie's big band for the Middle East trip. Dizzy had nothing to do with putting the band together, because he was in Europe with JATP, so Quincy arranged the personnel. As far as playing lead alto, Jimmy Powell and I split the book. I played lead on the bebop things, and he took over on the more traditional stuff. It was weird because, seventeen hours after leaving Charlie's Tavern, we were in an opium den in Iran. They were halcyon days for sure. Dizzy and I were dear friends to the end, and his band might not have had great intonation, but what spirit! I think he was in his prime then and at the peak of his powers. He would plant his feet in front of the band as if to say, "You'd better do something great back there, because the Maestro is getting hot!" He had to send Joe Gordon home when we went to South America because Joe had a drug problem, so he sent for Lee Morgan, who was only about eighteen years old. Lee was so good that he got the break on "Night in Tunisia," and Dizzy didn't give that up to just *anybody*!

In 1957 I played on a Manny Albam date called "The Jazz Greats of Our Time," and the rest of the saxes were Al Cohn, Zoot Sims, and Gerry Mulligan.[5] I remember the session started with me sitting next to Gerry, who I loved, but he was a stickler for detail. He'd say, "Are we going to make these notes short, long, long or long, long, short?" and I'd think, "How the hell do I know?" Eventually I said, "I think the saxes would sound better if we put the alto between the two tenors, and Gerry said, "Yeah, you're right," so I moved over and put Zoot next to Gerry. Now you try asking *Zoot* whether it was going to be "short, long, long" or "long, long, short" and you'd get a much more barbed comment than you would from me. Gerry liked to mark the part, and he was probably right, but I was young and it was driving me crazy.

Towards the end of the fifties I worked with Buddy Rich in his quintet with Willie Dennis, John Bunch, and Abdul Malik. I took Sonny Criss's place, and I loved playing with Buddy, who was a sweetheart, despite what you hear. If you couldn't cut the mustard, he'd be all over you, but otherwise he'd just say, "Wear a clean shirt, play your ass off, stop treating me like the leader, and buy me a drink!" Willie was a wonderful player who was married to Morgana King. She still sings, and I see her once in a while.

In 1962 I did a tour of Russia with Benny Goodman, who wasn't the greatest human being I've ever met, but what a great artist. You could say I loved the band but hated the leader! Also, ten weeks over there was a bit dour.[6] Before we left, Mel Lewis said, "Don't worry. I've got Benny in my pocket," but Benny would kick off one tempo and Mel would go to another. There was a constant thing between the two of them until some of the guys said, "Come on, Mel, whose pocket are we in here?" For the concerts we all had red jackets, which I thought was a nice touch, and when we played in Moscow, everyone watched Krushchev. If he applauded, they applauded.

I remember a party in the room Jimmy Knepper and Jerry Dodgion shared when the vodka was flowing and I got pretty high. I went out on the balcony and yelled to the elements, "Fuck you, King!" Guess who was on the balcony below? That's right, the King himself, Benny Goodman. He recognized my voice, immediately called a rehearsal for the next morning, and the first number was "Blue Skies." "Just the saxophones," says Benny, so we all know what's coming. He pointed to me and said, "Play your part." Then after a while, "No, not like that. Play along with me," and he stuck the damn clarinet right in my ear and the band sat there while I played with him. Then he said, "I'm getting kinda sick and tired of you thinking you're the only one who can swing on this band." Now I don't ever remember saying that, but Benny just had to put me in my place in front of everyone. Eventually Zoot told Benny to lighten up, and Benny said, "What's it to you?" Zoot replied, "He's my roomski"—what you might call a gift for languages—and that was the end of the rehearsal.

The only time I was really in doubt about my playing was when Benny said to me, "It's starting to sound pretty good, kid," because by then I had tamed the bebop approach and got more into the "Hymie Schertzer" groove! When he died, and this shows how cold musicians can sometimes be, John Frosk phoned Jerry Dodgion and said, "The good news is that Benny Goodman died last night. The bad news is that he died in his sleep!"

Soon after I got back from Russia I subbed for Gene Quill in the Mulligan CJB. Gene had an accident at Birdland when he had his horn balanced on his knee with the mouthpiece close to his face. Somebody called him and, in turning quickly, the reed cut his eyeball. I was in the house that night, so I was called immediately. The CJB was a great band, which I loved, and I'm only sorry that I never recorded with it. There were wonderful writers like Brookmeyer, Mulligan, Holman, and Al Cohn—and for me, Al's chart on "Lady Chatterley's Mother" is the chart of charts. Mel Lewis was there, and any band Mel was on was a swinger. Of course the alto chair was mostly all clarinet, so there were several nights before I got a solo; then Gerry looked at me and said, "Oh yeah, you play alto!" Judy Holliday was in Birdland every night, and she was a lovely lady and a great jazz fan. I have that record she made with Gerry, and I love it because it is just charming and the arrangements are superb.[7]

You know, nobody played the instrument like Mulligan, because as Lee Konitz said about Parker, "It's too hard." He was the complete musician, and although there have been many other baritone players, very few have changed the course of music like he did with his first pianoless quartet. He was the first to leave out the piano, and now that technique is taught in every university. It's called the "Guide Tone Principle," and it frees improvisers from the tyranny of the piano dictating what's played. It was revolutionary in its time, and when those first records came out, we used to listen to them by the hour—we loved them. I saw Gerry just before he died, when he was playing on a jazz cruise on the SS *Norway* in November 1995. Gene Lees and Johnny Mandel were there, and we all hung out with Gerry and had a great time, even though we realized it might be the last time we saw him. He was playing beautifully, more poignantly than ever. He was a lovely writer, and he played some of his new tunes, and the group with Ted Rosenthal, Dean Johnson, and Ron Vincent sounded great. He performed from a chair, and I'm sure he knew it might be his final performance, but he was playing so well and finding new ways. I'd love a tape of that concert, because there wasn't a dry eye in my part of the house.[8]

In 1968 I moved to Europe, and right off the bat I opened at Ronnie Scott's in London, which is where I met Gordon Beck, who had the house trio. Someone from the club collected me from Heathrow, and they didn't realize I had my family with me and our forty-eight cardboard boxes of matching luggage, because they took us to a hotel in Piccadilly which served hot and cold running hookers! I hadn't been playing much jazz in the States and had pretty much got sucked into the studio scene.[9] We moved to Paris, and that's where I formed the "European Rhythm Machine" with George Gruntz, Henri Texier, and Daniel Humair, but later Gordon Beck took over from George on piano. That group lasted for four years and was an important part of my life.

When I got back to New York in 1974, I recorded an album called *Musique Dubois*,[10] which was named after my father. He came from Quebec and "Dubois" was his surname, but he never officially changed it. Jaki Byard was on piano, and he is also a great saxophone player.[11] In 1975 I played on the Billy Joel hit "Just the Way You Are," and I hear that solo in the darndest places all over the world. Billy didn't know me, so it was thanks to the producer Phil Ramone that I was on the record, and I actually overdubbed my part after the vocal was done. At the same session, I overdubbed a solo for Phoebe Snow, and I did both records for $700.

On my 1988 album *Evolution*,[12] I wrote a song for Al Cohn called "Alvin G." We were roommates on the 1956 Birdland tour, and he was one of my favorite arrangers, and he, Zoot, and I were all really good friends. Al could be very funny. He was once in Copenhagen and someone said, "Have you tried the Elephant beer?" Al replied, "No, man. I drink to forget!" I miss those guys, because these days, the youngsters in their three-piece suits don't quite have that panache.

NOTES

1. Phil Woods, *Live at the Wigmore Hall with Gordon Beck*. JMS (F) 083-2 CD.
2. Phil Woods. OJC CD052–2 and Fresh Sound FSR CD 182.
3. Phil Woods, *New Jazz Quintet*. OJC CD 1881-2.
4. George Wallington, *Jazz for the Carriage Trade*. Prestige LP 7032.
5. Manny Albam, *The Jazz Greats of Our Time*, vol. 1. Coral CRL 57173.
6. When the band returned to the States, Zoot Sims was asked what touring Russia with Benny Goodman was like. He replied, "*Every* gig with Benny is like touring Russia."
7. Judy Holliday, *Holliday with Mulligan*. DRG SL 5191.
8. The Caribbean Jazz Cruise on the SS *Norway* in November 1995 was the last time that Gerry Mulligan performed in public. He died on January 19, 1996.
9. The work situation during the sixties had become so difficult for jazz musicians that Phil Woods was quoted at the time as saying he couldn't even get *arrested* with his own quartet in New York.
10. Phil Woods, *Musique Dubois*. 32Jazz CD32016.
11. Jaki Byard was an amazing multi-instrumentalist. Paul Desmond was once listening to him playing piano in a club. At the end of his solo, Byard switched to the tenor sax, which he played really well. Desmond turned to a companion and said, "I wish he'd mind his own business!" Jaki Byard died on February 10, 1999.
12. Phil Woods Little Big Band, *Evolution*. Concord Jazz CCD 4361.

Bibliography

Balliett, Whitney. *American Musicians: 56 Portraits in Jazz.* Oxford University Press. 1986.

Balliett, Whitney. *American Singers: Twenty-Seven Portraits in Song.* Oxford University Press. 1988.

Balliett, Whitney. *The Sound of Surprise.* William Kimber. 1960.

Carey, Gary. *Judy Holliday: An Intimate Lifestory.* Robson Books. 1983.

Catalano, Nick. *Clifford Brown: The Life and Art of the Legendary Jazz Trumpeter.* Oxford University Press. 2000.

Clancy, D. William, with Audree Coke Kenton. *Woody Herman: Chronicles of the Herds.* Schirmer Books. 1995.

Clarke, Donald. *Wishing on the Moon: The Life and Times of Billie Holiday.* Penguin Books. 1994.

Cohen, Noal, and Michael Fitzgerald. *Rat Race Blues: The Musical Life of Gigi Gryce.* Berkeley Hills Books. 2002.

Crow, Bill. *From Birdland to Broadway: Scenes from a Jazz Life.* Oxford University Press. 1992.

Crow, Bill. *Jazz Anecdotes.* Oxford University Press. 1990.

De Valk, Jeroen. *Chet Baker: His Life and Music.* Berkeley Hills Books. 1989.

Easton, Carol. *Straight Ahead: The Story of Stan Kenton.* Da Capo. 1973.

Enstice, Wayne, and Paul Rubin. *Jazz Spoken Here: Conversations with 22 Musicians.* Da Capo. 1994.

Feather, Leonard, and Ira Gitler, eds. *The Biographical Encyclopedia of Jazz.* Oxford University Press. 1999.

Gavin, James. *Deep in a Dream: The Long Night of Chet Baker.* Chatto and Windus. 2002.

Gelly, Dave. *Stan Getz: Nobody Else but Me.* Backbeat Books. 2002.

Gioia, Ted. *West Coast Jazz: Modern Jazz in California 1945–1960.* Oxford University Press. 1992.

Gitler, Ira. *Jazz Masters of the '40s.* Macmillan. 1966.

Gitler, Ira. *Swing to Bop: An Oral History of the Transition in Jazz in the 1940s*. Oxford University Press. 1985.

Goldberg, Joe. *Jazz Masters of the 50s*. Macmillan. 1965.

Gordon, Robert. *Jazz West Coast*. Quartet Books. 1986.

Hall, M. Fred. *It's about Time: The Dave Brubeck Story*. University of Arkansas Press. 1996.

Hentoff, Nat. *The Jazz Life*. Panther. 1964.

Hoogeveen, Gerard J. *Meet Mr. Gordon: A Discography of Bob Gordon*. Micography. 1987.

Horricks, Raymond. *Gerry Mulligan's Ark*. The Owlet Press. 2003.

Horricks, Raymond. *Gil Evans*. Spellmount. 1984.

Horricks, Raymond. *These Jazzmen of Our Time*. Victor Gollancz. 1960.

Jewell, Derek. *Duke: A Portrait of Duke Ellington*. Sphere Books. 1977.

Jones, Patti. *One Man's Blues: The Life and Music of Mose Allison*. Quartet Books. 1995.

Kernfield, Barry, ed. *The New Grove Dictionary of Jazz*. Macmillan. 1991.

Kirkpatrick, Ron. *Stan Getz: An Appreciation of His Recorded Work*. Zany Publications. 1992.

Klinkowitz, Jerome. *Listen: Gerry Mulligan: An Aural Narrative in Jazz*. Schirmer Books. 1991.

Lees, Gene. *Leader of the Band: The Life of Woody Herman*. Oxford University Press. 1995.

Lees, Gene. *Meet Me at Jim and Andy's: Jazz Musicians and Their World*. Oxford University Press. 1988.

Lord, Tom. *The A–Z Jazz Discography*. 25 volumes. North County Distributors. 1992–2001.

Maggin, L. Donald. *Stan Getz: A Life in Jazz*. William Morrow. 1996.

Meeker, David. *Jazz in the Movies: A Guide to Jazz Musicians 1917–1977*. Talisman Books. 1977.

Palmer, Richard. *Stan Getz*. Apollo. 1988.

Pepper, Art, and Laurie Pepper. *Straight Life: The Story of Art Pepper*. Schirmer Books. 1979.

Ramsey, Doug. *Jazz Matters: Reflections on the Music and Some of Its Makers*. University of Arkansas Press. 1989.

Shapiro, Nat, and Nat Hentoff. *Hear Me Talkin' to Ya: The Story of Jazz by the Men Who Made It*. Penguin Books. 1955.

Simosko, Vladimir. *Serge Chaloff: A Musical Biography and Discography*. Scarecrow Press. 1998.

Sjogren, Thorbjorn. *Chet: The Music of Chesney Henry Baker*. JazzMedia. 1993.

Sparke, Michael, with Peter Venudor. *Stan Kenton: The Studio Sessions*. Balboa Books. 1998.

Urso, Joe. *The Upper Register*. Joe Urso. 1999.

Vail, Ken. *Birds's Diary: The Life of Charlie Parker 1945–1955*. Castle Communications. 1996.

Voce, Steve. *Woody Herman*. Apollo. 1986.

Williams, Martin. *Jazz Heritage*. Oxford University Press. 1985.

Index

Novak, Kim, 111, 125
Nut Club, 216
"Nutmeg," 138

O'Brien, Hod, xiii, 186–192
Ocean's Eleven, 211
O'Day, Anita, 100, 102
"Ode to Billy Joe," 10
O'Farrill, Chico, 175
O'Hara, John, 138
Oliver, Lynn, 6
Oliver, Mert, 180
Oliver, Sy, 38
On Golden Pond, 28
One Man's Blues, 15n2
"One Room Country Shack," 14
"Only the Lonely," 97
The Onyx (club), 104, 130
Open Door (club), 63, 119
"Opus in Chartreuse," 177
The Orchid Room (club), 104
Ørsted Pedersen, Niels-Henning, 20, 96
Osborne, Mary, 100
Otis, Fred, 24–25, 154
Orrison, Ted, 81n2
"Out of Nowhere," 89, 209
Overton, Hall, 39n12, 188

Pacific Jazz Records, 14, 19, 140, 159
The Pad (club), 187
Page, Patti, 24
Page Three (club), 110
Page, Walter, 38n1
Paich, Marty, 28, 79, 80, 140, 196, 201
"Parchman Farm," 14
Parker, Chan, 216
Parker, Charlie, ix, x xii, 3, 11, 34, 41,
    49–50, 51n2, 57, 61, 68, 83–84, 86–89,
    96–97, 98n2, 106, 108, 111, 114–116, 120,
    122, 124, 129–134, 141, 170, 171n2, 175,
    177–178, 180, 184, 190, 194, 203, 205,
    207, 215–216, 219
Parker, Leo, 131
"Parker's Mood," 97
Parlan, Horace, 9
Pass, Joe, 179, 190
Payne, Cecil, 36, 57, 184
Payne, Freda, 102
Payne, Sonny, 17
Peacock Alley (club), 138

Peacock, Gary, 30, 202
Peacock Lane (club), 138
Pell, Dave, 81, 141n3, 156
Peña, Ralph, 23, 25, 44–45, 159
"Pennies from Heaven,"177, 179n4
"Pennies in Minor," 87
"Pennsylvania 6-5000," 5
Peplowski, Ken, 96, 144, 178
Pepper, Art, 23, 29, 31n8, 33, 80, 81n5, 88,
    93–94, 135–140, 145, 156, 174, 177,
    195–196, 199–200, 210
Pepper, Diane, 94
Perkins, Bill, 28, 79, 136–137, 175, 177,
    179, 184, 193–200, 203, 207
Perlow, Steve, 71n3
Persip, Charlie, 177, 182
Peterson, Oscar, 25, 31n3, 119, 132, 175, 178
Pettiford, Oscar, 14, 16–17, 33, 44, 51n9,
    125, 130, 134, 164, 166, 186–188, 205,
    207–208
"Phil & Quill," 188
Phillips, Flip, 109, 130, 175
Pierce, Dick, 95
Pierce, Nat 7, 90, 181
The Pink Pussycat (club), 95
Pisano, John, 29
Pizza Express (club), 10, 180
"Planet of the Apes," 28
The Playboy Club, 69, 120
Playboy Jazz Festival, 102
Playboy Magazine, 27, 202
"Playing Jazz," 98
"Polka Dots and Moonbeams," 167
Pollard, Terry, 100, 120
Polo, Danny, 144
"Poor Little Rich Girl," 3
Porcino, Al, 2, 45, 82–83, 203, 208
Potter, Tommy, 36
Potts, Bill, 215
Powell, Bud, 14, 15n2, 30n2, 86, 96, 134,
    186, 217
Powell, Jimmy, 217
Powell, Seldon, 36, 210
Powell, Specs, 33
Powell, Teddy, 122
Prell, Don, 24
Presley, Elvis, 28
Prestige Records, 12, 145, 187
"Pretty," 139
Preview Lounge (club), 17

About the Author

Gordon Jack was born in Watford, England, in 1941. He took up the tenor saxophone in his late teens, playing in rehearsal bands that concentrated on arrangements by people like Neal Hefti, Gerry Mulligan, and William Russo. In the mid-sixties he switched to the baritone, joining a James Brown–like rhythm 'n' blues band that was resident at London's 100 Club. When the gigs dried up he started contributing regular CD and book reviews to *Jazz Journal International*, as well as the occasional article to *Crescendo & Jazz Music*. He was also responsible for a Gerry Mulligan discography in Raymond Horricks's book on Mulligan, published by the Owlet Press in 2003.